Ancient Egyptian Technology and Innovation

BLOOMSBURY EGYPTOLOGY
Series editor: Nicholas Reeves

Burial Customs in Ancient Egypt
Wolfram Grajetzki

Court Officials of the Egyptian Middle Kingdom
Wolfram Grajetzki

**Hidden Hands: Egyptian workforces in Petrie
excavation archives, 1880-1924**
Stephen Quirke

**The Middle Kingdom of Ancient Egypt:
history, archaeology and society**
Wolfram Grajetzki

Performance and Drama in Ancient Egypt
Robyn Gillam

ANCIENT EGYPTIAN TECHNOLOGY AND INNOVATION

Transformations in Pharaonic Material Culture

Ian Shaw

B L O O M S B U R Y

LONDON · NEW DELHI · NEW YORK · SYDNEY

Bloomsbury Academic
An imprint of Bloomsbury Publishing Plc

50 Bedford Square
London
WC1B 3DP
UK

1385 Broadway
New York
NY 10018
USA

www.bloomsbury.com

First published in 2012 by Bristol Classical Press an imprint of Bloomsbury Academic
Reprinted by Bloomsbury Academic 2013

British Library Cataloguing-in-Publication Data
A catalogue record for this book is available from the British Library.

ISBN: 978-0-7156-3118-8

Library of Congress Cataloging-in-Publication Data
A catalog record for this book is available from the Library of Congress.

Typeset by Ray Davies
Printed and bound in Great Britain

Contents

This book is dedicated to Barry Kemp, Janine Bourriau and John Ray, who taught me Egyptian archaeology, texts and material culture in the 1980s, and have continued to inspire me with their work ever since.

Preface

My overall approach in this book is similar to that of Serafina Cuomo in her recent study of technology and culture in the Greco-Roman world (Cuomo 2007); thus, my initial discussions of the general sources and problems of science and technology in Egypt (in the first three chapters) are followed by a series of case-studies seeking to understand certain aspects of the dynamics of ancient Egyptian technology, culture and society. The case-studies deal with various specific technical areas: medicine, writing, stone-working, monumental construction, mummification, glass-working, and weapons manufacture. Like Cuomo (2007: 5), I have tried to organise each chapter around one or more areas of debate, using particular technological topics to provide more general theoretical insights into the cultural dynamics of technology and innovation in ancient Egypt.

Although the principal aim of this book is to bring together the basic evidence for many different aspects of change and evolution in Egyptian technology, it will also include some consideration of the wider cognitive and social contexts. What was the Egyptian propensity for mental creativity and innovation? How rapidly did Egyptian technology change in comparison with other African, Mediterranean or Near Eastern states? The various chapters will include consideration of those aspects of Egyptian society that made it predisposed (or, in other instances, actively opposed) to certain types of conservatism or innovation in material culture. Examples are also given of the idea that technological change is not necessarily a continuous succession of innovations – it can also involve maintaining the status quo or even entirely viable and justifiable reversions to earlier techniques and equipment. The penultimate chapter is a discussion of the ways in which the practice and development of Egyptian technology interrelated with Late Bronze Age urban society as a whole, using the city at Amarna as a case-study.

Acknowledgements

I would like to thank Nick Reeves for initiating this book, and Deborah Blake for ensuring that it finally appeared. I would also like to thank over ten years of Liverpool University undergraduate and postgraduate students for helping to maintain my enthusiasm for ancient Egyptian technology and material culture. Thanks to Ann for several of the line drawings.

Parts of Chapters 7, 8 and 9 have previously appeared as Shaw 2001, 2010b, and 2004 respectively.

List of Illustrations

Figures

ix

List of Illustrations

List of Illustrations

Tables

Chronology

This chronology has been compiled on the basis of a number of different criteria, ranging from the interpretation of ancient texts to the radiocarbon dating of excavated materials. The dates for prehistory (*c.* 700,000-3000 BC) are approximations based on a combination of stratigraphic information, seriation of artefacts, radiocarbon dates and thermoluminescence dates. The dates for the majority of the pharaonic period (*c.* 3000-664 BC) are based mainly on ancient king-lists, dated inscriptions, and astronomical records. When the dates for two or more dynasties overlap (principally in the Second and Third Intermediate Periods), this is because their rule was accepted in different parts of the country.

PREHISTORY

Palaeolithic	*c.* 700,000-10,000 BP
Epipalaeolithic	*c.* 10,000-7000 BP
Neolithic	*c.* 5300-4000 BC
Maadi-Buto Cultural Complex (north only)	*c.* 4000-3200 BC
Badarian period	*c.* 4500-3800 BC
Amratian (Naqada I) period	*c.* 4000-3500 BC
Gerzean (Naqada II) period	*c.* 3500-3200 BC
Naqada III/'Dynasty 0'	*c.* 3200-3000 BC

PHARAONIC/DYNASTIC PERIOD

	c. 3000-332 BC
Early Dynastic period	3000-2686 BC
1st Dynasty	3000-2890 BC
2nd Dynasty	2890-2686 BC
Old Kingdom	2686-2181 BC
3rd Dynasty	2686-2613 BC
4th Dynasty	2613-2494 BC
5th Dynasty	2494-2345 BC
6th Dynasty	2345-2181 BC
First Intermediate Period	2181-2055 BC

7th and 8th Dynasties	2181-2125 BC
9th and 10th Dynasties	2160-2025 BC
11th Dynasty (Thebes only)	2125-2055 BC
Middle Kingdom	2055-1650 BC
11th Dynasty (all Egypt)	2055-1985 BC
12th Dynasty	1985-1795 BC
13th Dynasty	1795-after 1650 BC
14th Dynasty	1750-1650 BC
Second Intermediate Period	1650-1550 BC
15th Dynasty (Hyksos)	1650-1550 BC
16th Dynasty (minor Hyksos)	1650-1550 BC
17th Dynasty (Theban)	1650-1550 BC
New Kingdom	1550-1069 BC
18th Dynasty	1550-1295 BC
Ramessid period	1295-1069 BC
19th Dynasty	1295-1186 BC
20th Dynasty	1186-1069 BC
Third Intermediate Period	1069-664 BC
21st Dynasty	1069-945 BC
22nd Dynasty	945-715 BC
23rd Dynasty	818-715 BC
24th Dynasty	727-715 BC
25th Dynasty (Kushite period)	747-656 BC
Late Period	664-332 BC
26th Dynasty (Saite period)	664-525 BC
27th Dynasty (1st Persian period)	525-404 BC
28th Dynasty	404-399 BC
29th Dynasty	399-380 BC
30th Dynasty	380-343 BC
2nd Persian period	343-332 BC
PTOLEMAIC PERIOD	332-30 BC
Macedonian Dynasty	332-305 BC
ROMAN PERIOD	30 BC-AD 311

1

Introduction: towards an explicitly anthropological analysis of technological change and innovation in ancient Egypt

Technology has not generally been a revolutionary force; it has been responsible for keeping things the same as much as changing them (Edgerton 2008: 212).

The archaeologists and anthropologists classify things by their uses, having first separated material and mental culture, or things and ideas (Kubler 1962: 2).

The title of this book refers not only to technology but also to the process of innovation, since the intention here is not simply to discuss some of the means by which Egyptians created the materials and artefacts that they needed (many of which are particularly characteristic of their culture) but to consider the ways in which changes in material culture took place in the Nile valley, and also to consider how the development of particular types of artefact both reflected and instigated specific processes of cultural and mental change.

However, it is also crucial to bear in mind the view, eloquently argued by Edgerton (2008), that technological change – whether premodern or comparatively recent – is not always a progressive sequence of innovations, but can also be characterised by continued use of traditional methods or artefacts, and even the surprisingly frequent re-introduction of techniques that might be assumed to have become outmoded. As Edgerton (2008: xiii) puts it, 'alternatives exist for nearly all technologies: there are multiple military technologies, means of generating electricity, powering a motor car, storing and manipulating information, cutting metal or roofing a building. Too often histories are written as if no alternative could or did exist.' In other words, the traditional polarised view of cultures as *either* innovative *or* conservative in their technology ignores the fact that processes of change in material culture are frequently multifaceted and multi-directional.

Thus, as we will see in the discussions of Egyptian medicine, magic, mummification and glass-working below (Chapters 4 and 6), certain aspects of pharaonic science and technology could be heavily influenced simultaneously by both traditional and progressive viewpoints. As Lemonnier (1993: 22) puts it: 'Every technical system is continually evolving and is subject to a mixture of conservation and change.' This applies to the overall technological system in a society, but even within a specific area of material culture or technology there can be very subtle combinations of traditional and innovative approaches. The case-study focusing on medicine and magic, below, makes it clear that the study of some forms of ancient technology can become problematic, because of the partial or flawed nature of the evidence itself, especially when our main sources are textual rather than physical or artefactual. When we seek to understand sequences of cultural development, including periods of rapid or gradual technological advance and decline, we primarily do so via the partial survival of the material results of human actions. It has frequently been pointed out that archaeology is virtually always an attempt to understand human prehistory and history via the study of those physical things that have survived rather than the totality of the original event or phenomenon.

Several edited volumes over the last decade (notably Shortland 2001, Bourriau and Phillips 2004, Mathieu et al. 2006) have explored different aspects of the social context of Egyptian technology, from pottery-making to faience production, but the primary aim here is to explore Egyptian technology as an integral and embedded part of ancient Egyptian society, 'taking material culture for what it is, a social production' (Lemonnier 1993: 26). Wengrow (2006: 66) has already demonstrated the importance of treating Egyptian technological change as a fundamental part of social and cultural change in his study of the Nile valley during the Neolithic period, in which he concludes that 'new empirical knowledge may be generated or assimilated through the performance of a whole range of social activities that we might be tempted to classify as "symbolic" or "ritual"'. This is certainly the case with Egyptian mummification, as discussed in Chapter 6 below.

The current state of Egyptian technological studies

The study of ancient Egyptian technology is vibrant and progressive, with research being conducted by a wide diversity of scholars throughout the world. This book analyses many different types of technology, and the ways in which they affected and sometimes transformed Egyptian society and economics; in doing so, it draws not only on traditional archaeological and textual sources of Egyptological data but also on the results of scientific analyses of ancient materials and sources of experimental and ethno-archaeological information.

Although ancient Egypt tends to be conventionally caricatured as one of the most conservative and intractable of civilisations, even the briefest study of the material culture of the Nile Valley shows that the Egyptians had an enormous capacity both to absorb new modes of production and innovative techniques and to exploit new materials when necessary. John Ray (1986: 307-8), argues that 'Egypt's role was that of perfecter of ideas, rather than an inventor; most of the innovations in the ancient Near East come from outside Egypt, but Egypt, once it adopts a new idea, produces a form of it which is often more effective than it was in its original home'. Later in the same article Ray also suggests that, as far as the emergence of the hieroglyphic writing system was concerned, its failure to develop into an alphabetic system should not be regarded as a major flaw or as an indication of 'Oriental conservatism' but as a direct result of hieroglyphics being well-tailored to the expression of the ancient Egyptian language: 'when Egyptian is found written in an alphabetic script, as in Hellenistic and Roman texts where the Greek alphabet is applied to the language, the result, perversely enough, is extremely difficult to follow, and the advantages of the native script become clear' (Ray 1986: 315). Similarly, the nature of the Egyptian political and social systems – both of which seem to have been remarkably rigid and enduring – should not blind us to the vitality and flexibility of much of their material culture, the rough chronology of which is summarised below.

Technological time-line

Most of our knowledge of Egyptian technology during the earliest periods of Egyptian prehistory (the Palaeolithic period) centres on the production of stone tools and weapons (Fig. 1.1), and the earliest known chert quarries, such as those at Nazlet Khater and Saqqara (*c.* 40,000 BP). However, a much more varied range of crafts have survived from the Neolithic period. Apart from the domestication of plants and animals and the emergence of pottery (the two factors that tend to characterise this phase in most cultures), there are also surviving indications of basketry, rope-making and bone-working.

By the Predynastic period, the Egyptians' irrigation techniques had improved, thus expanding the agricultural capacity of the Nile Valley. By this time they were also producing large numbers of stone vessels and making pottery on an unparalleled scale (particularly between 3800 and 3500 BC at Hierakonpolis). From at least the Naqada period onwards, they were brewing beer and cultivating grapes. They were also

Fig. 1.1. Lower Palaeolithic handaxe from the desert near Thebes (Garstang Museum, University of Liverpool, E6581; 14 x 10cm); this artefact is typical of the earliest phase of tool use in the Nile Valley, *c.* 400,000-300,000.

1. Introduction

Fig. 1.2. Bird's eye view of a ground loom, from the Middle Kingdom tomb of Khnumhotep III (BH3) at Beni Hasan.

able to build wattle and daub buildings, smelt copper (by 4000 BC), mine gold, and work lead, gold and silver into artefacts. Some of the weaving techniques developed in basketry and rope-making had begun to be applied to textile production, using linen. The earliest depiction of a ground (or 'horizontal') loom dates from the Badarian period (*c.* 4500-3800 BC); the painting, executed on a pottery vessel, shows four corner pegs holding two beams, one at either end, with the warp running between them; three bars depicted in the middle of the loom may perhaps be the laze rod, heddle rod and some form of beater (see Fig. 1.2 for a Middle Kingdom depiction of a ground loom). It was also around this time that the first faience was being manufactured, initially for simple beads and later for small animal figurines (Fig. 1.3). By the Naqada period, or perhaps even as early as the Badarian period, certain forms of artificial mummification had been introduced – the question of precisely when this process first began to take place depends very much on how we define mummification itself (see Chapter 6, which deals with questions of definition in relation to both mummification and the production of glass artefacts). Mud-brick buildings began to be constructed at least as early as the Naqada I, or Amratian, phase (*c.* 4000-3600 BC), at a number of sites in Upper Egypt (e.g. sites 29 and 29a at Hierakonpolis, see Holmes 1992; Hoffman 1980), although Kemp (2000: 79) notes that

5

Fig. 1.3. Protodynastic figurine of a baboon in efflorescence-glazed faience, holding a cone on its knee, from Hierakonpolis (Petrie Museum, University College London, UC11002; h. 5.2cm).

wattle and daub structures continued to be widely made several centuries after the introduction of mud brick. Evidence from such sites as Maadi and Tell el-Farkha indicates that mud-brick architecture had spread to Lower Egypt by about Naqada IId (*c.* 3400-3300 BC)

However, the Predynastic development that most obviously foreshadowed the pharaonic period was the increasing use of images and symbols that are assumed to be the forerunners of hieroglyphics. By the 4th millennium BC, the Egyptians' use of pictorial symbols had evolved into the earliest stage of a sophisticated writing system (see Chapter 3 below). The oldest surviving sheet of papyrus – unfortunately uninscribed – was found in a 1st-Dynasty tomb at Saqqara (*c.* 3000 BC). In the Early Dynastic period the first élite tombs incorporating stone masonry were built, the granite quarries at Aswan began to be exploited, and specialised copper tools began to be used for wood-working. Other Early Dynastic developments were the introduction of dyed threads and dyed cloth, and the earliest evidence for wine production.

From the 3rd Dynasty (*c.* 2686-2613 BC) onwards, limestone quarries began to be exploited on a huge scale, primarily for the construction of pyramid complexes. From this date we also have the earliest evidence for the laminating of sheets of timber. By the 4th Dynasty (*c.* 2613-2494 BC), a form of frit called 'Egyptian blue' had begun to be used both as a sculpting material and as a pigment, and the earliest surviving faience workshop (at Abydos) had come into existence. By approximately this date, mummification techniques, for the élite at least, began to include evisceration and treatment with drying agents. By the 5th Dynasty (*c.* 2494-2345 BC) the potter's wheel had been introduced (Fig. 1.4), although it was not until the First Intermediate Period (*c.* 2160-2055 BC) that it began to be widely used.

From the 11th Dynasty (*c.* 2055-1985 BC) onwards, sandstone quarries began to be exploited for building and sculptural material. By the Middle Kingdom (*c.* 2055-1650 BC), excerebration (removal of the brain) had become part of the mummification process, which had by now spread to the 'middle classes'. Techniques of gold granulation were also introduced at this date. The earliest surviving texts presenting mathematical problems and their solutions date to the Middle Kingdom (e.g. the Mathematical Leather Roll, BM EA 10250), but earlier depictions of scribes as accountants indicate that a fairly sophisticated system of mathematics was already in use, primarily for accounting and architectural purposes, from at least the beginning of the Old Kingdom (see Imhausen 2007). The earliest surviving medical texts also date to the Middle Kingdom (see Collier and Quirke 2004: 54-64). From the early New Kingdom we have the earliest examples of Egyptian wood turning, and the introduction of tapped-slag furnaces for copper processing. At around 1500 BC the first vertical loom is attested in Egypt. Unlike the horizontal loom, which was pegged out across the ground, the vertical (or 'two-beamed') loom was usually placed against a wall, with weavers working upwards from its base; the lower beam was either set into a

Fig. 1.4. Scene from the tomb of Ty at Saqqara (no. 60), showing a potter using a wheel to fashion a vessel.

shallow hollow in the ground or resting on grooved blocks, examples of which have survived in some New Kingdom houses (see Fig. 1.5). By at least the reign of Thutmose III (*c.* 1479-1425 BC), glass was being processed (and perhaps even manufactured) by Egyptians, probably adopting techniques developed at an earlier date in the Near East (Fig. 1.6).

By the Late Period (664-332 BC), specialised techniques of gold refinement had been developed, and, from about 600 BC onwards, iron-working became fairly widespread. In a temple of the early Ptolemaic period (4th century BC) we have the first *representation* of a wooden object being turned on a lathe (Fig. 1.7), although the lathe had almost certainly already been introduced as early as the New Kingdom. It was around this date that artificial mummification became more widespread throughout all levels of the population. During the Ptolemaic period stake-and-strand basketry was introduced, and lime mortar began to be used in mud-brick buildings. By the Roman period, silver-working had become more common, and by the 1st century AD, cotton was in general use for textiles, gradually beginning to replace linen.

Fig. 1.5. Vertical looms depicted in the 18th-Dynasty tomb of Thutnefer at Thebes (no. A6).

Fig. 1.6. Blue and yellow core-formed glass vessel probably dating to the reign of Thutmose III, one of the earliest examples of worked glass in Egypt (Harrow School, HE121, h. 64cm).

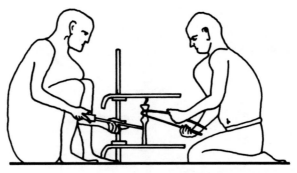

Fig. 1.7. Scene showing a carpenter turning wood on a lathe,
in the early Ptolemaic tomb of Petosiris at Tuna el-Gebel.

One of the crucial elements of the technological time-line above is its reliance on the earliest physical, visual or textual evidence for changes and innovations in technology. It goes almost without saying that these attestations must invariably be later than the actual developments themselves, therefore, in most areas of material culture, we can probably assume that changes took place earlier than the evidence currently suggests, and future research will invariably tend to reveal earlier instances or provide evidence of gradual processes of transition and development. Chronology, however, is only part of the picture, and much of the discussion in the rest of this book attempts to focus on the 'why' and the 'how' rather than the 'when'. As Bauchspies et al. (2006: 17) put it: 'When we talk about science, truth, logic, technology and related ideas, we are always talking about social relations.'

2

Analysing Egyptian technological dynamics: was Egyptian technology underpinned and framed by 'science'?

We must accept that from time to time the Egyptians produced figures of great intellectual ability responsible for major changes in traditions. Yet the Egyptians remained without the means to conceptualise this. Past innovators were remembered, but as 'wise men' (Kemp 2006: 159).

Part of the basis of modern technology was already set out by Greek 'mechanicians' (Gille 1980) at Alexandria in the 3rd century BC, and the surviving fragments of writings by these scholars suggest that something approximating 'science' had already begun to provide a theoretical framework and backdrop for technological developments. This raises the question of whether the mechanicians and their contemporaries – based as they were in the Egyptian Delta – were building on a tradition of ancient Egyptian thought that could also be regarded as scientific in something like the modern sense of the term. Opinions differ considerably as to how science should be defined, particularly in an ancient, 'pre-Greek' context (see, for instance, Cunningham and Wilson 1993). Ancient Egyptian, like other ancient languages, had no word that refers explicitly to science, although the root rh (to know, knowledge) is probably the closest approximation, and of course a similar situation applies to many other modern cultural designations, such as 'art' and 'religion' (but the two latter clearly existed in ancient Egypt, without actually being described directly by any specific noun).

It is not simply that the ancient Egyptian language, and therefore perhaps the Egyptian mindset, did not include a word that is equivalent to the modern concept of scientific enquiry. There is also a crucial cultural difference in these 'pre-Greek' times, in that the concept of a single individual thinker, such as Archimedes or Pythagoras, being credited with crucial intellectual, scientific or technological advances seems not yet to have come into existence to any great extent. The idea of the exceptionally talented thinker as the prime agent of progress was not entirely absent from Egyptian culture – such individuals as Imhotep and Amenhotep son of Hapu were remembered as great men, whose achievements resulted in the very unusual situation of their being deified (see Wildung 1977). However, as Kemp (2006: 158) observes, no matter how much these comparatively rare individuals might be admired, they could not be acknowledged as innovators by their contemporaries because 'the ancient myth that whatever was new and admirable was in fact true to the past allowed no room for recognition of individual genius'. Lemonnier (1993: 19-20) has come to the same conclusion in a more cross-cultural context: 'mythology legitimates the origin of particular technical operations, and a tool may be worshipped in lieu of a goddess. In short, technical variants are diversely embedded in the larger symbolic framework that underlies the hierarchy of ... society'. In other words, the pre-science era prioritised, and even mythologised, the development of craft or technology itself rather than the craftsmen or thinkers who shaped it. This automatically increases the difficulty involved in examining the scientific framework within which Egyptian technology developed.

There seems to be little or no evidence that the Egyptians investigated the natural world with techniques that approximate to experimentation or analytical research, and indeed a number of ancient textual sources suggest that they expected to find knowledge recorded almost magically in written documents – thus, for instance, there are a number of texts that refer to written knowledge transcribed by a god (usually Thoth) and hidden in a box. This so-called Book of Thoth (which was usually thought to contain everything that was known about the physical world, the divine system of laws, magic, and the nature of the afterlife) features heavily in such Ptolemaic narrative cycles as the tales of Setna Khaemwaset and Neferkaptah (see Lichtheim 1980: 125-51).

Geoffrey Lloyd (2004: 13) points out, however, that, 'even when the most up-to-date science does not need to refer directly to earlier ideas, they belong nevertheless to the same field of enquiry in so far as they tackled the problems of understanding presented by the same general phenomena'. In other words, the entire history of science is marked by the continual replacement of incorrect or inappropriate methods and data with new techniques or paradigms. On this basis even the so-called pseudo-science of the pre-Greek civilisations (and indeed the work of the early Greeks) can be regarded as 'true' science by broadly defining scientific enquiry as the pursuit of knowledge and understanding, regardless of the precise methodology employed.

The best-documented aspects of Egyptian investigation and speculation are in the areas that would now be described as mathematics, medicine and astronomy, which were perhaps already recognised in some sense as separate independent disciplines. However, in the case of medicine and astronomy there is distinct overlap with the areas of culture that would now be described as magic and religion respectively. There are therefore crucial differences in the relationships between these early 'scientific' areas and the Egyptian cultural and social contexts.

There is one problem that all scholars of ancient science encounter when they seek to understand pre-modern and/or non-western science: whether to attempt to understand it in our own terms or in terms that would have been recognised and understood by the ancient 'scientists' themselves, or their contemporaries (see, for instance, Lloyd 2004: 8-11). Both approaches can lead to misconceptions and confusion – thus, the use of modern terminology can perhaps erroneously imply that not only the terms but also the associated meanings and systems of thought already existed. Conversely, if we attempt to describe Egyptian mathematics or medicine purely through the media of the ancient vocabulary we encounter difficulties in adequately translating, defining or contextualising the ancient terms and ideas. It is not even simply a question of translating more or less accurately and precisely, since the actual system of thought underlying certain vocabularies may differ from that to which we are accustomed, as Lyons (1995) has demonstrated, for example, in the field of colour terminology, in that many cultures use 'colour' terms that refer to luminosity rather than hue.

The relationship between science and technology

On the basis of the above discussion of ancient Egyptian areas of specialised knowledge, it can be argued that something roughly corresponding to the modern concept of science did exist, but that it was not overtly recognised as such. To what extent, then, might this early science have sustained and activated the technology of ancient Egypt? A closely related question of course is the extent to which science was a prerequisite for ancient technology. How much of ancient Egyptian technological innovation emerged out of sustained periods of scientific investigation, and how much of it simply arose in the form of *ad hoc* solutions to practical problems? A potential answer to this (although one which, to some extent, sidesteps the main issue), is to apply to Egypt the arguments deployed by Cuomo (2007) in her monograph on the material culture and technology of ancient Greece and Rome, in which she discusses at length the diverse meanings and implications of the Greek term *technê* ('craft' or 'art') and its Latin equivalent *ars*; as she points out, 'both carpentry and medicine were *technai*; a rhetorician, capable of turning opinions around in the minds of his audience, and a sculptor, capable of turning a block of marble into the statue of a god, both qualified as technicians'. This holistic interpretation of *technê*, whether it is translated as 'craft', 'art' or 'skill', suggests that the modern distinctions between science and technology barely existed in the ancient world. Can the same be said then of the ancient Egyptian term *ḥmwt*, which is often translated as 'craftwork' but which actually probably encompasses some of the senses of 'art' and 'skill' too (see, for instance, Drenkhahn 1976)?

To what extent did Egyptians even consciously divide such aspects of technology as architecture, structural engineering and the decorative arts into separate entities? Kemp (2006: 158) suggests an ancient Egyptian 'lack of awareness or interest in abstract divisions of knowledge'. This is perhaps reflected not only in the tendency towards anonymity of master-craftsmen but also in the creation of lexicographical lists that seem to represent more of a continuum of knowledge rather than a rigid division into distinct categories. The classic word-lists or onomastica (Gardiner 1947, Nims 1950, Osing 1981), were composed from at least the Middle Kingdom onwards (the fragmentary Ramesseum Onomasticon, now in

Berlin, being the earliest). The introduction to the classic example of this genre, the *Onomasticon of Amenemope* (the main physical copy of which is the Golenischeff Papyrus, at the Puskhin Museum in Moscow), states that it is the 'beginning of the teaching for clearing the mind, for instruction of the ignorant and for learning all things that exist ...' (Gardiner 1947: 1). Gardiner claims that it is not merely a list but an attempt to classify phenomena, given that the order runs from such major entities as sky, water and earth, at one extreme, to choice cuts of meat at the other. Within each section there is also a tendency to list from highest/largest down to lowest/smallest, but this hierarchical listing is not particularly informative. In reality these onomastica seem thrown together rather than representing a serious attempt to arrange knowledge coherently and logically together. It is notable that no attempt is made by the text's original author or any of the subsequent scribal copyists to add any explanation or commentary concerning the individual terms, restricting the value of the onomasticon generally to that of a vocabulary list or aide-mémoire for scribes. As Kemp (2006: 71) puts it: 'Ancient knowledge, when not of a practical nature (of the kind: how to build a pyramid and how to behave at table), was essentially the accumulation of names of things, beings and places, together with their associations. "Research" lay in extending the range of associations in areas which we would now term "theology".'

This situation must partly derive from the fact that many of the surviving texts on ostraca and papyri relate to scribal education, which was evidently concerned not only with teaching the writing and reading of the hieratic script but also with the immersion of the scribally trained officials in the official ideology of the royal court; as Assmann (2002: 124) puts it, 'Cultural knowledge, in its central sense as binding norms of behaviour, was encoded in written form. Learning to write meant more than learning to plan, organise and administer; it meant – in a very broad sense – learning to live.'

Papyrus Anastasi I (BM EA1024; Fischer-Elfert 1986), the so-called *Satirical Letter*, allegedly written by a scribe named Hori, suggests that New Kingdom scribes were also expected to have the ability to accomplish a number of complex technological tasks, including the transportation of an obelisk, the excavation of an artificial lake, the construction of a ramp and the erection of a colossal statue. This, in theory at least, elevates the

Egyptian scribe – who may, after all, be the closest equivalent in ancient Egypt to a scholar or scientist – from a mere bureaucrat to a renaissance man sitting at the interface of ancient 'science' and technology.

Egyptian mathematics and scribal education

The surviving examples of ancient Egyptian mathematical texts seem to have been virtually all created as part of the education of apprentice scribes. As Imhausen (2007: 8) puts it: 'These papyri contain collections of problems and their solutions to prepare the scribes for situations they were likely to face in their later work ... While mathematical papyri are extant from two separate periods only, depictions of scribes as accountants (and therefore using mathematics) are evident from all periods, beginning with the Old Kingdom.'

The scribes needed to master not only writing itself but also the basics of accountancy and administration, which would be crucial to them in various aspects of their later careers as bureaucrats, administrators and technical overseers (see Imhausen and Ritter 2004: 72) – grain, land and labour were three aspects of the Egyptian economy during the pharaonic period that frequently had to be quantified by scribes. It is important here to note that mathematics and arithmetic seem not to have been regarded as arcane separate areas only for specialists but as part of the overall scribal 'skilling' process. There is therefore a definite parallel with Cuomo's discussion of *technê*, when she talks about the essential 'teachability' of *technê* in classical Athens: 'The rationale is that, although when it comes to actions experience is not different from *techne*, and *techne* is acquired through experience, unlike experience *techne* has knowledge of the universal and can be taught' (Cuomo 2007: 13). Plato's *Timaeus* conceives of the universe as having been created by *technê*, through the action of the divine craftsman or Demiurge, for which Egyptian myth has a fairly close parallel in the so-called Memphite Theology, preserved on the Shabaqo Stone (*c.* 705 BC, British Museum EA 498), a basalt slab bearing a hieroglyphic inscription in which Ptah, the patron deity of craftsmen, creates all things by pronouncing their names (see Allen 1988).

Egyptian mathematics was evidently taught by means of numerous examples rather than by the use of abstract formulae, so that problems were usually broken down into a repetitive series of smaller calculations.

What kinds of texts have survived? In physical terms, the texts take the form of hieratic papyri, ostraca and one leather document (the Egyptian Mathematical Leather Roll, see Glanville 1927) from the pharaonic period, and a number of demotic papyri from the Ptolemaic period (332-30 BC; see Parker 1972). Most of the more famous individual examples, such as the Rhind and Moscow mathematical papyri (see Robins and Shute 1987 and Struve 1930, respectively, and see Fig. 2.1 here for one

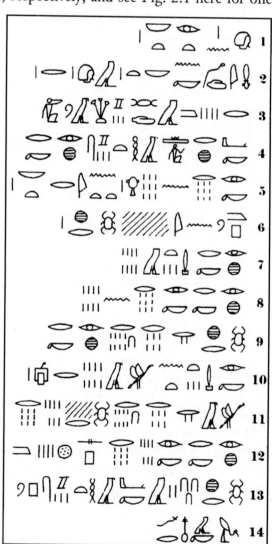

Fig. 2.1. Problem no. 10 in the Moscow mathematical papyrus, showing the method for calculating the area of a semi-circle.

17

of the Moscow problems), were obtained via the art market rather than by excavation, and in fact the set of seven fragments of papyri from the Middle Kingdom settlement of Lahun (Imhausen and Ritter 2004) are the only properly provenanced examples, as they derive from Flinders Petrie's excavations at the site. Shute (2001: 348) remarks that 'the scantiness of the surviving material ... undoubtedly fails to cover the full extent of their knowledge'.

There are two different kinds of Egyptian mathematical texts: 'procedure/problem' types and 'table' types. The procedure texts begin by setting out a specific mathematical problem and then go on to solve it in a series of stages essentially corresponding to the modern concept of an algorithm. In contrast, table texts constitute two-dimensional arrays of numbers that can be assumed to have been used either as aids to the procedure texts or as part of one or more specific real acts of calculation. These tables could in theory have been used repeatedly to look up the answers to individual mathematical problems. In other words, in the absence of formulae, Egyptian scribes learned their mathematics by copying out set examples, replacing the figures with their own. Unlike the Mesopotamian mathematicians perhaps, the Egyptians seem to have been more interested in practicalities than in theory. Nevertheless, certain calculations in the Rhind Papyrus end with the short phrase *mitt pw* ('it is equal'), which is used where calculations could not be exactly matched to proofs.

The Egyptian numerical system was a combination of the decimal and the repetitive. It lacked a symbol for zero, but scribes occasionally left a gap between numbers as though such a sign existed. Numbers were written from the largest to the smallest. The Egyptians' calculation of whole numbers was relatively simple: to multiply by ten, for example, the appropriate hieroglyphs were changed for the next highest, so that ten, for instance, could become one hundred. In other calculations, a sum equal to the desired multiplier was reached by a process of doubling, while the multiplicand was itself doubled as many times as necessary for the multiplier.

Thus the sum 13×19 would be calculated by first deriving the multiplier from the table below, in which $8 + 4 + 1 = 13$:

multiplier		multiplicand			
1	x	19		19	3
2	x	19		38	
4	x	19		76	3
8	x	19		152	3
Total **13**	**x**	**19**		**247**	

Once a number was reached which was equal to half or more of that desired (i.e. 8, in this case, is more than half of 13), no further doubling was needed. The scribe would then tick the relevant lines in the table and add them up, 152 + 76 + 19 = 247, which is the equivalent of 13 × 19. Multiplication tables were therefore replaced by simple tables of duplication, and division was achieved by the reciprocal method, i.e. the repeated halving of the multiplier.

The use of fractions appears to have caused more difficulties, particularly as the Egyptians recognised only those in which the numerator was one, all of which were written by placing the hieroglyph *r* above the relevant number. There were, however, also some special signs for such commonly used fractions as two-thirds, three-quarters, four-fifths and five-sixths, and the Rhind Papyrus is exceptional in presenting a table of fractions in which the numerator is two. Complicated fractions were written by reducing them to two or three separate fractions, the first of which had the smallest possible denominator. Thus two-fifths was written as one-third + one-fifteenth. In calculations fractions were broken down and thus treated as whole numbers.

Mathematics, pyramid building and the calculation of *skd*

Modern surveys of pharaonic and Greco-Roman monuments have enabled much to be deduced concerning the Egyptians' practical use of mathematics, and – at least since the time of Petrie's survey of Giza in 1880-82 – it has been clear that the principles and methods involved in setting out the pyramid complexes (constructed during the period *c.* 2700-1650 BC) were pragmatic rather than mystical (Petrie 1883). From a relatively early date, the Egyptians developed geometrical knowledge on the basis of observation of practical situations. The surviving texts indicate, for instance, that they knew that they could calculate the area of a rectangle by multiplying its length by its width

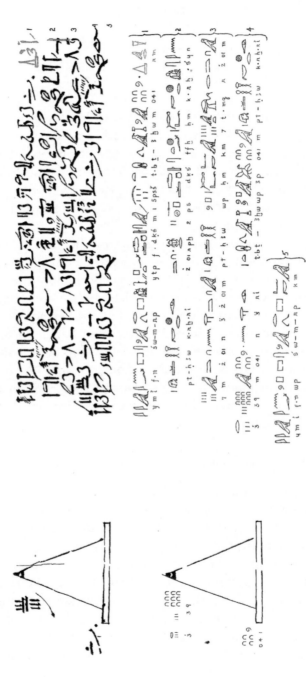

Fig. 2.2. Problem no. 57 in the Rhind Mathematical Papyrus: the height of a pyramid is calculated from the base-length and the *sḳd* (slope).

(which is one of the mathematical problems presented in the Moscow Mathematical Papyrus, see Struve 1930: 37-8). Similarly, they knew that if a triangle was drawn inside the rectangle, having the same length as its sides and the same height as its width, then its area would be half that of the rectangle. Arguably, however, their most significant achievement in geometry was the recognition that the diameter of a circle could be used to calculate its area (problem no. 50 in the Rhind Mathematical Papyrus, see Robins and Shute 1987: 44-6; Gillings 1972: 139-43). They did so by squaring eight-ninths of the diameter's length, thus providing an approximate notional value for π of 3.16 (although opinions differ as to whether Egyptian scribes were aware of the concept of π itself – see, for instance, Robins and Shute 1987, who assume that the Egyptians did know π, and Rossi 2004: 65-7, who argues not only that the Egyptians did not conceive of π but that even Archimedes 'did not think in terms of π as we do today' since much of even Greek mathematics, up to the 2nd century BC, was 'non-arithmetised'). The Egyptians were also able to reckon volumes of many three-dimensional shapes (including the cylinder and pyramid, even when truncated) by using a series of smaller calculations, which, although they lack the elegance of formulae, nevertheless produce correct solutions (e.g. problem no. 10 in the Moscow Mathematical Papyrus, calculating the curved surface of a hemisphere, according to Gillings 1972: 194-201, or a semi-cylinder, according to Miatello 2010).

Mathematics and ancient Egyptian construction engineering

The above discussion centres on the papyri and ostraca that allow us to study Egyptian mathematical exercises, but another approach, taken by Corinna Rossi (2004), is to compare such texts with Egyptian construction engineering, asking the fundamental question: what impact did mathematics have on Egyptian architecture. Rossi's study of the mathematical basis of the pyramids does its best to restrict the mathematics to that which can be proven to have been known in ancient Egypt: the calculation of the volume and the *skd* (slope) of pyramids), especially on the basis of the Rhind and Moscow mathematical papyri (see Fig. 2.2). The *skd* is specifically discussed in problems 56-60 of the Rhind Mathematical Papyrus (Chace et al. 1929: pl. 79), and Gillings

(1972: 212) defines it as 'the inclination of any one of the four triangular faces to the horizontal plane of its base ... measured as so many horizontal units per one vertical unit rise'. Physical proof of the process of planning a specific angle of slope was discovered by Petrie (1892: 11-13, pl. 8) on the corners of Mastaba 17 at Meidum. He found four L-shaped mud-brick walls constructed below ground level at the corners of the monument, each serving as a means of checking the mastaba's slope: the mud-brick walls effectively allowed the architects to first create a zero-line (given the unevenness of the ground on which the mastaba was built), and then draw lines on the walls that showed projections of the correct slope. Rossi (2004: 191-2) points out how this basic set of diagrams ultimately allowed the architects to enlarge the mastaba while maintaining the same slope: 'At some point, two other lines were drawn parallel to the first pair, and the mastaba was enlarged by the short distance between them. In this way, regardless of the depth of the rock bed, the masons could start the construction of a sloping side which would reach the surface at the "right" point.'

Rossi restricts her overall hypothesis concerning pyramid construction to a limited set of aims, allowing her to present a set of basic constructional factors that apply as well to the Great Pyramid as to the small mud-brick pyramidia on New Kingdom private tomb-chapels. Her basic thesis is that the variations in pyramidal form can essentially be related to the choices made by architects between different triangular forms. The value of this approach in terms of the study of the Bent Pyramid of Sneferu at Meidum is that it allows the three basic stages of this engineering project to be viewed objectively as mathematical solutions with common parameters rather than simply as a series of unrelated attempts to achieve a 'true pyramid'. Indeed the concept of the 'true pyramid' as the ultimate aim of Egyptian architects is rendered redundant by adopting the viewpoint that the choice of base-length and slope were essentially mathematical decisions, revolving around about eight 'triplets' (such as the Pythagorean 3-4-5 triplet).

Rossi is not arguing that mathematics dictates the forms of the pyramids, but that the evolution of pyramidal shape and slope can actually be boiled down to a series of simple mathematical choices. This makes it a little more likely that at least one practical aspect of Egyptian technology – architecture and structural engineering – was fundamentally rooted in their scientific knowledge and techniques (primarily mathematics). The distinction between science and technology is sometimes characterised as being analogous to the differences between basic and applied knowledge respectively, but it is surely the case that all knowledge is 'applied' to some degree or other – the crucial thing perhaps is the extent to which developments in knowledge are able to have significant impacts on wide areas of society or economics.

3

Writing: human communication as social technology

More than any other single invention, writing has transformed human consciousness (Walter J. Ong 2002: 77).

The Americans have need of the telephone, but we do not. We have plenty of messenger boys (Sir William Preece, chief engineer, British Post Office, 1878, quoted in Wilkinson 2008: 112).

Introduction

The appearance of *Homo sapiens* is currently dated to around 100,000 BP, and the earliest forms of writing appear to have been developed by the Sumerians at around 3500 BC, so the 'oral' phase of human development was at least twenty times longer than the 'literate' phase. The first writing systems developed by the people of Mesopotamia, Egypt, the Indus valley, Crete and China were more than just the making of meaningful marks, as rock art or cave paintings had been, but the emergence of sufficiently complex codes to allow the spoken word to be physically preserved, recorded and communicated. Walter Ong (2002: 83) suggests that, 'The critical and unique breakthrough into new worlds of knowledge was achieved within human consciousness not when simple semiotic marking was devised but when a coded system of visible marks was invented whereby a writer could determine the exact words that the reader would generate from the text.'

Writing systems are forms of technology that have been so firmly embedded in most human cultures for so many millennia that we can take them for granted to some extent, and fail to give them their full status as extremely sophisticated early technological developments in their own

24

right, quite apart from their enormous implications for the development and dissemination of other technologies. As Jack Goody (1968: 1) points out in one of his earlier discussions of literacy and its consequences: 'even where writers are specifically investigating the differences between "simple" and "advanced" societies, peoples, mentalities, etc., they have neglected to examine the implications of the very feature which is so often used to define the range of societies with which they claim to be dealing, namely, the presence or absence of writing'.

A considerable body of scholarship, particularly in applied linguistics, sociolinguistics and literary studies, has been devoted to the identification and analysis of differences between mental and social structures and behaviour, both before and after the introduction of some form of written script. A real pioneer in this area was Eric Havelock (1963), who discussed the ancient Greek transition from orality to literacy, arguing that this only fully took place with the work of Plato (see also Goody 1977, 1986, 1987, on 'technology of the intellect' in a variety of ancient and modern cultures, as well as Foley 1980 and Chafe 1982). Such crucial areas of culture as religion, law, administration and economics were hugely transformed and shaped by the ability to use writing, even if, as seems likely in the case of Egypt, the literate élite constituted a tiny minority of the population (see Baines and Eyre 1983). According to Goody (1987: 298), 'writing is a mechanism that permits us to change the format of our creative endeavours, the shape of our knowledge, our understanding of the world, and our activities within it'. A good ancient example of the latter was the gradual creation of canonical texts documenting religious rituals (such as the Edfu temple inscriptions in which the daily temple rituals are laboriously recorded, see Fairman 1954), which presumably contributed significantly to the degree of standardisation of state religion throughout Egypt, allowing the same rituals to be performed in different temples throughout the country.

In all kinds of respects, the development of writing in ancient cultures transformed the ways in which individuals observed and understood the particular space and time in which they were situated – place and date automatically acquire greater significance and meaning with the development and proliferation of written documents. One example of this phenomenon, which is discussed at some length by Ong, is the way in which purely orally based cultures appear to have a lack of interest in the measurement of time and the precise dating of people or events: 'Persons whose world view has been formed by high literacy need to remind themselves that in functionally oral cultures the past is not felt as an itemized terrain, peppered with verifiable and disputed "facts" or bits of information. It is the domain of the ancestors, a resonant source for renewing awareness of present existence, which itself is not an itemized terrain either. Orality knows no lists or charts or figures' (Ong 2002: 97). In the context of 'listing' as a precondition or essential component of writing, it is interesting to note that some of the decorated late Predynastic stone palettes seem to prefigure the register composition of early Egyptian art (Davis 1976), signalling a transition from the less coherent organisation of earlier prehistoric art to the codified forms of decorum in the art and writing of the pharaonic period.

Baines (1983: 593) also stresses the impact of the invention of writing systems on the process of memorising and communicating data: 'The initial impact of writing is a huge increase in and elaboration of memory. The literate can extend their communication in space and time, and their memory in compass and duration.' He goes on to argue, however, that literacy is more of a *response* to rapid cultural change than a stimulus to it. Whereas others have stressed the roles that ancient scripts must have played in the development of early states and economies, Baines suggests that the capacity for writing to serve as stimulus for major change is severely limited in ancient cultures, and that it is only in comparatively modern times that the cultural and social effects of the use of the written word have been fully exploited and experienced. Nevertheless, this is simply to state that writing, like many other inventions, was not necessarily instantly influential on its cultural contexts – the full impact of writing was perhaps always more apparent in *mature* literate cultures rather than in those that were still developing at the time that they passed from orality to literacy.

In many of the cultures in which the earliest writing systems developed, the emergence of the full-blown grammatically organised script seems to have been preceded by a phase during which the basic elements of the system were beginning to appear as symbols (and primarily, initially, as logograms or ideograms of various types). This pre-writing (or perhaps even quasi-writing) phase is particularly well-attested in Neolithic Mesopotamia, where three-dimensional clay tokens seem to have initially been used in early economic transactions (see Amiet 1966, Schmandt-Besserat 1978; 1992). The possible link between this early accounting system and the early cuneiform script takes the form of small clay containers (or bullae), originally attached to bales of merchandise, within which sets of clay tokens were sometimes placed; the outer surfaces of the bullae bore impressed signs, some of which corresponded to the tokens and could also be to some extent equated with early Sumerian cuneiform signs (Schmandt-Besserat 1996: 55-85). Schmandt-Besserat's theory has been criticised by some scholars on several grounds, such as the fact that it cannot be clearly proven that anything other than the numbering system actually links the tokens with the earliest writing (i.e. few symbols actually seem to occur in both systems), and the fact that some of the earliest texts actually pre-date some of the tokens. Yoffee (1995: 286) points out that 'While Schmandt-Besserat has certainly demonstrated that the system (or probably several systems) of tokens conveyed meaning in Mesopotamian prehistory, she has not appreciated the difference between these (highly specific) aides memoires and writing as a communication of speech acts. ... Although the first writing in Mesopotamia shows the important, but not exclusively economic, context in which it was devised (i.e. for keeping track of commodities), a cursory look at the cross-cultural evidence provides little justification for a single, simple, and linear progression from various complex iconographic systems to writing.' It can certainly be argued, however, that the initial impetus to create visual symbolic systems seems often to derive from the logistics of economic transactions. Even if Schmandt-Besserat's theory were entirely correct for the origins of writing in Mesopotamia, there is little surviving evidence for any similar process having occurred in ancient Egypt (i.e. no equivalent tokens or bullae have survived from the Predynastic period), although recent evidence from late Predynastic funerary material at Abydos suggests that the early use of Egyptian writing was primarily connected with the counting and labelling of objects (see Postgate et al. 1995).

Abydos and the origins of the Egyptian writing system

For many years it was assumed that the Sumerian cuneiform writing system, the proto-cuneiform version of which emerged in southern Iraq at least as early as 3400 BC (Nissen 1986), preceded Egyptian hieroglyphs, and that the relatively sudden appearance of writing in Egypt, at the end of the fourth millennium BC, was therefore probably the result of increased contact with Near Eastern peoples. Although it seemed unlikely that the Egyptian writing system had evolved directly out of cuneiform, many scholars believed that the basic *idea* of pictographic writing might have come from Mesopotamia by so-called 'stimulus diffusion' (see, for example, Ray 1986, Bard 1992 and Schmandt-Besserat 1981: 323-4).

However, archaeological discoveries at Abydos have provided insights into the early emergence of the Egyptian writing system, suggesting not only that the origins of the script almost certainly lie much further back than was previously thought, but also that the purpose they initially served was economic rather than ritualistic. In 1988, the German Archaeological Institute excavated tomb U-j at Abydos, the impressive burial of an early élite individual (probably a local ruler who held the name Scorpion) dating to the early Naqada III period (*c.* 3200 BC; see Boehmer et al. 1993 and Dreyer 1993), which was by far the largest tomb in the late Predynastic Cemetery U. As with the majority of the earliest inhumations at Abydos, the wood, matting and mud-brick superstructure of the burial had largely deteriorated, but its substructure comprised a large (9.1 x 7.3m) rectangular mud-brick-lined pit containing twelve individual chambers separated by mud-brick walls. The surviving material in one of these rooms included about 150 small labels carved from wood, bone and ivory, which appear to bear clearly recognisable hieroglyphs consisting of numbers, commodities and possibly also place-names or royal agricultural estates (see Fig. 3.1). The importance of these hieroglyphic labels is that they are almost certainly not just pictorial signs ('ideograms/logograms'), which would represent a much more basic stage in the history of the script; many of them are representations of sounds in the spoken language ('phonograms'), a stage in the development of the script that was not thought to have occurred until at least the 1st Dynasty (see, for instance, Kaplony 1963, for this earlier view). The labels have been identified as phonetic symbols because some of them appear to spell out the names of well-known towns frequently mentioned in later inscriptions, such as Buto and Bubastis (Dreyer 1998). It therefore seems that the bureaucrats employed by the earliest rulers at Abydos – at least 200 years before the 1st Dynasty

Fig. 3.1. Inscribed labels from tomb U-j at Abydos, *c.* 3200 BC (Egyptian Museum, Cairo, each measuring 1-2cm²).

– were already using a sophisticated form of Egyptian script involving phonetic signs as well as ideograms (Kahl 2002-4, Morenz 2004).

Early potmarks – is an *aide-mémoire* a writing system?

Another category of evidence that has been regarded as potentially relevant to the 'prehistory' of the Egyptian writing system is the corpus of Predynastic and Early Dynastic potmarks that have survived on sherds excavated at many early sites in both Upper and Lower Egypt (see Helck 1990, van den Brink 1992 and Bréand 2005). The earliest of the potmarks appear at some sites in the Naqada I period (*c.* 4000-3600; see, for instance, Bréand 2005: 17 for a discussion of early examples from Adaïma) and the latest date to the end of the 1st Dynasty. Although there is not yet any general consensus as to the purpose and meaning of these early potmarks, some scholars have argued that they may have functioned as *aides-mémoire* applied by Predynastic and Early Dynastic potters in order to control the production of certain vessels. As Bréand (2009: 61) proposes, 'Within the framework of the contemporary emergence of hieroglyphic writing – which is concomitant with the formation of a central court that uses an official system of counting, which the tags containing numerals in Tomb U-j attest – this example of a non-official system of counting has evolved as an alternative

Selected Gebel el-Asr non-numerical marks

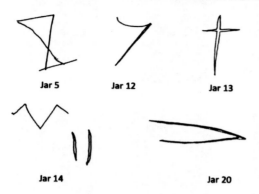

Jar 5   Jar 12   Jar 13

Jar 14   Jar 20

Fig. 3.2. A selection of five potmarks on Middle Kingdom Marl-C storage jars from Quartz Ridge, Gebel el-Asr.

system of communication which cannot be deciphered outside of its context of use, and therefore cannot be considered as a transcription of hieroglyphic signs.' In other words, the system of symbols incised on late Predynastic pots before firing cannot be regarded as an early stage in the development of the hieroglyphic writing system because it appears to be a largely separate and distinct method of communication. More than 7000 late Predynastic and Early Dynastic potmarks are currently known; although they include some signs that are very similar to contemporary hieroglyphs, most appear to be non-linguistic signs and they never seem to be used to represent spoken language. Potmarks, which continue in use throughout the pharaonic and Greco-Roman periods, always appear to be a parallel system of symbols existing alongside hieroglyphics, with only very small areas of overlap (see, for instance, Aston 2009, Gallorini 2009, Shaw 2009; see Fig. 3.2).

Writing as a technological choice in Egypt and elsewhere

It may often seem that writing was a single inevitable visual communication strategy for many early cultures, yet the *khipu* system of communication developed by the Inca (comprising knotted cords containing numeric and other values encoded in a base ten positional system), for instance, suggests that there have certainly been other possible trajectories, and that the emergence of written sign-based forms of communication was a technological choice rather than a given. It is also clear that other forms of visual communication have thrived in certain circumstances alongside the canonical writing systems, sometimes using different media, as we have already seen with the late Predynastic and Early Dynastic potmarking system above (see Haring and Kaper 2009 and Andrassy et al. 2009 for discussions of other Egyptian 'non-textual marking systems', such as quarry marks and textile marks during the pharaonic period); this re-emphasises the fact that forms of communication emerge and adapt in response to cultural and technical needs, and that different methods of communication are generally deliberately chosen, while others may have been rejected. Since new technologies are usually created or adopted in order to solve particular problems or to enhance existing equipment and expertise, we must ask: for what purpose was the Egyptian hieroglyphic script initially used?

While there has been general agreement for some time that the Mesopotamian cuneiform system was developed primarily as an accounting and administrative tool (and this is simply reinforced by Schmandt-Besserat's demonstration of the possible links between early tokens and the emerging cuneiform signs, even if this only constitutes *functional* rather than evolutionary overlap), there has been less consensus on the initial roles played by other writing systems, such as those used by the Egyptians and the early Chinese. Postgate et al. (1995), however, present a persuasive argument, bearing in mind all the possible problems posed by the varying survivability of different writing materials, that at least four of the major early scripts (from Mesopotamia, China, Egypt and Mesoamerica) have primarily utilitarian origins, although they admit that, in addition 'some components of the different scripts may have originated in ceremonial symbols, or that written texts may have served to display the agenda of a political élite' (Postgate et al. 1995: 479).

'Craft literacy': the mobility and exploitation of scribes as technicians

As noted above, in the introduction to this chapter, a great deal has been written about the social restrictions surrounding the writing systems of ancient Egypt, primarily in terms of the likely limited audience for early texts, given the potentially small percentage of the population that could read or write, even at the height of pharaonic culture (Baines 1983, Baines and Eyre 1983). There is however a more directly technological sense in which the hieroglyphic, hieratic and demotic writing systems may have been culturally and socially circumscribed. Havelock (1963) noted that, in many cultures, the introduction of writing quickly leads to the development of 'craft literacy', whereby a professional scribe can be hired by others to write a particular document, just as a carpenter might be hired to make a chair or coffin. A much more recent example of this form of craft-literacy is provided by the West African kingdom of Mali, where *karamokos* (effectively professional writers/teachers) plied their trade from medieval times until the 20th century (Goody 1968: 169-71). As Ong (2002: 93) points out, 'At such a craft-literacy stage, there is no need for an individual to know reading and writing any more than any other trade. Only around Plato's time in ancient Greece, more than three centuries after the introduction of the Greek alphabet, was this stage transcended when writing was finally diffused through the Greek population and interiorised enough to affect thought processes generally.'

Another situation in which scribes can be perceived not simply as writers but as a group of élite craftsmen creating what might be defined as a luxury product, is the context of diplomatic contacts between the royal courts of the ancient Near East. The complex system of international correspondence that had developed in the Near East by the Late Bronze Age, primarily using the Akkadian cuneiform script as a *littera franca*, was influential not only in taking written communication onto another level (particularly in terms of translation to and from different languages and scripts), but also as part of a process by which scribes, and the documents they produced, effectively mediated between different élite groupings. Inevitably, some scribes – like doctors, sculptors, and other in-demand professionals – were sent from one royal court to another, in order to facilitate the reading and writing of foreign scripts. In the Maya culture, the capture of scribes from defeated groups was part of the process by which they were rendered ungovernable – this emphasises the degree to which ancient states and polities in many cultures relied on élite scribes and bureaucrats generally for basic functioning, in situations of highly restricted literacy (see Johnston 2001).

For the Late Bronze Age, there is a great deal of archaeological and textual evidence for communities of scribes transplanted into a foreign royal court. The majority of the 380 clay cuneiform tablets (e.g. Fig. 3.3)

3. Writing: human communication as social technology

Fig. 3.3. Cuneiform letter from Amarna, written by Tushratta, ruler of Mitanni, to Amenhotep III of Egypt, 18th Dynasty, *c*. 1360 BC; unusually, it is annotated in hieratic for archival purposes, indicating that it dates to year 36 of an unspecified ruler, presumably Amenhotep III (British Museum, WA29793, 9 x 7cm).

in the well-known archive found in and around the Records Office at Amarna were letters forming part of the royal diplomatic correspondence with other states in western Asia and the east Mediterranean (in the period from *c*. 1360 to 1334 BC). Shlomo Izre'el, however, has published the 32 so-called 'scholarly tablets' from the archive, providing some of the strongest evidence for the existence of a group of 'cuneiform scribes' living within the community at Amarna, perhaps on a semi-permanent basis (Izre'el 1997). The tablets include such genres as lexical lists, syllabaries, vocabularies, myths, and historical or literary narratives. The scribes who produced this range of texts must either have been Egyptian scribes who had acquired a close familiarity with the cuneiform script and associated languages through direct contact with foreigners, or perhaps non-Egyptian scribes sent to Amarna by their respective royal employers. In particular, Izre'el (1997: 12) argues that 'The main site of scribal learning is, as far as we know, the site of the Records Office, where tablets – including letters – were kept ... it is here that students exercised cuneiform writing, learned Akkadian words and phrases, and were trained in reading Akkadian literature'. In addition, Izre'el (1997: 9) points out that several blank, uninscribed clay tablets (now at the Ashmolean and the British Museum) were also found in the central city at Amarna, providing further evidence that an Akkadian-literate scribal community was located there, rather than just an archive.

Izre'el (1997: 12) also argues that, in addition to Egyptian scribes learning Akkadian, there must have been 'guest students from abroad' sent by other Near Eastern courts, and that there were almost certainly also 'local cuneiform schools in Canaan' (Kossmann 1994, Izre'el 1995). Von Damow (2004) proposes that such cuneiform-literate scribes were not writing the Akkadian language but simply using Akkadian signs to represent what was essentially their own Canaanite language, while Wilhelm (1984) has suggested that similarities between the texts on cuneiform tablets found at Amarna and Hattuša perhaps indicate that Hittites were at least partially responsible for teaching Akkadian cuneiform to Egyptian scribes.

The petrographic analyses of about 300 of the Amarna tablets by Yuval Goren et al. (2004) have also been highly influential in filling in some of the cultural context of such groups of 'expatriate' scribes. Using highly specialised forms of petrography, designed specifically to minimise damage to the tablets, Goren has tracked down the provenances of the tablets, demonstrating in addition that some letters, made of local Egyptian clay, were probably archival duplicates of those actually received or sent. As far as the 'scholarly tablets' are concerned, Goren has been able to show that they were primarily made from Egyptian clay – although this does not solve the question of whether the scribal school was populated primarily by Egyptian scribes or by foreign counterparts, it at least indicates the extent to which Egyptians embraced the cuneiform technology that was so alien to their traditional use of papyrus and brush.

Such mobility and versatility, although relatively new to Egyptian scribes, as Egypt fully entered the cosmopolitan world of the Near East in the New Kingdom, was undoubtedly already much more a part of the routine of Near Eastern scribes, given the more heterogeneous nature of western Asiatic cultures and empires – certainly by the Assyrian period it became common to see depictions of pairs of scribes, one writing cuneiform script on a tablet or board and the other writing Aramaic on a sheet of papyrus (see, for instance, Wiseman 1955: pl. III.2), and the term *sepiru* – borrowed from Aramaic – was used in Babylon at this date to refer to bilingual administrators (Pearce 1999). It should not be forgotten, however, that clay tablets incised with cursive hieroglyphic script, have been found at Ayn Asil, an Old Kingdom settlement in the Dakhla oasis, indicating that surprisingly, about a thousand years earlier than the Amarna correspondence, at least one group of Egyptians had flirted with this alternative writing medium (see Soukiassian 1997). Intriguingly, there is also some evidence for the adoption of a set of exotic symbols incorporated into some Assyrian inscriptions dating to the reigns of Sargon II and Esarhaddon (e.g. British Museum WA 91027: 'Lord Aberdeen's Black Stone', from the time of Esarhaddon), which may be an attempt by the Assyrian scribes and élite to imitate hieroglyphic writing (see Finkel and Reade 1996). As Radner (2009: 225) puts it 'The hieroglyphs ... cannot have failed to impress the members of a cultural environment that highly valued tradition and exclusivity in a writing system as a parallel to their own ancient cuneiform tradition, especially at a time when palaeography was a favourite and lively discipline of Assyrian cuneiform scribes'. The other side of this particular coin is demonstrated by the 19th-Dynasty London Medical Papyrus, which includes six incantations in northwest Semitic languages and one said to be in some form of Minoan language, transcribed into a syllabic form of Egyptian (see Grapow et al. 1958: 360, 434-5, Steiner 1992). These foreign spells were properly understood and integrated into the papyrus itself, as demonstrated by the interpolation of some Egyptian sentences amid the Semitic sections. The degree of religious integration here, between Egyptian and Syro-Palestinian ritual is indicated by a reference in one of the Semitic spells to the god Amun as *rabunna* ('our lord') associated with 'my mother Ishtar'. The reason for this particular combination of Egyptian and Asiatic protective spells is perhaps indicated by the fact that the disease itself is described by the Semitic word *ḥmktw* ('strangulation'), which suggests that the affliction may have been encountered outside Egypt, thus requiring powerful Asiatic rituals to deal with it effectively.

For the early Iron Age, Radner (2009) discusses the reasonably extensive evidence for Egyptian scribes resident in the Assyrian court from the 8th to 6th centuries BC. One important source for this period is a set of documents from Nimrud listing wine rations from the reign of Adad-

Nirari III to that of Shalmaneser IV (*c.* 810-773 BC), which includes references to many Egyptian craftworkers, including scribes, 'exported' to Assyria, even before Egypt had been conquered by Ashurbanipal in the early 7th century BC (Kinnier Wilson 1972, Zaccagnini 1983). From the reigns of Esarhaddon and Ashurbanipal alone, there are more than 1300 surviving examples of letters and reports received by the Assyrian court, which suggests an extremely busy bureaucratic centre (Radner 2009: 221). It is interesting to speculate how Egyptian scribes would have ended up at the Assyrian court at this date, and although Kinnier Wilson (1972: 93) suggests that they were somehow prisoners of war captured during Assyrian campaigns in Syria-Palestine, Zaccagnini (1983: 260) puts forward the more likely explanation that individual Egyptian artisans, including scribes, were already 'possibly fleeing from their original work-place in search of better jobs abroad', thus suggesting a degree of spontaneous personal mobility, rather than the enforced movement that is usually assumed. Zaccagnini (1983: 260) goes on to suggest that the situation in terms of mobility of artisans and professionals may have constituted a state of transition in the 1st millennium: 'From a series of scattered sources, all we can propose with a reasonable degree of confidence is that in the course of the first millennium BC there was an emērgence of new forms of the organization and employment of professional labor which do not seem to have existed in the third and second millennia BC.'

One Assyrian text dated to the period shortly after Esarhaddon's defeat of Egypt in 671 BC comprises a list of specialised scholars resident at the Assyrian court, including astrologers, physicians, exorcists, diviners, and lamenters, who (according to Radner 2009: 223) represent the five traditional branches of Mesopotamian scholarship. The list also includes three 'bird-watchers' (i.e. augurers, probably Syro-Anatolian in origin), three Egyptian scribes, and three *ḫarṭibē* (the latter being an Assyrian term for Egyptian ritual experts of some kind). The *ḫarṭibē* only seem to appear at the Assyrian court after Esarhaddon's conquest of Egypt, and indeed a list of specialists moved to Assyria after the defeat of Memphis includes 'exorcists, *ḫarṭibē* [...], veterinary surgeons, Egyptian scribes, [...], snake charmers' (Onasch 1994: I, 31-2). On the basis of these lists, it seems that the Egyptian specialisms that were most appreciated and exploited at the Egyptian court were dream interpretation (perhaps contributing to the increase in dream oracles in Ashurbanipal's reign) and magico-medical expertise. As Radner (2009: 225) puts it: 'While structurally the approach of Egyptian and Mesopotamian ritual experts had much in common, we can take it for granted that the Egyptian way of purifying and divining will have differed in detail from the routines of the Assyrian and Babylonian experts but most important of all the language in which incantations and prayers were performed was of course Egyptian, as were the gods the prayers were addressed to.'

This well-attested exchange of documents and scribes across the Near East would surely have not only formed part of the process of technology transfer in the late 2nd and 1st millennia (see Moorey 2001 and Shortland 2004), but would also presumably have been the means by which a great deal of technical know-how was communicated and disseminated, i.e. via texts and highly educated scholars rather than simply by the physical import and export of skilled craftworkers, as was probably the case in the 2nd millennium BC.

Discussion

Writing, therefore, can be seen to be initially fundamental as a kind of 'enabling' technology in itself, during the emergence of Egyptian civilisation in the late 4th millennium BC, providing the intellectual basis for later innovations and technological adaptations. But it can also be recognised as an important component in the process by which Egyptians exchanged ideas with other cultures in western Asia and the east Mediterranean, particularly at the beginning of the Late Bronze Age, when technologies and craftsmen were spreading more widely across western Asia and north Africa. As Moorey (2001: 6) points out, language and writing clearly reflect this process in the lexicography of technology: 'The impact of the technology of one region on that of another is likely to be most vividly indicated by the technical terms of foreign origin'. This observation is borne out by the work of archaeologists in the Nabta Playa-Kiseiba region of the eastern Sahara, in southwestern Egypt – sites in this area have yielded sherds from early Holocene pottery vessels, which are among the earliest ceramics in Africa. They make the point that 'the terminology associated with cattle raising in the northern Sudanic division of the Nilo-Saharan languages was established before

8500 BC, perhaps around the same time that the first pottery-making registered in the lexical data' (Jórdeczka et al. 2011: 112). Even before language survives in written form, it forms an integral part of cultural packages associated with the spread of certain types of material culture, technology and subsistence pattern (see, for instance, Ehret 1978 and 2006). However, it is only with the emergence of large quantities of textual evidence in the Late Bronze Age that the written word begins to provide crucial insights into technology transfer and the mobility of craftworkers in northeast Africa and the eastern Mediterranean.

Medicine, magic and pharmacy: the fusion of science and art

Without art, science would be as useless as a pair of high forceps in the hands of a plumber. Without science, art would become a crude mess of folklore and emotional quackery. The truth of art keeps science from becoming inhuman, and the truth of science keeps art from becoming ridiculous (Raymond Chandler, 19 February 1938; published as Chandler 1976: 7).

Problems in interpreting ancient medical systems and texts

This chapter examines the fields of medicine, magic and pharmacy in ancient Egypt, and explores the degree to which a single area of Egyptian technical ability and thought incorporated several aspects of culture that would appear, to modern eyes, to be incompatible – science, religion and magic. To what extent can Egyptian medicine be regarded as a coherent, organised system of thought rather than a largely arbitrary mass of traditional remedies and superstitions? Longrigg (1998: 18), for instance, argues that Egyptian and Mesopotamian physicians regarded diseases as 'manifestations of the anger of the gods', in contrast to the 'rational and theoretical systems of medicine free from magical and religious elements' practised by the Greeks. Weeks (1976-8: 297), on the other hand, points out that 'The arrangement and combination of drugs in P. Ebers suggest that drugs were systematically applied in the treatment of medical disorders by persons whose knowledge of *materia medica* was more sophisticated than some writers on ancient medicine have previously thought ... They reflect a higher degree of rational and empirical thought than we have given them credit for.'

The field of ancient Egyptian medicine might appear to have been well covered by publications from the mid- to late 20th century, which are primarily compendia of less than a dozen major texts identified as medical in nature (e.g. Grapow et al. 1954-73 and Bardinet 1995), as well as by more popularly targeted publications (e.g. Nunn 1996 and Halioua and Ziskind 2005). However, this area of Egyptian technology, in its broadest sense, remains a potentially fruitful source of potential insights into Egyptian thought and 'science'.

The so-called 'medical' papyri

A number of surviving papyri (fourteen relatively complete examples and several fragments) provide information concerning the Egyptians' knowledge of healing and the nature of the human body (see Bardinet 1995 for the most recent translations of each; in the discussion below, earlier translations are also cited). Such texts may have been housed in temple archives (the *pr ʿnḫ*, or 'house of life'), although the only evidence for this is the assertion of the Greek physician Galen (*c.* 129-99 AD), in volume two of his *De compositione medicamentorum*, that the ancient temple archives at Memphis were being consulted by Greek and Roman doctors of his own time (Ghalioungui 1973: 66).

The earliest surviving example of an Egyptian medical text is the 12th-Dynasty Lahun Medical Papyrus (Petrie Museum, UC 32057; *c.* 2100-1900 BC; Griffith 1898: 5-11, pls 5-6, Collier and Quirke 2004: 58-64), which may also be the original source for the later Ramesseum IV-V and Carlsberg VIII papyri (Gardiner 1955 and Iversen 1939 respectively). It deals mainly with gynaecological ailments, particularly issues relating to the womb, fertility and contraception. The Kahun settlement has also yielded a few other papyri relating to the healing process, including one comprising prescriptions for treating animals (UC 32036; Collier and Quirke 2004: 54-7).

The 18th-Dynasty Ebers Medical Papyrus (University of Leipzig; *c.* 1555 BC) is the longest and probably also the best-known textual source for Egyptian medicine; it was originally over 20m long and consisted simply of a list of some 876 prescriptions and remedies for such ailments as wounds, stomach complaints, gynaecological problems and skin irritations. The Ebers Papyrus would appear to have already been well translated and analysed by such scholars as Wreszinski (1913), Ebbell

(1937), Ghalioungui (1987) and Bardinet (1995: 251-374), but in reality recent research suggests that more can be extracted from this document by using innovative techniques of analysis. Fukagawa (2011), for instance, has taken a statistical approach to its terminology, signalling the need to deal with these fragmentary texts relating to Egyptian medicine in a more consciously 'scientific' and positivist fashion.

The early 18th-Dynasty Edwin Smith Medical Papyrus (New York Academy of Medicine; *c.* 1600 BC; Westendorf 1966, Bardinet 1995: 493-522), possibly deriving from the same tomb as the Ebers Papyrus, was once thought to be the work of a military surgeon, but recent opinion suggests that its author may have been a doctor associated with a workforce concerned with stone masonry construction (e.g. Brandt-Rauf and Brandt-Rauf 1987). The text deals mainly with such problems as broken bones, dislocations and crushings, dividing its forty-eight cases into three classes: 'an ailment which I will treat', 'an ailment with which I will contend' and an 'ailment not to be treated'. The symptoms of each case are described and where possible a remedy prescribed. Although it cannot be claimed that the writer fully understood the concept of the circulation of the blood, he clearly recognised that the condition of the heart could be judged by the pulse (as with section 854a of the Ebers Papyrus, quoted above): 'The counting of anything with the fingers [is done] to recognise the way the heart goes. There are vessels in it leading to every part of the body ... When a Sekhmet priest, any *swnw* doctor ... puts his fingers to the head ... to the two hands, to the place of the heart ... it speaks ... in every vessel, every part of the body' (Smith Papyrus, section 1: Bardinet 1995: 493-4).

The 18th-Dynasty Hearst Papyrus (University of California; *c.* 1550 BC; Wreszinski 1912, Bardinet 1995: 375-408) is inscribed with 260 prescriptions, a number of which deal with broken bones and bites (including that of the hippopotamus). Prescriptions such as those described in the papyri listed here were made up in proportions according to fractions based on parts of the eye of Horus, each part symbolising a fraction from 1/64 to 1/2.

The 19th-Dynasty Berlin Papyrus (Berlin 3038; *c.* 1250 BC; Wreszinski 1909; Bardinet 1995: 409-36), which comprises over 204 paragraphs, was discovered in a pottery vessel buried over 3m below the surface of the sand in the Saqqara region. Consisting, like the Kahun papyrus, primarily of gynaecological remedies and diagnoses, it is the only surviving medical text that preserves a reference to the scribe who composed it, described as 'scribe of the sacred writings, chief of excellent physicians (*swnw*), [who made] the book'. A smaller, slightly earlier, medical papyrus at Berlin Museum (Berlin 3027) dates to the 18th Dynasty and has the title 'book of protection for mother and child'.

The 30th-Dynasty Brooklyn Papyrus (Brooklyn Museum 47.218.48 and 47.218.85; Sauneron 1989, Bardinet 1995: 523-46) deals with snake bites and scorpion stings at great length, while the Chester Beatty VI Papyrus (British Museum; *c.* 1200 BC; Bardinet 1995: 455-60) is concerned only with ailments relating to the anus. The London Medical Papyrus (Wreszinski 1912, Bardinet 1995: 483-92) is one of the best examples of the Egyptian three-pronged approach to healing, which might be described as holistic in modern terms. It consists of a combination of magical spells, rituals and practical prescriptions, all of which would have presumably been considered equally essential to the recovery of the patient.

Interpreting Egyptian 'medical' texts

One of the main problems with the surviving texts concerning Egyptian medicine is that the majority essentially seem to list prescriptions rather than providing direct insights into medical thinking and principles, including such features as pharmacotherapy, diagnosis, prognosis, pathology, and aetiology. This, however, takes us back to the fundamental problem discussed at the beginning of Chapter 2: should we analyse ancient scientific or technological texts by means of modern terms (which might be considered inappropriate or anachronistic) or should we attempt to discuss them via the ancient terms and ideas (which we may be misunderstanding or misinterpreting). How legitimate or feasible is it to attempt to locate or identify such recently defined phenomena as diagnosis and aetiology in an ancient medical system, when such terms might not be applicable or relevant to the cultural construction being studied?

The problem is expressed very clearly by Fukagawa (2011: 18) when he discusses Greek, Chinese and Ayurvedic medicine in an attempt to place ancient Egyptian medicine in a broader cultural context: 'The notion of bodily vital force, that also plays an important role in the medicines of the three cultures, is called *pneuma* in Greek, *qi* in Chinese and *prana* in Ayurveda. There are similarities among these, but misconceptions may occur when the significance of their differences is not understood. The translation of these terms into the western concept of "energy", for instance, can lead to obvious misunderstandings for someone who has no access to ancient or traditional culture.' In other words, cross-cultural comparisons or interpretations of ancient systems of medicine must be based not only on secure translations but also on a sufficiently deep knowledge of the full cultural context of each medical system, so as to avoid erroneous assumptions concerning similarities or differences in medical approaches.

Lloyd (2004: 30) has also discussed this issue with regard to ancient Chinese and Greek medical science and knowledge, pointing out that 'where the Greeks generally focused on the study of structures and organisms, in China the emphasis was more often on processes, on interaction, on resonances'. In other words, this is not simply a terminological problem. It delves much deeper into the basic approaches that ancient and modern cultures take to the human body, the way that the body operates, and such important concepts as the 'well-being' of the body, which medicine usually seeks to maintain or achieve, but which may be defined very differently in different cultures' medical systems (themselves inevitably influenced by idiosyncratic beliefs and attitudes, see Rautman 2000, Meskell and Joyce 2003). A good instance of this kind of difficulty in the study of Egyptian medicine is the question of how the Egyptian terms *mt* (pl. *mtw*) and *wḫd* (pl. *wḫdw*) should be translated. The term *mtw* appears in the Ebers, Hearst and Berlin papyri and is frequently translated as 'vessels', although it also appears in contexts suggesting that it refers not only to blood vessels but also to tendons, muscles, and perhaps nerves, as well as other ducts passing through the body. The fact that it refers to conduits of some kind is suggested partly by the fact that disease and various physical substances (air, semen, water, blood and urine) are said to pass through the *mtw*. The term *wḫdw* is also frequently used in the Ebers Papyrus, and the most common translation is 'corruption'; thus Ritner (2000: 107-8) translates the title of the Berlin Medical papyrus 3038 as 'Book for driving out corruption (*wḫdw*) from all the limbs of a man'. The ways in which these two crucial terms are translated vary from one scholar to another, since their evident specificity within the Egyptian conceptualisation of the human body and disease makes it extremely difficult to find modern equivalents.

The nature of Egyptian medicine

Egyptian medicine was a mixture of magical and religious spells with remedies based on close study of patients, and any attempt to impose the modern distinction between 'magic' and 'medicine' is likely to confuse the picture. Thus, modern western cultures tend to distinguish clearly between the use of prayers, medicine or 'magic', whereas in ancient Egypt these three categories were regarded as overlapping and complementary. The Egyptians might attempt to solve a single problem, whether a disease or a hated rival, by using a mixture of magical rituals or treatments (*sšꜥw*), medicinal prescriptions (*pḫrt*) and religious texts (*rw*). This combination appears strange from the perspective of modern western chemo-therapeutic medicine, but the latter has only become the dominant paradigm for medicine in relatively recent times. As Ritner (2001: 326) has pointed out, the dearth of holistic studies of Egyptian magico-medicine derives at least in part from blinkered Egyptological attitudes to the topic: 'rational treatments have been the focus of detailed study, while magical aspects are often marginalised and their significance to the ancient audience is undervalued'.

Although Greek and Roman medical systems began to lay the foundations for modern scientific medicine, they were to some extent rooted, like much of ancient medicine, in a world-view whereby science and religion were not yet regarded as opposites, but rather as complementary means to understanding the nature of humanity and the cosmos. Brisson (2000: 45) points out the importance of the temple as home to a central tradition of Greek medicine: 'Moreover two aspects helped to reconcile "rational" medicine and temple medicine. The priests used medications, dietary prescriptions and phlebotomy. Certain "rationalist" doctors, for their part, used some of the same terms that also appeared in religious contexts, for example "purification".'

In the Ptolemaic period (332-30 BC) Greek forms of medicine appear to have been combined with those of the Egyptians, leading to a huge upsurge of medical knowledge in Alexandria in particular, evidently fuelled in part by royal patronage. Ptolemy II and III seem to have been particularly instrumental in providing bodies of criminals for vivisection, thus aiding the studies of anatomists such as Herophilus and Erasistratus (see Lloyd 1975, von Staden 1989 and Vallance 2000: 96-7), who were able to identify the nervous system and the blood-vascular system. However, a crucial distinction needs to be made between 'rational' medicine and truly scientific medicine, given that the kind of rational medicine promoted by Herophilus in the first half of the 3rd century BC not only continued in very much the same way until late antiquity but also still incorporated many aspects of 'pre-scientific' medicine – advances in understanding of human anatomy and physiology were not easily converted into real achievements in therapy and treatment of ailments (Pellegrin 2000: 430-2). In other words, truly scientific medicine, in something like the modern sense of the phrase, did not begin to be practised until the time of Galen in the mid-2nd century AD.

It was also in the Ptolemaic period that the deified Imhotep, long closely linked with Egyptian medicine, became identified with the Greek god Asklepios, and the Asklepieion at Saqqara was established as a centre for healing. Patients sometimes also stayed overnight in so-called incubation chambers at such temples, as in the cult-place of Bes at Saqqara, in the hope of receiving a cure through divinely inspired dreams. From the Late Period (747-332 BC) onwards, sanatoria were often attached to major temples, such as the cult-centre of Hathor at Dendera (Daumas 1956).

Magic (ḥkꜣ) as an integral part of medical 'science'

A somewhat artificial distinction is usually made between the religious texts in Egyptian tombs and temples and the 'magical texts' or 'spells' that were intended to solve the everyday problems of individuals. Different types of Egyptian magical texts range from the Book of Gates in New Kingdom royal tombs (Hornung 1999, Wiebach-Koepke 2003) to curses inscribed on ostraca (e.g. O. Armytage 6-9, see Shorter 1936), or spells to cure such ailments as snake bites or scorpion stings (e.g. O. Colin Campbell 14, see McDowell 1993: 18-19, pls XVIII-IXa), but all of them would have presumably been regarded by the Egyptians as roughly comparable methods of gaining divine/supernatural assistance for human problems. All employed *ḥkʒ* (which can be defined as something like divine energy and knowledge of magic), a force that was manifested in the form of the god Heka (Velde 1970). The latter was one of the three aspects of primeval potency (Heka, Hu and Sia) that empowered the creator-god at the beginning of time.

The royal uraeus, perhaps the most vivid symbol of the pharaoh's power, was sometimes described as *wrt ḥkʒw*: 'great of magic', while the king himself, from at least the Old Kingdom onwards, was thought to resemble the gods in having access to the power of Heka, Hu and Sia (Silverman 1991: 65). Probably the best-known literary description of the practice of magic in Egypt is a fictional narrative composed in the Middle Kingdom (2055-1650 BC) and preserved on the 18th-Dynasty Papyrus Westcar (P. Berlin 3033, Blackman 1988). This text describes various marvels performed by the magicians Djadjaemankh and Djedi at the courts of Sneferu and Khufu in the 4th Dynasty (2613-2494 BC). Whereas magic, in the modern sense of the word, has become relatively peripheral to the established religions, in ancient Egypt it lay at the very heart of religious ritual and liturgy. This, however, has not always been properly recognised, and as Ritner (1993: 4-5) points out: 'Bounded by religion on the one hand, and on the other by medicine, magic has been considered inferior to both and has often received only perfunctory treatment in the study of either.'

Since magic was above all the means by which the restoration of all forms of cosmic order and harmony could be ensured, it was not surprisingly considered to be essential to 'medical' restoration of human well-being. As in many other cultures the techniques employed by Egyptian magicians and physicians were frequently based on the idea of imitation – the belief that the replication of a name, image or mythical event could produce an effect in the real world (see Shirakawa 2006). The imitation of names meant that verbal trickery, such as puns, metaphors and acrostics, were regarded as powerful forms of magic rather than simply literary skills – according to Assmann (2001: 87), 'wordplay was regarded as a highly serious and controlled use of language'. In the case of the execration texts, the act of smashing ostraca or figurines bearing the names of enemies was considered to be an effective way of thwarting them. Similarly, the creation of statuettes or figurines of gods or enemies, which could then be either propitiated or mutilated, was regarded as an effective way of gaining control over evil forces. In a sophisticated combination of verbal, visual and physical imitation, it was believed that water poured over *cippi* of Horus (stelae depicting Horus the child defeating snakes, scorpions and other dangers) would confer healing on those who drank it (Jelinkova-Reymond 1956, Ritner 1989). The most common cure for maladies was probably the amulet or the magic spell rather than medical prescriptions alone (see Pinch 1994: 104-19), since many illnesses tended to be regarded as the result of malignant influences or incorrect behaviour.

Magico-medical practitioners

The overlap between science and religion in ancient Egypt is also apparent in the process of identifying individuals and professions connected with healing and bodily well-being. At least as early as the 3rd Dynasty (2686-2613 BC), there were already individuals who practised as healers of some kind, for whom the term *swnw* was used. One of the reasons that the term *swnw* is thought to come closest to the idea of a doctor or physician is that it survives with roughly this sense in the Coptic word *saein*. There are, however, also several texts in which the word would most rationally be translated as 'herbalist' or 'pharmacist' (e.g. Ebers Papyrus 188, see Bardinet 1995: 276). There are also a number of administrative titles (*ḫrp*, *ḥry*, *imy-r*, *sḥd* and *wr swnw*) suggesting a hierarchy among *swnw* from at least the Old Kingdom onwards.

The titles of Hesyra (Fig. 4.1), an official of the time of the 3rd-Dynasty ruler Djoser (2667-2648 BC), included the posts of *wr ibhy* ('chief of those who take care of teeth') and *wr swnw* ('chief of physicians'). His mastaba tomb (S2405), located to the north of the Step Pyramid at Saqqara, was discovered by Auguste Mariette in the 1880s, and re-excavated, about thirty years later, by James Quibell (see Quibell 1913). The earliest surviving mummified body of a *swnw* is that of the 6th-Dynasty royal physician Qar, whose mastaba tomb was excavated at Saqqara in 2001; his well-preserved burial included a selection of small copper tools that may well be surgical implements (Hawass 2003: 162-6).

There are several other titles associated with Egyptian magico-medical activity, the most important and frequent of which seem to have been

Fig. 4.1. One of the wooden funerary stelae of Hesyra, a medical official in the reign of the 3rd-Dynasty ruler Djoser (Egyptian Museum, Cairo, JE28504, h. of complete stele 114cm).

the *wꜥb*-priests of the goddess Sekhmet (see Jonckheere 1951), the *sꜣw* (literally 'protectors' or 'amulet-men'), and the *ḫrpw* (or *sꜣw*) *srḳt* ('administrators/controllers of the scorpion-goddess Selket'; see Känel 1984). Halioua and Ziskind (2005: 11) have suggested that there might be some grounds for paralleling the *swnw*, on the one hand, with the ancient Greek trained medical practitioner (*iatros*), and the *sꜣw*, *wꜥb*-priest and *ḫrp srḳt* on the other, with the Greek divinely inspired healer (*hiereus*), but this seems too simplistic a suggestion, given our lack of real understanding of the connotations and subtleties of any of these Egyptian terms/titles.

Additionally, it should be noted that there were quite a number of individuals from the Old Kingdom onwards who held two or three of these magico-medical titles simultaneously, such as the 4th-Dynasty *swnw* Iry (attested by his funerary stele at Giza, see Junker 1928: 63), who was also a *ḫrp srḳt*, and the 5th-Dynasty official Ptahhotep buried at Saqqara, who held the title 'overseer of the priests of Sekhmet of the palace, *swnw*' (see Boulu 1990: 55). Graffiti 15 and 21 at the Hatnub travertine quarries provide the names and attributes of two First Intermediate Period priests of the goddess Sekhmet: one called Heryshefnakht, who is also identified as an *imy-r ḥkꜣw* ('overseer of magicians') and *wr swnw n nsw* ('king's chief physician'), and another called Ahanakht, also apparently having medical skills (Anthes 1928: 33-5, 47, Tf19-20; Shaw 2010a: 147, 150).

Section 854a of the Ebers Papyrus (one of the most important 'medical' papyri discussed above) is particularly interesting in this regard, since it is a kind of gloss to the main text that specifically refers to the *swnw*, *wꜥb*-priest of Sekhmet and *sꜣw* as if they are broadly comparable as practitioners of medicine: 'There are vessels in him to all his limbs. As to these: if any *swnw*, any *wꜥb*-priest of Sekhmet or any *sꜣw* places his two hands or his fingers on the head, on the back of the head, on the hands, on the place of the heart, on the two arms or on each of the two legs, he measures the heart because of its vessels to all his limbs. It speaks from the vessels of all the limbs.' As well as implying that all three of these healers' titles are comparable, this passage of course has also been interpreted by some scholars (e.g. Nunn 1996: 113) as evidence for the Egyptians' awareness of the heart beat, the pulse and the links between the two.

To what extent did Egyptian medical knowledge and practice derive from the process of mummification, and the existence of individuals skilled in certain aspects of dissection? It is often stated that the Egyptians must have gained some of their medical experience as a byproduct of funerary processing of human and animal corpses. It is clear, however, that it would be incorrect to suppose that this long history of dissection (of a kind) provided the Egyptians with a good knowledge of the workings of the human body. The purpose of numerous organs remained unknown; for example, although it was known that brain damage could cause paralysis, it was not realised that the brain had anything to do with the act of thinking, an activity which the Egyptians ascribed to the heart. The purpose of the kidneys was also unknown, and the various appearances of the term *mtw* suggest a belief that all bodily fluids, such as blood, urine, excrement and semen, were constantly circulating around the body.

Egyptian doctors appear to have been mainly men, since there is only one possible attestation of a woman doctor (Peseshet, in the 5th/6th Dynasty), although this evidence may well be biased, given that the principal sources are inscriptions on funerary monuments, most of which were created for men rather than women. Peseshet's stele, found in the tomb of Akhethotep (perhaps her son) at Giza, identified her as *imy-r swnwt*, and opinions differ as to how this title should be translated: 'chief of female physicians' seems most likely, but it is also possible that she was a female overseer of male physicians (see Ghalioungui 1983: 18-19 and Nunn 1996: 124-5).

The Greek historian Herodotus, writing in the 5th century BC, claimed that Egyptian doctors each had their own specialisations, such as gynaecology or osteopathy, and there is certainly some evidence for titles indicating some degree of specialism in the Pharaonic period. Nunn (1996: 118-19) notes that there are many officials holding the title *swnw* followed by a body part, such as *ḫt* (body – perhaps in this context specifically the abdomen) or *irty* (eyes). The role of the *ḫrp srḳt*, or 'controller of the scorpion goddess Selket', seems to have been primarily concerned with the treatment of scorpion stings and snake bites – as often in Egyptian culture, the deity chosen to protect from a phenomenon is actually the one that personifies it (just as *wꜥb*-priests of Sekhmet combat disease precisely because the epithets and myths of the lioness-goddess Sekhmet suggest that one of her main functions is to spread pestilence). The early Ptolemaic (or perhaps 30th-Dynasty) Brooklyn Museum papyrus (Brooklyn 47, 218.48 and 47, 218.85; see

Sauneron 1989 and Bardinet 1995: 523-46) provides some context to the *ḥrp srḳt* title, since it consists of two sections: the first dealing with the identification of different types of serpent and the second providing advice on the treatment of patients suffering from snake bites or scorpion stings. In the titular section, paragraph 39, at the beginning of the second part of the papyrus, specific reference is made to the *ḥrp srḳt* as the main individual involved in providing such treatment: 'Compendium that serves to prepare the remedies to extract the venom of each male and each female snake, each scorpion, each tarantula (?), each reptile; compendium that is in the hands of the *ḥrp srḳt*, and that serves to drive away all reptiles and render their mouths ineffective' (see Bardinet 1995: 528). Some of the subsequent remedies (e.g. paragraphs 42 and 44) include references to the intervention of a *ḥrp srḳt* as an important part of the process. Both the snake descriptions and the remedies comprise a combination of rational data and magical or religious associations.

The sense of 'healing technology' as an Egyptian science in which several radically different strategies were employed is clearly exemplified by the magico-medicinal contents of the shaft tomb of a priest of the late Middle Kingdom (*c.* 1700 BC) excavated from beneath the Ramesseum in western Thebes (Quibell 1898: 3). The funerary equipment found in this tomb incorporated 'religious' and 'magical' artefacts alongside medical papyri. The artefacts included a female fertility figurine, a bronze cobra-wand, a statuette of a woman wearing a lion mask and holding two snake-wands, an ivory clapper, and a fragment of a magic rod. There was also a wooden box containing papyri inscribed with a wide range of religious, literary and magical texts, including three medical documents (Gardiner 1955). This single collection of equipment clearly demonstrates the wide spectrum of strategies that could have been involved in Egyptian medicine and magic, enabling an individual practitioner to utilise divine and physical resources in order to achieve several different aims. It thus provides physical artefactual evidence to back up the impression given by study of the titulary alone.

Conservatism and innovation in Egyptian magic and medicine

One of the most crucial aspects of ancient Egyptian science and technology, and one that is also central to the study of Egyptian medicine, is the question of ancient attitudes to change and progress. To what degree were these medical practitioners open to innovation, or were their methods quintessentially rooted in tradition and previous convention? At least two of the surviving 'medical' papyri include sections that essentially spell out their pedigree as ancient documents, in much the same way as some of the Book of the Dead papyri (see Ritner 1993: 202). There can therefore be little doubt that most magico-medical texts were considered to draw much of their potency from their longevity and archaism – the older the spell or medicinal recipe the more likely that it could be drawing to some extent on the original primordial magic associated with Heka, Hu and Sia, the three manifestations of divine potency. It is clear, however, that some of the surviving texts not only pay lip-service to this idea but in fact are genuinely copied from much earlier documents – the Edwin Smith Papyrus (Breasted 1930), for instance, dates to *c.* 1500 BC but it includes occasional grammatical features that indicate an original source text dating back to the Old Kingdom, perhaps as much as a millennium earlier. Although only fourteen examples of medical texts have survived from a period of two thousand years, the whole magico-medical genre seems to be based on a combination of archaism and genuinely ancient 'wisdom'.

Ritner (2000), however, has explored this issue in an intriguing article, in which he argues that the Egyptian texts concerned with healing have an innate tendency to stress adherence to longstanding traditions and ancient learning, but that they also sometimes contain evidence to suggest that innovation was both permissible and desirable. First he points out the frequent references made to other sources (e.g. the phrase 'another book says'), indicating a scholarly comparing of ideas by the medical practitioners, allowing them to choose proactively between different possibilities, while still maintaining of course that these sources are all embedded in ancient wisdom. Secondly he cites the London Medical Papyrus (discussed above in Chapter 3) as a good example of the Egyptians' readiness to adopt foreign incantations in order to create the most efficacious remedy for a particular affliction.

Thirdly, discussing the general tendency for Egyptians to disseminate and absorb medical (and other) ideas at the Assyrian and Persian royal courts, he turns to the latest surviving Egyptian medical text: the so-called Crocodilopolis Medical Book (P. Vienna 6257) for its instances of

Fig. 4.2. Relief depiction of surgical instruments on the inner face of the enclosure wall of the temple of Horus-the-elder and Sobek at Kom Ombo, dating to the Roman period.

new/outside influences on Egyptian medical practice (see, with caution, Reymond 1976). Written in demotic and dating to the 2nd century AD, this papyrus includes a large number of plant and mineral ingredients that are not previously mentioned in the earlier corpus of documents; Ritner (2000: 113) argues that this pharmaceutical expansion owes more to the international trade (encouraged initially by the Achaemenid empire) than to specific Classical influences. Fourthly, he notes that the famous depiction of surgical instruments on the inner face of the enclosure wall of the temple of Horus-the-elder and Sobek at Kom Ombo (Fig. 4.2), which also dates to the 2nd century AD, incorporates some artefacts that are clearly Roman rather than Egyptian (e.g. scalpels and a sponge, see Nunn 1996 for discussion and bibliography). The point that Ritner makes is that, rather than arguing that this adoption of Roman medical equipment necessarily indicates Egyptian technological decline and conservatism, it should instead be interpreted as evidence of Egyptian doctors' openness to fresh ideas and innovative utensils: 'Like the Demotic Vienna Papyrus, the Kom Ombo relief seems proof of innovation and adaptation but within a still vibrant medical tradition' (Ritner 2000: 114).

Stone-working: the synthesis of traditional *chaînes opératoires* and ideological innovations

Egyptian conservatism should not be misconstrued as resistance to new or different ideas but recognized instead as a reluctance to discard completely society's valued, older conceptions. As with Egyptian religious speculation, notions both old and new were preserved for scholarly consideration (Robert Ritner 2000: 110).

Architectural types were less amenable to mechanical production, and had a more complex evolution. They had a very real existence in the minds of the Egyptians, but gave rise to broader scope in their realization as structures and buildings. Even more than with art, Pharaonic architecture reveals how tradition was invented (Kemp 2006: 142-3).

The earliest traces of hominid technology tend to survive in the form of knapped stone tools, and indeed the first known artefacts found in Egypt are large stone Acheulean-style hand-axes, currently dated to the Lower Palaeolithic (*c.* 400-300,000 BP; see Hendrickx and Vermeersch 2000: 18-20, and see also Fig. 1.1 above), and probably produced by groups of *Homo erectus*. According to Hikade (2010: 2) 'it remains surprising that the handax was so long-lasting, and dominated flint tools for several hundreds of thousands of years. One reason for this conservatism may have been the inability of early humans to fully integrate knapping skills and toolkits with knowledge of the environment.' The traces of stone procurement also go back to an unusually early date in the Nile valley, with the earliest known chert and flint mines, in the Qena region of Upper Egypt, dating to the Middle Palaeolithic period (*c.* 50,000 BP, Vermeersch and Paulissen 1997).

The long history of the working of stone in ancient Egypt represents a considerable trek from the chipping and flaking of flint and chert hand-held tools to the gigantic masonry of the limestone, granite and basalt funerary complexes of the Old Kingdom (Stocks 2003b, Romer 2007), and, many centuries later, the vast stone Greco-Roman temples at such sites as Edfu and Dendera (Arnold 1999). For the first few hundred thousand years of human history in northeastern Africa, the principal craft products to have survived were stone tools of two different types: ground stone and chipped stone.

Ground stone lithics, such as axes, adzes, pounders and picks, were primarily made from such hard stones as granodiorite, gneiss and dolerite, and the functions they performed were mostly as heavy-duty tools for such tasks as quarrying and wood-working. Chipped stone lithics, on the other hand, mostly comprise flint or chert, shaped into core, flake or blade tools; they were used for lighter tasks such as food preparation, leather-working, harvesting and drilling. Both ground and chipped stone lithics continued to be utilised many centuries after the conventional end of the Neolithic, being used for numerous utilitarian and ritual purposes, alongside the copper alloy tools more readily associated with the pharaonic period (see, for instance, Hikade 2002 for the lithic industries of Old Kingdom Elephantine, and Tillmann 1992 for the lithics of New Kingdom Qantir). A scene in the 12th-Dynasty tomb of Amenemhat at Beni Hasan shows flint knives being produced en-masse by a group of workers (BH2; Griffith 1896: 33-8, pls VI-X, Snape and Tyldesley 1983; see Fig. 5.1), and numerous Old Kingdom tomb scenes show the use of large flint knives for animal slaughtering (e.g. the 5th-Dynasty tombs of Ptahhotep and Ty at Saqqara, see Davies 1901: pl. XXIII (Ptahhotep), and Junker 1953: Abb. 88a (Ty); see Fig. 5.2). There are many examples from different times, cultures and places of the relatively harmonious juxtaposition of radically different stages of technology, as Cuomo (2007: 55) points out: 'The co-existence of different stages of a technology is an extremely common phenomenon, and it does not require more explanation ... than the fact that, as of 2006, despite the introduction of the internet-connected mobile phone, many people still write letters by hand on paper.'

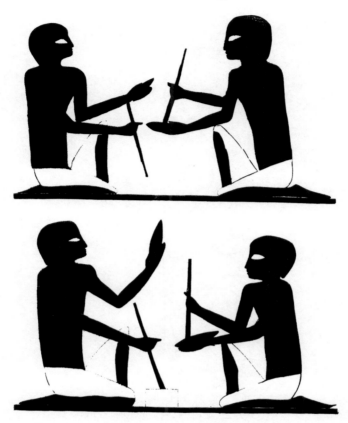

Fig. 5.1. Scene in the 12th-Dynasty tomb of Amenemhat at Beni Hasan (BH2) showing flint knives being produced.

Some of the specialised stone tools produced in the late Predynastic and Early Dynastic period are among the finest examples of Egyptian craftwork of any period and in any material (Holmes 1992, Hikade 2010). It appears that flint-knapping in the late Predynastic period was gradually transformed from a fairly widespread technology to one that was practised by highly specialised knappers producing prestigious items for the emerging élite of the Naqada II and III periods. Grave 66 at Kadero, dating to the Khartoum Neolithic (*c.* 4500-3500 BC), yielded the body of a man aged 18-25 years along with a complete set of tools for knapping quartz tools, suggesting that the idea of stone-working specialists in northeast Africa can be extended back as early as the 5th millennium BC (Kobusiewicz 1996: 354).

Fig. 5.2. Scene of butchery in the 5th-Dynasty tomb of Ptahhotep at Saqqara.

Ripple-flaked knives, sometimes with gold or ebony handles, have virtually always been found in either funerary or religious contexts and were therefore almost certainly used for ritual purposes; their elaborate production process involved shallow unifacial surface retouch, edge retouch, fine seriation at the cutting edge, and polishing of one face (Midant-Reynes 1987). The scale of some of the ritual ripple-flaked knives produced in the late Predynastic and Early Dynastic periods is, on occasion, quite colossal, as in the case of a 50-cm-long knife excavated at Tell el-Farkha in the eastern Delta (Cialowicz et al. 2007: 28, fig. 36b) and a 72-cm-long knife excavated from the funerary complex of the 2nd-Dynasty ruler Khasekhemwy at Abydos (Hikade 1997).

Pressure-flaked 'fishtail knives/lance heads' (almost certainly the prehistoric precursors of the *psš-kf* knife used for the 'opening of the mouth' ritual in the pharaonic period) are also recognised as complex and gracefully crafted artefacts (see Hikade 2003, and see also the discussion of the material culture of mummification ritual in Chapter 6 below). Some examples (e.g. Harvard 13.3915, dating to Naqada IIa, from tomb 825 at Mesaeed, see Harvey 1988) incorporated protrusions to allow attachment of a haft, and a Naqada II example found in tomb N7625 at Naga ed-Dêr had a 9-cm-long wooden haft still in place (Lythgoe and Dunham 1965: 409, fig. 184). Since the fine denticulations along the cutting edges of these knives seem to be rarely worn or broken on surviving examples (see Fig. 5.3), it seems likely that they were used for purely ritual purposes, and many seem to have been deliberately broken at the time of burial (Lythgoe and Dunham 1965: 309-10). Flint examples of this artefact are rare after the 1st Dynasty (and only one surviving flint fishtail knife later than the 6th Dynasty has survived, see van Walsem 1978-79: 231), but the shape is imitated in other materials, including other types of stone (particularly limestone and travertine, see van Walsem 1978-79: 224-5).

In late Predynastic Hierakonpolis, particularly at the late Predynastic religious structure HK29A, this flowering of flint-working took the unusual form of a group of about fifty pressure-flaked animal sculptures (representing cows, goats, hippopotami, ibex and dogs), probably used as votive offerings (Friedman 2000). These impressive, and uniquely Egyptian, flint animal forms are echoed not only by the theriomorphic greywacke and siltstone palettes that feature in funerary assemblages

Fig. 5.3. Flint 'fishtail knife', dating to the Predynastic period, from Hierakonpolis (Garstang Museum, University of Liverpool, E6560, h. 13cm).

from late Naqada I onwards (see Stevenson 2009), but also by the theriomorphic and plant-form stone funerary vessels that began to be produced.

There is a sense in which, from the perspective of Bronze Age Egyptians, traditional stone-working is culturally privileged. As a form of craftwork with such a long history, it is respected not for ingenuity or innovation but for its inherent conservatism. It seems likely, therefore, that ancient Egyptian pharaonic culture from the Early Bronze Age through to the Iron Age continued to incorporate some forms of stone-working technology for two quite differing reasons – some tools survive at the lower end of the socio-economic scale on the basis of cheapness and convenience of material (and perhaps also sterility, in the case of freshly knapped flint blades used for such medical purposes as circumcision – see Nunn 1996: 165), but another set of tools, such as the ripple-flaked blades or funerary vessels, continued to be manufactured because stone-working acquired deep associations with permanence and sacredness. In this context, certain aspects of stone-working survived technologically primarily because they – and the materials themselves – were so inextricably associated with rituals stretching back for thousands of years. Stone-working moved from widespread use simply as a convenient and versatile material in the prehistoric period, to a new role as a symbol of permanence and sacredness in the pharaonic period.

If the flint knapping, the carving of stone palettes and the making of stone vessels are all taken into account, there are good grounds for arguing that, across stone technology as a whole, a distinct pattern of production and consumption – from the Naqada II phase through to the Early Dynastic period (i.e. from the mid-4th millennium through to the early 3rd millennium BC) – can be perceived. This might be characterised in the following way: (1) standardisation, (2) élite specialisation, and (3) invention of tradition. Hikade (2004) has clearly demonstrated in the case of one type of stone tool (the ubiquitous scraper) that local flint-knappers throughout Egypt, during the Naqada II phase, produced a wide range of flint scrapers of different types, sizes, weights and functions, but that, with the onset of the protodynastic period and increasing political unification (Naqada IIII and Dynasty 0), a degree of mass production of certain types (e.g. triangular scrapers and bitruncated oval and rectangular blades) began to take place, but also more specialised production for élite patrons, using particular distinctive kinds of flint, in workshops associated with the nascent royal courts at Naqada, Hierakonpolis and Abydos. New, élite forms of blade, such as the ripple-flaked knives, were by this date being produced at these workshops and traded throughout Upper Egypt.

In the Early Dynastic period these two long and overlapping phases of centralised control, imposing both degrees of standardisation and specialisation (Hikade 2004: 58), became the norm for stone-working, in the production of many different types of stone product. Stevenson (2009: 4), for example, makes the following observation about stone palette production towards the end of the Predynastic: 'Palettes became progressively rarer towards the end of the Predynastic period, from Naqada IIIA2-B onwards, possibly because the source of the material used to make them had been appropriated by the elite and was exploited for other purposes, such as the production of bangles, stone vessels ... and, in particular, ceremonial palettes'. She also points out that the

increasing simplicity of the standard palettes making up the majority of
the examples from the protodynastic period, is in contrast to the growing
elaboration of the élite ceremonial palettes and mace-heads (of which the
early 1st-Dynasty Narmer Palette, Cairo JE32169, from Hierakonpolis, is
the classic instance, see Shaw 2004: 1-7 and passim). This whole process
of polarisation identified by Stevenson seems to exemplify a phenomenon
characterised by Baines (1989: 476-7) as 'aesthetic deprivation of the
non-elite', which is essentially the flip-side of the process by which
production of ceremonial greywacke palettes primarily in temple
contexts, and vast quantities of stone vessels in funerary contexts, express
and solidify the emerging symbolism of Egyptian kingship, and invention
of associated traditions. Specialised stone-working was thus utilised as
a driving force (and also one of the principal surviving expressions) of
the major social and ideological transformations of the Early Dynastic
period and Old Kingdom. In the areas of ceremonial stone artefacts and
the emergence of stone masonry and sculpture, the accepted canonical
view of Egyptian kingship necessarily involved a degree of invention of
tradition. Kemp (2006: 111) describes the process by which official élite
use of stone mobiliary art – and later also monumental stone architecture
– consolidated a particular view of the past and the cosmos: 'When well
established, a great tradition may have an influence that is felt throughout
society. But to reach this stage it has to expand at the expense of other
traditions. It has to colonize the minds of the nation. Whatever does not
succumb, becomes "folk culture".'

Stone vessel making technology and its physical and social contexts

The working of stone into vessels of various shapes and sizes was one of the
earliest specialised forms of craftwork in ancient Egypt, and thus became
firmly established as one of the most characteristic aspects of Egyptian
technology from the early Predynastic period onwards. Ironically, it
seems to have been at a relatively early stage (the Predynastic through
to the Early Dynastic) that many of the most impressive hard-stone
vessels were produced; by the late Old Kingdom fewer stone vessels were
being made, and most of these were carved from the softer stones. The
precocity of Egyptian craftworkers in this area of technology appears to

Fig. 5.4. Scene showing workers drilling out the interiors of stone vessels (and also a stone sculptor, on the right-hand side), on the west wall of room A in the 12th-Dynasty tomb of Pepyankh at Meir.

be confirmed by the fact that the Egyptian term for 'craftsman' (*ḥmwty*) is written with a determinative sign in the form of a drill, and was therefore not only initially used only to refer to producers of stone vessels, but also implies that the concept of craftwork took stone vessel production as its blueprint (see Drenkhahn 1995: 338).

If one aspect of Egyptian technology were to be characterised as 'conservative' and 'traditional' then stone vessel-making would surely be it. The earliest stone vessels, dating to the Badarian period (*c.* 4500-3800 BC) seem to have been created using some form of basic grinding stone, operated either by hand or in the form of a primitive type of drill. During the pharaonic period depictions of vessel-making workshops (see Fig. 5.4) suggest that the principal drilling implement changed at about the end of the Middle Kingdom, but in other respects the basic process remained very much the same from the late Predynastic onwards (see Stocks 2003a).

In 1972, the discovery of a crescent-shaped tool by a French archaeological surveyor working in the southwest corner of the mortuary temple of Ramesses II (the Ramesseum) in western Thebes, led to Fernand Debono's excavation of a 19th-Dynasty gypsum vessel-making workshop (Debono 1993-4). Extensive traces of stone vessel production processes have also survived at a number of Egyptian quarrying sites of many different dates. Some partially worked fragments and piles of debris have survived *in situ* at the Hatnub travertine quarries (Shaw 2010a: 27-30), but travertine workshops often seem to have been situated in urban areas rather than in the desert locations where the stone was extracted (e.g. a workshop in the Royal Adminstrative Building in the Heit el-Ghurab settlement on the Giza plateau, see Lehner et al. 2009: 61). This is in quite striking contrast to the situation at the Umm el-Sawwan alabaster gypsum quarries, in the northern Faiyum, surveyed and excavated in 1928 by Gertrude Caton-Thompson. The quarries yielded numerous tools and partially drilled and fashioned vessels in working areas scattered across the region (Caton-Thompson and Gardner 1934). The tools at Umm el-Sawwan principally comprised crescent-shaped flint borers used to carve out the interiors of cylindrical alabaster gypsum vessels. This particular tool type was initially published by Jacques de Morgan in 1897 (de Morgan 1897: 114) and John Garstang (1903), but it was at Umm el-Sawwan that flint borers were first found in large numbers.

A number of insights into processes of hollowing out the interiors of stone vessels have been provided by ethno-archaeological and experimental studies (see Hester and Heizer 1981 for the former, and Stocks 2003a for the latter). The initial stages of soft stone vessel production, from the Predynastic period onwards, clearly consisted of a process by which the fragment of stone was roughly shaped and smoothed with stone tools (probably flint chisels, punches and scrapers). The next stage of the *chaîne opératoire* has been greatly illuminated by the experimental work undertaken by Denys Stocks, who took as the basis of his work such pictorial evidence as hieroglyphic symbols representing boring tools (Stocks 1993: fig. 3) and depictions of the use of the so-called twist-reverse-twist drill – labelled TRTD by Stocks – in various tombs, including that of Mereruka at Saqqara (6th Dynasty; Duell 1938), that of Pepyankh at Meir (12th Dynasty; Fig. 5.4), and those of Rekhmira at Thebes and Iby at Thebes (18th Dynasty and 26th Dynasty; see Stocks 1986: fig. 1). On the basis of such depictions, Stocks succeeded in creating modern replicas of the figure-of-eight stone borer and the TRTD, thus producing an experimental limestone vessel. With a height of 10.7cm and a diameter of 10cm, the vessel took 22 hours and 35 minutes to make (including the exterior shaping, interior tubular drilling and stone boring). Stocks found that bow-driven tubes produced a tapering drill core, whereas the use of the TRTD resulted in a parallel-sided core, as in the case of an un-catalogued alabaster gypsum vase in the Petrie Museum. Although bow-driven tubes would have been five times faster than the TRTD, they would have provided insufficient leverage and control, and Stocks' experiments showed that the vessels could actually be broken by the additional mechanical stresses involved in using a bow.

5. Stone-working

Different toolkits seem to have been required for the drilling of different rock types, thus travertine and alabaster gypsum, although very similar in appearance, are 3 and 2 respectively on the Mohs scale of hardness (4.5 and 1.25 on the 'absolute' scale of hardness). Modern experimentation involving the attempted drilling of gypsum and travertine vessels with flint or chert crescent-shaped borers has demonstrated that such tools would not have been capable of drilling harder stones such as travertine, which are instead likely to have been hollowed out with a reed tubular drill in the earliest periods, and later with a copper tubular drill (Stocks 2003a: 139-40). With travertine vessels, the brittleness of the stone would have presented an additional difficulty to the use of flint borers.

Although great progress has been made in the understanding of the skills and tools used to produce stone vessels in the pharaonic period, far less is known about the social and economic framework within which the production of stone artefacts took place, from small cosmetic items up to colossal statuary. One means of beginning to understand this context is to identify and study workshops at settlements both in association with quarries and in the vicinity of the towns, temples and tombs that were the primary destinations of high quality worked stone.

Where were stone-working ateliers located?

Opinions differ as to the amount of stone-sculpting or vessel-making that took place at ancient Egyptian quarry sites (as opposed to such work taking place at royal and temple workshops/studios in cities such as Memphis or Thebes), and in practice it seems likely that *in situ* sculpting varied according to date, material and location, and perhaps through other factors too. The survival of debris from vessel-making, including occasional unfinished vessels, indicates that the quarry-workers transformed a certain amount of the travertine into vessels *in situ* at the Hatnub quarries (Shaw 2010a: 55-9, figs 2.2-3), but there is no real evidence of the creation of any large-scale objects, such as statues, at Hatnub. In addition, recent work by the Katholieke Universiteit Leuven Mission to Deir el-Bersha has revealed a New Kingdom travertine vase-making workshop at the Maghara Abu Aziz travertine quarries, midway between Sheikh Said and northern Amarna (Harco Willems, personal communication).

One type of evidence for the extent to which items were carved in advance of transportation takes the form of a number of surviving depictions of the movement of statues, the best-known being the scene in the early 12th-Dynasty tomb of Thuthotep at Deir el-Bersha, showing a colossal statue of the deceased being dragged along by lines of workers pulling on ropes (Newberry 1893: 17-26, pl. 15). The principal difficulty in interpreting such scenes, however, is the well-known problem that pharaonic-period artists often portrayed objects in their finished form even when, in reality, they were still incomplete – this is particularly evident from the many scenes in which objects are being manufactured in temple workshops. It is therefore uncertain as to whether Thuthotep's travertine statue was actually completely carved at the Hatnub quarries, or simply shown in its finished state as an artistic convention. Badawy (1963) refers to the text accompanying the Thuthotep scene, and specifically the description of the statue as *ist twt pn ifd*, arguing that this implies that the statue was only a squared block until it reached Hermopolis Magna (or Deir el-Bersha). Bryan (1992: 138-9), however, argues that 'statues were largely completed in or near quarries and ... shipped to distant sites', pointing out, for instance, that there were 'chief sculptors among Ramesside quarry expedition personnel' and also that 'calcitic works are homogeneous as a stylistic group and were very likely sculpted in or near the quarries'. The archaeological evidence for some quarry-site carving of *hard-stone* items is reasonably widespread, with the survival of near-complete colossal statues in the southern granite quarries on the east bank at Aswan, an inscribed obelisk of Seti I at the Gebel Gulab quartzite quarries (Habachi 1960; see Fig. 5.5), and a statue of an unknown 25th-Dynasty king in the Tumbos granite gneiss quarry (Dunham 1947).

On the other hand, evidence does exist for the large-scale working of stone at the point of use, as opposed to the quarries. Saleh (1974) excavated a set of apparent workshops southeast of Menkaura's pyramid at Giza, consisting of a large open courtyard and several small house-like buildings (Saleh 1974). A large collection of fragments of travertine (including an unfinished column base) was found in the courtyard, and it seems likely that these were being carved and polished for use in the nearby pyramid complex of Khafra, particularly in the Valley Temple. Rainer Stadelmann (1981: 67) has suggested that the structures excavated

Fig. 5.5. The inscribed tip of an unfinished obelisk of Seti I at the Gebel Gulab quartzite quarries.

by Saleh may perhaps correspond to the so-called *ḥmwt-smit*, 'desert workshop', which is mentioned in workmen's graffiti on the granite wall-blocks of Khafra's Valley Temple (Reisner 1931: 277).

A workshop for granite vessels has also been excavated on the island of Elephantine in the eastern part of the Old Kingdom town (Kaiser et al. 1999: 71-81), providing evidence for the techniques used to produce large numbers of vessels from the local granite in the 3rd and 4th dynasties. This workshop suggests that funerary stone vessel-making may have been extensively undertaken at provincial towns, close to the actual quarries, rather than being focussed primarily on workshops near the Memphite necropolis, like the Menkaura one described above (see

Arnold and Pischikova 1999: 129, n. 23). The fact that the Elephantine granite vessel workshop included numerous individual courtyards and working areas, and covered an area of up to 600m², suggests that it was operating at a scale considerably higher than household production.

The overall picture of state-organised stone vessel and sculpture production seems to involve workshops based at a number of different types of location, perhaps largely dependent on the type of stone being worked, and the nature, function and manoeuvrability of the end products. The archaeological data discussed above can of course be contextualised to some degree by textual and visual evidence. Eyre (1987) has provided a detailed study of the principal sources of textual evidence for the organisation of labour in the Old and New Kingdoms, which includes a great deal of data relating to quarrying and building (particularly covering such questions as the composition, management and remuneration of the workforce involved in procuring, transporting and working stone, as well as the timing of quarrying and construction projects). This leads on logically to the consideration of the major logistical factors, in terms of technology and labour management, and resource procurement, that would have been involved in the construction of the Old Kingdom royal pyramid complexes and sun temples.

Stone masonry as the monumentalisation of ideology

When royal funerary monuments began to be built in stone rather than mud brick, in the early 3rd millennium BC, the transition was as much ideological as technological. Whereas late Predynastic and Early Dynastic temples and tombs were largely constructed from mud brick, from around the time of the late 2nd Dynasty onwards it is clear that stone began to be regarded as the primary material for divine or funerary constructions, in contrast to the more ephemeral medium of soil/mud. There are some parallels here with the primacy ascribed to stone vessels as opposed to pottery, which was already deeply entrenched in Egyptian thought, long before the change to stone architecture. As Kemp (2006: 144) points out, however, stone masonry also evolved to some extent out of another ephemeral method of construction – that using wooden frames, wooden panels and sheets of matting. In fact, it is arguable that the latter exerted an influence on stone architecture that was stronger and more lasting than that of mud-brick structures. Mud bricks had been used frequently for tombs and funerary chapels from the late Predynastic to the 3rd Dynasty, whereas wood and reeds seem to have been typically employed for religious buildings, and particularly shrines.

Old Kingdom royal funerary architecture as the pinnacle of stone-working technology

Since at least the time of the ancient Greeks there has been considerable debate concerning the means used by the Egyptians to construct the Great Pyramid. However, since very few Egyptian textual records referring to their engineering and architectural methods have survived, experimental archaeology has often turned out to be the principal means of proof for many recent theories. There are still numerous unanswered questions concerning the quarrying, dressing and transportation of the stone blocks, let alone the processes of precisely levelling the base and aligning the sides.

Between 1880 and 1882, Petrie undertook several seasons of careful survey work on the Giza plateau, site of the pyramid complexes of the 4th-Dynasty rulers Khufu, Khafra and Menkaura (Petrie 1883). The results of this work suggested to him that the Egyptians had levelled the area intended for the Great Pyramid and its successors by cutting a grid of shallow trenches into the bedrock, and flooding them with water, then reducing the intervening 'islands' of stone to the necessary height. For most of the 20th century there was surprisingly little archaeological work concerned with the pyramids at Giza, but in the 1980s Mark Lehner began to produce a meticulous new map of the plateau, incorporating the various holes and trenches cut into the rock around the pyramids (Lehner 1985a, 1985b). On the basis of this mapping project, Lehner argued that the Egyptians had in fact not levelled the whole area intended for the pyramids, but simply ensured that narrow perimeter strips around the edges of each pyramid were as perfectly horizontal as possible.

Egyptian architects, surveyors and builders used two specialised surveying tools, the *mrḫt* ('instrument of knowing') and the *bꜣy* (a sighting tool probably made from the central rib of a palm leaf), to allow them to lay out straight lines and right angles as well as orienting the sides of and corners of structures in accordance with astronomical alignments. It is

Fig. 5.6. Granite door-jamb from Hierakonpolis, dating to the reign of the 2nd-Dynasty king Khasekhemwy (Egyptian Museum, Cairo, JE33896, 155 x 120 x 60cm).

clear that the Egyptians were already utilising astronomical knowledge to assist their architectural projects from the very beginning of the pharaonic period, since the ceremony of *pḏ šs* ('stretching the cord') is first attested on a granite block of the reign of the 2nd-Dynasty king Khasekhemwy (Cairo JE 33896, *c.* 2650 BC, see Fig. 5.6). In later periods, the process of 'stretching the cord' continued to be depicted in the texts and reliefs of temples such as that of Horus at Edfu, but it gradually appears to have become more of a ritual than a practical technique, since these later temples were aligned much less precisely, often simply with reference to the direction of the river.

But how did this astronomically-based surveying actually work in practice? Edwards (1993: 247-51) suggested that true north was probably found by measuring the place where a particular star rose and fell in the west and east, then bisecting the angle between these two points. More recently, Spence (2000) argues that the architects of the Great

Pyramid sighted on two stars rotating around the position of the north pole (Kochab and Mizar) which would have been in perfect alignment at around 2467 BC, the date when Khufu's pyramid is thought to have been constructed. This hypothesis is bolstered by the fact that inaccuracies in the orientations of earlier and later pyramids can be closely correlated with the degree to which the alignment of the two aforementioned stars deviates from true north. Rawlins and Pickering (2001), however, point out an error relating to 'inter-star line drift' which leads them to suggest a different pair of circumpolar stars: Thuban and Draconis. Whatever the intricacies of the arguments, there seem to be good grounds for assuming that the practical logistics of pyramid construction in the Old Kingdom were accompanied by astronomical observations that not only assisted the architectural work but also demonstrated an equally highly developed level of achievement in astronomy; as Rawlins and Pickering put it: 'Thuban passed within 0.1 degrees of the pole in 2800 BC, a chance event that may have stimulated the historical flowering of celestially based surveying, which was unquestionably used for the pyramids built soon after that at Giza'.

What were the basic engineering techniques underlying the construction of Old Kingdom pyramid complexes?

Most archaeologists agree that some kind of system of ramps must have been used in order to drag the millions of stone blocks into their positions in Old Kingdom pyramid complexes and other monumental constructions (e.g. Edwards 1993: 261-6, Arnold 1991: 79-108). No such ramps have actually survived at the Great Pyramid itself (although small, quasi-embankments made of rocks and tafla clay may have been used for the preliminary raising of stone blocks at ground level, see Lehner 1997: 217), but enough traces have survived around some of the other Old Kingdom pyramids (and at other, much later monuments, such as the first Pylon of the Karnak temple, see Fig. 5.7) to suggest that at least five different systems might have been used. The most straightforward method would have been the so-called linear ramp, which was perhaps used in the 3rd-Dynasty pyramid of Sekhemkhet at Saqqara (Goneim 1957). Such ramps, however, were probably rarely used because they would have had to be very wide. An alternative would

Fig. 5.7. The remains of a mud-brick construction ramp against the inner face of the first pylon of the Temple of Amun at Karnak.

have been the 'staircase ramp', a steep and narrow set of steps leading up one face of the pyramid, traces of which have been found at the Sinki, Meidum, Giza, Abu Ghurob and Lisht pyramids (see Dreyer and Swelim 1982 for evidence of ramps at the small Sinki 3rd-Dynasty pyramid). The construction of a 400m-long and 30m-high 'spiral ramp' is perhaps described in a 19th-Dynasty 'satirical letter' (Papyrus Anastasi I, British Museum EA10247), although the translator, Gardiner (1911: 16-17), makes the point that this is a very complex text: 'the technicalities of these passages are such that the modern Egyptologist is placed in a far worse quandary than this ancient scribe; so far from being able to supply the answers, he is barely able to understand the questions'. The principal objection to the spiral ramp, in the form suggested by Wheeler (1935) and Dunham (1965), is the question of what it would have rested on and how corrective calculations and checks could have been made from the corners if most of the pyramid was continually covered up (see Arnold 1991: 100).

The 'reversing ramp', a zigzag course up one face of a pyramid, would probably have been most effective for the construction of step pyramids, although, frustratingly, there are no signs of its use on the step pyramids at Saqqara, Sinki and Meidum. Traces of 'interior ramps' have survived inside the remains of the 5th-Dynasty pyramids of Sahura, Nyuserra and Neferirkara at Abusir and of Pepi II at Saqqara, but some kind of exterior ramp would still have been needed after the interior was filled in (although see Brier and Houdin 2008 for the theory that an interior ramp alone was sufficient). It has been suggested that the terraced nature of the pyramid core would often have made it more convenient to use a series of much smaller ramps built along the sides of the pyramid from step to step (e.g. Edwards 2003); the remains of these would no doubt have been lost when the outer casing was applied. It is also possible that the causeway connecting the pyramid/mortuary temple to the valley temple might originally have served as builders' ramp from quay to construction site (the quay being connected with the Nile by canal).

Apart from the question of the types of ramps that were employed, debate has also tended to centre on the methods by which individual stone blocks were raised into position. Since the Egyptians made no use of block and tackle methods or cranes, it is usually assumed that wooden and bronze levers were used to manoeuvre the blocks into position. Stocks (2003b) has discussed the engineering issues relating to such factors as friction and angle of slope, with regard to dragging blocks up ramps on sledges, while Parry (2004) has undertaken experimental work and analysis to explore the possibility that sets of four full-size versions of the model wooden 'rockers' frequently known from foundation deposits (e.g. Naville 1908: pl. 168, Hayes 1959: 85-6, fig. 47) (see Fig. 5.8), might have been fitted around stone blocks to allow them to be rolled up ramps. Such rockers are conventionally assumed, as the name indicates,

Fig. 5.8. Three wooden model 'rockers' from a foundation deposit of the temple of Hatshepsut at Deir el-Bahri (Museo Archeologico, Florence, 2325-7).

to have simply been used to allow stone blocks to be manoeuvred more easily (see Petrie 1917: 41), or perhaps to physically rock casing blocks into place in monuments (e.g. Fitchen 1978: 3-9), although, as Arnold (1991: 272) points out, 'The fall of a loaded rocker would have wiped out all working teams below ... One might suggest, therefore, that rockers could have been used only on particularly wide and specially equipped steps – that is, on a staircase that was never provided by the pyramid itself, but only by masonry added at a lesser angle from outside the pyramid slope.'

As far as the internal chambers of the Great Pyramid were concerned, the level of structural engineering was equally high; indeed the roof of the so-called Grand Gallery was the Egyptians' earliest attempt at corbel-vaulting on a colossal scale. The architects surmounted particularly difficult logistics in the creation of the corridor leading up to the main burial chamber of the Great Pyramid (the so-called King's Chamber). The corridors in other pyramids are all either level or sloping downwards, whereas this one slopes steeply upwards, which would have presented particular problems when it came to blocking the passage with heavy granite plugs, after the king's body had been placed in the chamber. It is clear from the fact that the plugs in this 'ascending corridor' are an inch wider than the entrance that the plugs must have been lowered into position not from the outside, as was usually the case, but from a storage position within the pyramid itself (perhaps in the Grand Gallery). It is also clear that the design had to allow the workmen who pushed the plugs into position to be able to escape down a shaft leading from the Grand Gallery down to the 'descending corridor', through which they could then exit.

Discussion

When Scarre (1994: 77) argues that the Egyptian pyramid complex 'does not represent a house or building, but an abstract concept', he is primarily concerned with the use of Egyptian architectural symbolism as a possible way of gaining insights into prehistoric European monumental architecture. Almost inadvertently, however, he highlights perhaps the most crucial aspect of ancient Egyptian monumental architecture – the fact that, like many other ancient ritual monuments, it represents a highly distinctive meeting point of engineering expertise and ideology. In John Romer's monograph on the nature and construction of the Great Pyramid at Giza, he suggests that 'the physical process of making this Great Pyramid was in itself a kind of thinking' (Romer 2007: 150). There are fruitful areas to explore at the interface between the Egyptian belief system and the emergence of distinctive forms of architecture, given the extent to which these two areas of ancient Egyptian culture shape one another.

As already noted above, in the last section of the discussion of the science and technology of healing in Chapter 4, the Egyptians seem to have developed new methods of construction engineering while striving to maintain the illusion that the thinking behind pyramids was deeply traditional and rooted in the past. Thus Kemp (2006: 158) points out that 'religious architecture well illustrates the Egyptian genius for clothing change in traditional costume'. A text at Edfu suggests that the architecture of the temple of Horus derived ultimately from the work of Imhotep, the 3rd-Dynasty official associated with the construction of Djoser's step pyramid (Sethe 1902: 15-18), despite the gap of several thousand years, and the very different characteristics of the stone structures involved. This deliberate invoking of the past may have been intended to demonstrate the authenticity of the Edfu temple architecture by rooting it in a much earlier era, but it perhaps also sought to stress a degree of continuity in Egyptian architectural elements, styles and proportions. Architects and engineers were allowed to innovate, but their innovations, like those of artists and poets, were embedded strictly within the elaborate system of decorum that had been laid down in the Early Dynastic period, when the officially approved 'traditions' of newly unified state and its royal court were established through careful selection of élite materials, techniques and products. Baines (2007: 17), discussing the nature and effects of ancient Egyptian decorum, suggests that visual and written aspects of Egyptian culture 'changed slowly, in phases of significant reformulation rather than progressively' – this seems to have been the case with Egyptian stone-built monuments, which were fundamentally cosmological in form and purpose.

Mummification and glass-working:
issues of definition and process

The reasons for artificial mummification, and the date when it was first introduced in Egypt, cannot yet be confirmed (Rosalie David 2008: 12).

The question of the establishment of either glassmaking or regular glassworking is a vexed one, and there has been a general consensus that glass comes to Egypt as a developed craft (Paul T. Nicholson 2007: 3).

Defining and dissecting technologies

The artificial preservation of human and animal bodies and the production of glass are not, at first glance, connected to any great degree (although, technically speaking, both made some use of 'natron' as a raw material). They are however closely linked by certain issues encountered in reconstructing their emergence as technologies within Egyptian culture. The origins and nature of Egyptian mummification and glass-working can only be properly understood if they are first clearly defined in terms of the processes and materials involved.

One frequent reason for unresolved debates about the timing of the first appearance of particular technologies in the Nile valley is the lack of a rigorous agreed characterisation of the craft or products in question. This is very much the case with mummification, which can of course be simply defined as the artificial preservation of human or animal tissues, but in reality requires more subtle definition, particularly if the specific cultural and environmental contexts of Egyptian mummification are to be taken into account. Discussing international analysis of human

77

mummified material in general, Aufderheide (2003: xiii) points out that 'the absence of consensus for a theoretical basis and mission tends to limit the coherence and directionality of its activities', and he admits that his own definition of a mummy ('a corpse with soft tissues sufficiently preserved to resemble a once-living person') is not scientifically ideal.

To some extent, the situation in Egypt (and elsewhere) is complicated by the fact that the climate and environment are highly conducive to 'natural/spontaneous mummification' (whereby burial in sand, in a hot, dry climate, has the effect of arresting decomposition and desiccating the body), as opposed to 'artificial' or 'anthropogenic' mummification involving application of a variety of materials in order both to prevent the corpse from decomposing and to enable it to retain some kind of life-like appearance. The desiccating effects of Egypt's deserts have ensured that, from the Palaeolithic onwards, human bodies have frequently been transformed into 'natural' mummies, through burial in the sand (see, for example, Wendorf 1968 for Palaeolithic examples). Examples of the naturally mummified type of corpse were excavated by Petrie at the Naqada and Ballas mid- to late Predynastic cemeteries (Petrie and Quibell 1896, Baumgartel 1970), where over three thousand burials had been made, usually with the body lying on its side in a flexed position. In a bioarchaeological analysis of the bodies from another Predynastic cemetery at Naga ed-Dêr, Podzorski points out that 'the state of preservation of the human remains was so good that skin and hair were often found completely intact' (Podzorski 1990: 85).

As far as artificial mummification is concerned, Mokhtar et al. (1973) have outlined a set of thirteen criteria that they regard as the essential components of fully developed Egyptian mummification in the New Kingdom:

1. putting the corpse on the operating table
2. extraction of the brain
3. extraction of the viscera
4. sterilisation of the body cavities and viscera
5. embalming the viscera
6. temporary stuffing of the thoracic and abdominal cavities
7. dehydration of the body
8. removal of the temporary stuffing material

9. packing the body cavities with permanent stuffing material
10. annointing the body
11. packing the face openings
12. smearing the skin with molten resin
13. adorning and bandaging the mummy

There are a number of reasons why the above list, however comprehensive it may seem, does not adequately define the full process of mummification as practised in Egypt. The first crucial point to be made is that such procedures as desiccation and embalming are only parts of mummification – the rest of the process belongs not so much to technology as to ritual, as modern observers would see it, although of course to ancient Egyptians the magical, ritualistic aspects of mummification would have presumably been considered to be integral elements of the technology. It is perhaps no accident that the only surviving ancient Egyptian text to provide any details on the process of mummification – the so-called 'Ritual of embalming', preserved in the form of two Theban hieratic papyri dating to the early 1st century AD (P. Boulaq III and P. Louvre 5.158; Goyon 1972, Sternberg-el-Hotabi 1988) – consists primarily of description of rituals rather than physical treatment of the corpse; it deals first with ceremonies to be performed on the mummy, secondly prayers and incantations to be recited, and thirdly methods of covering the body in linen wrappings and embrocations. In other words, it omits any discussion of such crucial procedures as desiccation and evisceration.

The second major problem with the itemised description provided by Mokhtar et al. is that it is based only on what had actually emerged and developed by the New Kingdom. It does not therefore take into account any of the blind alleys down which the technology strayed on several occasions on the road from the early Predynastic to the 21st Dynasty. Table 6.1 therefore takes a different approach – instead of dissecting the nature of fully developed mummification in the New Kingdom, it looks at the various stages the technology appears to have passed through, several of which were never incorporated into the final accepted definition of the process.

The practice of Egyptian mummification seems to have evolved initially simply to preserve the image of the body – thus some of the

Predynastic	Wrapping – bandages wrapped around whole or part of body
	Soaking of bandaging/body in resinous substances
	Use of linen bandaging/plugs to pad and mould the corpse
	Dismemberment
Early Dynastic	Use of natron/salt as preservative
	Soaking of bandages in stucco to create life-like appearance
Old Kingdom	Evisceration
First Intermediate Period	Funerary mask
	Inclusion of amulets in wrappings
Middle Kingdom	Removal of brain
20th Dynasty	Artificial eyes
21st Dynasty	Refinement of subcutaneous packing

Table 6.1. Possible stages in the development of Egyptian mummification.

early mummies of the 3rd millennium BC were painted or soaked with plaster, paint and/or resin, preserving the outer shell of the body but allowing the rest to decay away inside. Two good examples of the latter are (1) the 5th-Dynasty body of Ranefer, excavated by Petrie (1892: 15-17) in Tomb 9 at Meidum, which was encased in resin-soaked wrappings sculpted over the forms of the face and other anatomical features (Fig. 6.1), and (2) the 5th-Dynasty body of Waty (or perhaps Nefer) found swathed in plaster-impregnated linen strips, inside a wooden coffin in the tomb of Nefer and Ka-hay at Saqqara (Moussa and Altenmüller 1971, and see Rice 1990: pl. IX for an excellent colour image), and thus preserving the outer appearance extremely realistically.

The development of more sophisticated techniques meant that gradually more of the original body was retained, eventually reaching something of a peak in the late New Kingdom and Third Intermediate Period (*c.* 1200-900 BC). However, by the mid-5th century BC, when Herodotus wrote his detailed description of the process of mummification (*Histories* vol. 2, 86-8, see de Selincourt 1954), techniques are thought to have gone into decline, presumably partly in order to meet the demands of 'mass production' as mummification spread through larger numbers of the population.

Until the 1990s it was generally thought that the first *artificial* Egyptian mummies were those found at Early Dynastic cemeteries such as Abydos, Saqqara and Tarkhan, but in 1997 one of the non-élite Predynastic cemeteries at Hierakonpolis (HK43) yielded three intact burials containing female bodies with their heads, necks and

6. Mummification and glass-working

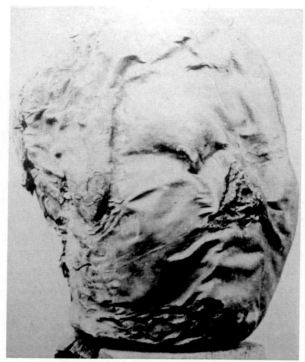

Fig. 6.1. Head of the 5th-Dynasty body of Ranefer, encased in resin-soaked linen wrappings. This body was excavated by Petrie from Tomb 9 at Meidum, and the head was brought back to London, but later destroyed when the Royal College of Surgeons was bombed in World War II.

hands wrapped in linen bandages, the whole of each of the corpses being swathed in linen and matting (Friedman et al. 1999; 2002; Figueiredo 2004: 18-19). The grave goods accompanying these bodies dated to around 3600 BC (the early Naqada II culture), therefore pushing back the earliest use of artificial mummification to a much earlier period than previously supposed, although opinions differ as to whether the simple bandaging of parts of a corpse can necessarily be described as mummification. Intriguingly, one of the women had her throat cut after death, suggesting that even at this date there might have been a sense in which the ritual dismemberment and reassembly of Osiris' body-parts was being acted out. This evidence raises the possibility that among the earlier versions of mummification was a set of procedures connected with dismemberment and reassembly of the body. Herodotus' very detailed account of Egyptian mummification describes the main practitioners as *paraschistai* ('slitters') and *taricheutai* ('picklers'), and, although the terms are somewhat irreverent, they convey well the two principal stages: the body must first be cut up and to some extent

81

dismembered by the slitters before it can be reassembled and preserved by the picklers. The Osiris myth is therefore a very accurate prototype for the practical process of physical preservation, but some of the evidence seems to suggest that the dismemberment theme initially dominated the process, only later being subordinated to the idea of physically preserving the body.

Further work by Jana Jones (2002) indicates that some form of artificial treatment of the body was even taking place much earlier in the 4th millennium, in the Badarian period (*c.* 4500-4100 BC). Jones' examination of thick, desiccated clumps of wrappings from the Neolithic cemeteries at Badari and Mostagedda has shown that resin-soaked bandages were already being applied to bodies in a similar way to the Hierakonpolis examples mentioned above (Jones 2002: 7); this suggests a period of at least a thousand years of experimentation in mummification before the 1st Dynasty, although, as Jones points out, 'Whether the act of wrapping the body in the very earliest periods indicates an intention to preserve it artificially, or whether it was another aspect of the funerary ritual, is uncertain.'

Issues of innovation and archaeological attestation: mummification as case-study

Each of the stages in Table 6.1 is of course just the earliest archaeological attestation of any specific innovation. There is no reason, for instance, why evisceration should not have occurred earlier than the 4th Dynasty but is from this date that the first relevant evidence survives: a travertine chest divided into four compartments (Reisner 1928: 80-1), which was excavated at Giza from the tomb of Hetepheres I, the mother of the 4th-Dynasty ruler Khufu, *c.* 2589-2566 BC (or perhaps from her re-burial cache, since her sarcophagus was found empty). Each compartment was found to contain a flat linen package with traces of organic material, and in three cases also traces of a 3% solution of natron, leading Alfred Lucas (1932) to argue that this was essentially a 'canopic' chest, and therefore evidence of the first known case of evisceration (see Dodson 1994 for detailed discussion of canopic equipment in relation to evisceration). Other types of evidence, however, may hint at less tangible evidence for evisceration at an earlier date. It has been suggested that the mastaba-style 'south tomb', forming part of 3rd-Dynasty royal funerary complexes, might have been intended to hold the viscera (on the basis that the room identified as the burial chamber is too small to hold an entire human corpse, see Edwards 1993: 50), but most scholars regard this as unlikely. A more reliable indication of the emergence of the practice of evisceration and separate preservation of the viscera occurs in the mastaba-tombs of high officials at Meidum in the reign of Sneferu (2613-2589 BC) at the beginning of the 4th Dynasty (i.e. either earlier than or roughly contemporary with Hetepheres I), some of which include niches located high in the wall, in positions which are similar to later canopic installations (see Petrie et al. 1912), and in the case of the 5th-Dynasty Tomb 9 at Meidum, belonging to the above-mentioned Ranefer, packages of viscera were found in such a niche, and described by Petrie (1892: 18) as follows: 'In the recess in the south end ..., there were parts of the internal organs embalmed, forming lumps of resined matter wrapped round in linen, and fragments of such were in Rahotep's recess ... There was no sign of these organs having been in jars or enclosures; and it seems as if these recesses in the tombs were intended to lay the internal parts on after embalming, before the use of jars for such was introduced.'

The same can be demonstrated for the so-called 'opening of the mouth' ritual. Certain aspects of this ritual have survived both in the textual and archaeological records. One of the most important objects used in the ritual of the 'opening of the mouth' (designed to instil life into mummies and funerary statues, see Roth 1992, 1993) was the *psš-kf*, probably originally a pressure-flaked flint knife with a bifurcated blade shaped like a fish tail (sometimes described as a fishtail lance-head, see Needler 1956 and van Walsem 1978-9; see also Chapter 5 and Fig. 5.3 above), many finely crafted examples of which have been excavated from Predynastic graves as early as the Naqada I period (*c.* 4000-3500 BC), thus probably indicating that a similar ceremony was already being used well before the first evidence for many other aspects of Egyptian funerary ritual (although it has also been argued that the blade may have been used to cut the umbilical cord at child-birth, see Roth 1992 and Harer 1994). Other implements relating to the 'opening of the mouth' process are described as *ntrwy*-blades (models of which have survived) and were principally made from meteoric iron, although occasionally other metals were used. The *nmst*-vessel was used for a form of ritual lustration, also in association with the opening of the mouth procedure. The so-called 'seven sacred oils' were used for anointing the deceased in the opening of the mouth ceremony (see Serpico and White 2000: 419, 461-2); some of the oils are known from 1st-Dynasty wooden and ivory funerary labels, but the group appears not to have been used collectively until the Old Kingdom (2686-2181 BC), when they were represented as part of the offering formula on the walls or false-door stelae of tombs. The earliest known actual set of the seven sacred oils is from the above-mentioned tomb/re-burial cache of Queen Hetepheres I at Giza. However, small stone tablets with depressions for these oils were sometimes placed in burials throughout the Old Kingdom. Examples of all of these items associated with the ritualistic aspects of mummification have survived in the archaeological record, and in the case of the *psš-kf*, the possible derivation from the fishtail knife suggests that at least some of these posthumous rituals can be traced back to a date prior to the emergence of most of the other elements of fully developed Egyptian mummification.

Glass-working or glass production?

By the time that the first glass artefacts appear in the archaeological record in Egypt, in the early 18th Dynasty, mummification – one of the quintessential technologies of the Nile valley – had already gone through most of the major stages of its development. Egyptian glass-working, in contrast, has very much the feel of a new technology introduced from the outside, like the chariot or the composite bow. A number of early scholars (e.g. Lucas 1926: 38-40) assumed that glass was actually produced in Egypt, using raw materials, from at least the Amarna period onwards, but more recently there has been considerable debate as to whether the production technology could have emerged locally at this date, as opposed to the importing of foreign ingots and/or foreign glass-workers. Newton (1980: 176), for instance, argues that 'the Egyptians could only melt other people's glass even though they could fabricate the most exquisite items from it ... the Egyptian court depended for their basic raw material, or for an essential ingredient thereof, on imports from Asia'.

In the case of early Egyptian glass-working, the definitional issues do not particularly focus on the nature and constituents of the product, since there is considerable agreement on what constitutes Bronze Age glass, e.g. Henderson (2000: 116): 'the working properties of the molten glass governed the composition of ancient glass which all during Antiquity remained a soda-lime glass ... with some 60% of silica, some 5% of lime, much alkali and several percents of impurities due to the natural ingredients used'. Henderson's general characterisation is fairly close to the definition of Egyptian glass in the Late Bronze Age, e.g. Nicholson (2007: 102): 'the general composition of Egyptian glasses is consistently based upon a soda-lime glass with minor concentrations of potash and magnesia'. Thus, although there are some disputes as to the precise nature of the 'minor concentrations' mentioned by Nicholson, the major issues in ancient Egyptian glass-working instead centre on the definition of production processes, and when it is that Egyptians can be said to be producing glass from the basic raw materials, as opposed to melting and re-working imported cullet or ingots of glass.

There had already been a long history of production of two other important vitreous products in Egypt – faience and frit (for clear definitions of which, see Nicholson 1993: 9-17). The best-known form of frit is the so-called 'Egyptian blue' material, which, according to Nicholson (1993: 16): 'appears to be an Egyptian invention and, though of much greater antiquity, is closely allied to glass'. This clear evidence for Egyptians' long history of producing these two other forms of vitreous product, makes it more likely either that they developed early glass roughly simultaneously with other Late Bronze Age cultures in the Near East, such as the kingdom of Mitanni, or that, at the very least, they were capable of quickly assimilating and adapting to this new technology, on the basis that they had been producing similar substances since the Predynastic period.

Early glass in Egypt: the fundamentals

The basic facts can be broken down into the following types of evidence: the surviving artefacts, the archaeology of urban glass-working, the textual evidence, and the chemical analysis of glass artefacts.

Artefacts and archaeology

The archaeological picture consists of two basic elements: examples of glass artefacts and examples of sites where glass may have been either made or re-worked. The earliest surviving glass artefacts from Egypt date from the early 18th Dynasty onwards (*c.* 1500 BC), initially appearing as exotic products primarily in élite funerary assemblages, such as the tomb of Thutmose I (see Roehrig 2005: 67) and the tomb of the foreign wives of Thutmose III in Wadi Qubbanet el-Qirud at Thebes, *c.* 1460 BC (and see Nicholson 2006 for discussion of the small group of known early 18th-Dynasty glass vessels; see also Fig. 1.7 above). Because these earliest examples of glass in Egypt already seem to be very technically accomplished, it has tended to be assumed that the technology must have been introduced from outside rather than being the result of a long-term evolution of technology (since, if the latter were true, we might expect to see more of a continuum of earlier examples of glass, gradually becoming more sophisticated and complex over time).

A small group of New Kingdom archaeological sites (Amarna, Qantir and perhaps Malkata and Gurob) incorporate the remains of areas of production and debris relating to glass-working and/or glass-making. The possible glass-working/making areas at Malkata and Gurob were excavated in the early 20th century, but lack of proper records or publication means that little can be said about this evidence at present (although see Hodgkinson 2010: 74-7 and Shaw 2011, for new work on the pyrotechnological area of the settlement at Gurob). At Amarna, however, the early discoveries of Petrie (1894: 15-16, 25) have been greatly enlarged by the excavations conducted by Paul Nicholson (2007),

62 Fritting Pans, supported in the furnace on jars inverted, down which the glaze runs. N.M.F.P.

Fig. 6.2. Petrie's line drawing depicting his interpretation of distinctive cylindrical clay vessels as 'fritting pans' used in the initial stage of glass production; Nicholson et al. 1997, however, have reinterpreted these 'pans' as glass ingot moulds.

focusing on site O45.1, where the presence of kilns, glass ingot moulds (see Fig. 6.2), and traces of fritted glass suggest that glass may have been produced from raw materials, and was probably also worked both here and in other parts of the city. At the Ramessid settlement of Qantir (ancient Piramesse), Edgar Pusch's excavations have revealed melting crucibles and frits, specifically connected with red glass, but not yet any kilns or signs of glass-working (Rehren et al. 2001, Pusch and Rehren 2007). According to Rehren et al. (2001: 235), 'the ... discovery of a complete crucible still filled with a powdery white calcium silicate material, probably badly corroded primary glass' is an indication that Qantir was the site of primary Egyptian glass production from raw materials in the Ramessid period (i.e. *c.* 1300-1000 BC).

Two further archaeological contexts that relate to glass-working in Egypt and elsewhere during the Late Bronze Age are the shipwrecks excavated at Cape Gelidonya (dating to *c.* 1200 BC, see Bass 1967) and Ulu Burun (*c.* 1305 BC, see Bass et al. 1989, Cline and Yasur-Landau 2007). The cargo of the Gelidonya wreck included a jar of glass beads, while the diverse contents of the more opulent Ulu Burun boat encompassed 100kg of cobalt blue glass ingots. Nicholson et al. (1997) have demonstrated fairly convincingly that ingot moulds excavated by Petrie at Amarna correspond closely to the shape and dimensions of the Ulu Burun ingots (see also Fig. 6.3 for a fragment of a bun-shaped, re-melted glass ingot from Amarna).

Fig. 6.3. Fragment of a glass ingot from Amarna (Garstang Museum, University of Liverpool, E5654, diameter 13.3cm).

Texts and images

Then there is the textual and visual evidence. Lexicographically some Egyptian texts refer to glass as *inr n wdḥ* (stone of casting) or *ʿt wdḥt* (stone that flows), but the equally frequent use of two foreign words for glass (the Hurrian term *ehlipakku* and the Akkadian term *mekku*) suggests strongly that New Kingdom glass was a foreign import rather than an indigenous invention. The word *ḥsbḏ* is also often used to refer to glass, although confusingly this is also the word for lapis lazuli, a substance that blue glass presumably was thought to replicate (and indeed the dark blue glass inlaid into Tutankhamun's gold mask has been mistaken by some scholars for lapis lazuli, e.g. Tiradritti 1998: 235). The term for glass-maker/worker was probably *irw ḥsbḏ*, and four individuals bearing this title are known, all dating to the New Kingdom (while, in addition, a craftsman in the 13th Dynasty holds the comparable title *imy-r ṯḥntyw*: 'overseer of faience-workers', see Shortland 2007: 264-5).

Glass features among the materials acquired by Thutmose III from Syria-Palestine and both listed and depicted in his *Annals* on the walls of Karnak temple (see Wreszinski 1935: Tf33a-b, Nicholson 2007: 3), and glass vessels imported from western Asia are also shown in the tombs of early 18th-Dynasty high officials Rekhmira and Kenamun in western Thebes (TT100: Davies 1943: 28; TT93: Davies 1930: 30-1; see Fig. 6.4). In addition, eight of the Amarna Letters (EA14, 25, 148, 235, 314, 323, 327 and 331) mention glass, usually as a commodity being imported into Egypt, although letter EA14 lists it among gifts sent by the Egyptian king to the king of Babylon (Moran 1992: 27-37).

A further relevant set of texts are a group of about a dozen cuneiform tablets, the earliest of which date to the late 2nd millennium and come from Hattuša and Babylon, but the majority derive from the library of the Assyrian ruler Ashurbanipal (668-627 BC) at Nineveh (although Oppenheim et al. 1970: 28 argue that the texts they bear are copies of Middle Assyrian originals dating back to the mid-2nd millennium) – they comprise 'recipes' for glass, copying and re-copying what appear to be Late Bronze Age methods and constituents of glass-making, probably because of the highly ritualised attitudes to stone types and therefore also to the artificial materials that imitated stone. The fact that some

Fig. 6.4. Glass vessels portrayed among the materials presented by foreign 'tribute' bearers to the vizier Rekhmira in his Theban tomb.

of the recipes included a high degree of ritual activity is a reminder that for ancient scribal 'scholars' in the Near East, like these in Egypt, religion and ritual could be regarded as integral elements of scientific and technological procedures, in the world of glass-making, just as in the world of healing (as discussed in Chapter 4 above). As Robson (2001: 54) puts it, 'For the scholars of Mesopotamia, coloured glass was not simply an attractive synthetic material but had powerful medico-magical properties ... the nature of coloured glass was that it resembled precious stone both physically and conceptually'. Nevertheless, the authenticity and efficacy of at least one of the Assyrian recipes, in terms of the practical methodology and ingredients, has been demonstrated by Brill (1970: 109-14), who succeeded in making '*zukû*-glass' according to the recipe given by one of the tablets (Oppenheim et al. 1970: 35, Tablet A).

Chemical analyses

Detailed chemical analyses have been undertaken on samples of glass from all parts of the eastern Mediterranean and Near East, and it is clear from these studies that, chemically speaking, there were probably at least three basic forms of glass being produced in the mid to late 2nd millennium BC: (1) a light blue/turquoise form that was made in Mesopotamia from a plant ash alkali and copper colorant, and (2) a dark blue plant ash alkali glass, with higher quantities of copper, giving it a colour resembling lapis-lazuli, and (3) a dark blue cobalt-natron glass made in Egypt. Shortland (2001: 221) provides a useful summary of the situation: 'There is good evidence that at least some of the earliest copper-coloured plant ash-alkali glass to be found in Egypt was imported from Mesopotamia, but, at the same time, small quantities of cobalt-coloured natron glasses are already being produced in Egypt by local workers exploiting local raw materials'.

Trace elements of certain chemicals in glass can also be examined, to allow similarities and differences in production methods and raw materials to be examined. The traces of magnesia and potassium oxide detected in Amarna glasses can be compared with those in glasses of similar date in other parts of the Near East and eastern Mediterranean (e.g. late 15th- to 12th-century BC samples from Pella in Jordan, 14th-century BC samples from Tell Brak in Syria, and 14th-century BC Minoan glasses). This demonstrates that Amarna glass samples are grouped quite tightly together compositionally, seemingly quite different to the samples from Tell Brak and the 13th- to 12th-century Pella glasses, but quite similar to the 15th-14th-century Pella glasses in terms of high magnesia content.

Nicholson and Henderson (2000: 220) point out that there is some variety in the composition of Egyptian glasses of different periods: 'although from an early period Egyptian glass displays signs of being a conservative technology ..., and to some extent this is also true of Amarna glass, there is nevertheless some compositional variation, with some relatively high alumina levels occurring in translucent non-cobalt glasses as early as the reign of Thutmose III'.

Current views on Egyptian glass

It seems, therefore, that, although glass was deliberately manufactured in western Asia from at least as early as *c.* 1500 BC, no definite evidence has yet been found for the fritting of glass from primary raw materials (the only certain evidence for primary glass-making) in either Egypt or Mesopotamia. Although the earliest glass has so far been found in Mesopotamia, it is not possible to rule out the possibility that glass was also fused from primary raw materials in Egypt, but perhaps at a slightly later date. An interesting suggestion has also been made by Peltenburg (1987), who argues that the production of glass may have involved technical input and expertise from metal-workers, who would have had the necessary experience to allow techniques for manipulating hot, viscous glass fluids into the form of vessels. He suggests therefore that the emergence of glass production in the Near East (and perhaps also in Egypt) by 1500 BC might have related to new Late Bronze Age economics and working practices, i.e. the emergence of large-scale craft production controlled by royal courts and temples (see Moorey 1989). Peltenburg's suggestion is perhaps reinforced by the close association between some form of glass-working or production and a 'copper-centred industrial complex' at Qantir (Rehren et al. 2001: 236).

Another issue that is perhaps peculiar to Egyptian glass-working is the clear tendency for their glass vessels – particularly the earliest exampes – to imitate the forms and appearances of the stone and faience vessels that preceded them as principal containers for cosmetics, oils and unguents. Lilyquist and Brill (1993) point out that the early glass vessels imported by the Egyptians tended to imitate their stone equivalents (such as those depicted in the 18th-Dynasty Theban tomb of Kenamun, apparently imitating marbleised stone, and thus typical of known Near Eastern glass vessels, see Davies 1930: 30-1, pl. XXII). There is also, however, a technological sense in which the early Egyptian glass vessels hark back to pre-glass technology, and perhaps also imply an initial failure to recognise the new, more malleable qualities of glass – four of the small group of vessels from the reign of Thutmose III were clearly cold-cut as if they were stone vessels, perhaps indicating that the (Egyptian?) craftsmen involved were unwilling or unable to fashion the glass with the 'correct' procedures. This also suggests that, rather than faience-workers or metal-workers being the obvious craftsmen to learn and develop the innovative new vitreous technology, it may actually have been stone vessel-makers that were initially involved, partly on the basis that they had previously been producing the main artefact that glass was first used for – the cosmetic vessel.

Intriguingly, Moorey (1994: 206) notes that glass-working in the early 1st millennium BC began to incorporate both casting and cold cutting, suggesting that the apparently conservative Egyptian glass-workers several hundred years earlier were, in another sense, ahead of their time – clearly both good examples of Edgerton's observation that 'In use-centred history, technologies do not only appear, they also disappear and reappear, and mix and match across the centuries' (Edgerton 2006: xii).

Chariot production: technical choice and socio-political change

You can't say civilization don't advance, however, for in every war they kill you in a new way (Will Rogers, *New York Times*, 23 December 1929).

You are brought into the armoury and workshops surround you – you do all that you have wished. They take care of your chariot so that it is no longer loose. Your pole is freshly trimmed and its attachments are fitted on. They put bindings on your collar piece ... and they fix up your yoke. They apply your ensign, engraved with a chisel, and they put a handle on your whip and attach a lash to it. You sally forth quickly to fight at the pass and accomplish glorious deeds (Papyrus Anastasi I; British Museum, EA10247; Gardiner 1911: 28).

Introduction

Although the pace of technological change in military hardware was generally considerably slower in the distant past, there nevertheless seem to have been crucial phases when certain cultures went through very rapid processes of 'catching up' with their rivals. The Second Intermediate Period and early New Kingdom seem to have constituted just such a phase for Egypt. Among the most crucial Egyptian innovations ascribed to the late Second Intermediate Period were the horse-drawn chariot (for which the Egyptian terms were *wrrt* or *mrkbt*, the latter probably being a Semitic loan word) and the composite bow. The chariot in particular was of paramount social and political significance in the early New Kingdom, quite apart from its value as a piece of military technology (Littauer and Crouwel 1979, Schulman 1980).

7. Chariot production

One of the Amarna Letters (EA22) includes a list of chariot components forming part of the dowry of a daughter of the Mitannian king Tushratta sent to marry Amenhotep III (Moran 1992: 51-61). Similarly, Papyrus Anastasi IV mentions 'beautiful chariots of *bri*-wood' and then goes on to list eleven chariot parts, each of which is followed by discussion of its material or place of origin (P. BM10249; Caminos 1954: 200-1). Finally, the so-called *Poem concerning the royal chariot*, preserved on an ostracon in Edinburgh and dating to the Ramessid period, includes a list of the various elements of the chariot and its associated weapons, and each of these individual pieces is linked with some particular aspect of the king's character, usually employing some kind of play on words (Dawson and Peet 1933).

Unusually (compared with other ancient civilisations) this rich body of textual information on Egyptian chariots is supplemented by reasonably extensive surviving physical evidence. It is true that the six chariots from the tomb of Tutankhamun constitute the majority of the surviving *complete* examples (see Littauer and Crouwel 1985), but large numbers of chariot components (sometimes comprising tiny fragments of ivory, bone or copper alloy) have survived. This repertoire has now been greatly expanded by the discovery, during the 1980s, of many more pieces from the area of the city of Piramesse (Qantir) identified by the excavators as the 'headquarters of the royal chariot-troops' (see Herold 1999, 2007).

The chariot was not only used in battle by the *snnyw*, an élite corps of the Egyptian army in the New Kingdom (see Fig. 7.1), but it was also regarded as an essential part of the royal regalia. Depictions of the king charging enemies in his chariot became a common feature of

Fig. 7.1. Two Egyptian soldiers in a chariot, New Kingdom.

Fig. 7.2. Ramesses III hunting wild bulls in a chariot, 1st pylon of Medinet Habu Temple, 20th Dynasty.

the exterior walls of temples as symbols of 'the containment of unrule' (Fig. 7.2), roughly comparable with the more ancient theme of the king smiting foreigners with a mace. In the context of the development of Late Bronze Age Egyptian and Near Eastern military technology, there are good grounds to believe that we are dealing with a very complex web of social and technological factors. A similarly elaborate scenario was encountered by Colin Renfrew in his reanalysis of the archaeological remains at Varna (a cemetery near the Black Sea coast of Bulgaria, dating to the late 5th millennium BC). In his discussion of the Varna material, Renfrew (1986: 146) argues that 'the decisive innovation in the development of a new commodity is generally social rather than technical. Often the technology is already there'. A similar point is made by Bryan Pfaffenberger (1988: 241), who argues that ancient technology should be regarded as 'a system, not just of tools, but also of related social behaviours and techniques'.

7. Chariot production

The tendency in the past has been to discuss the origins of various innovations in Egyptian warfare in the late Second Intermediate Period and early New Kingdom in terms of contact between different cultural groups resulting in the transmission of military ideas and hardware. Studies have therefore concentrated on trying to find out *when* weapons or ideas first appear in the archaeological record, and, if they do not appear to have evolved locally, *where* their likely source was located.

It is clear, however, that the process of innovation – or the means of adoption of new technology – is invariably much more complicated, involving not merely the acquisition of technological 'packages' or inventions but also, in each case, the emergence of a sympathetic set of social and economic conditions. In addition, it can be argued that military equipment and military strategy need to be seen as symbiotic and mutually influential – sometimes particular strategies are sparked off by the acquisition of new types of weapons, and sometimes the adoption of new methods of warfare result in the development or adoption of weapons that can enhance and facilitate such methods.

The emergence of Egyptian chariotry

The first Egyptian textual reference to chariotry is on the second Kamose stele, which mentions the chariots used by the Hyksos (Habachi 1972). The earliest examples of spoked wheels in Egypt are found on a small model carriage in the Theban tomb of Ahhotpe, mother of King Ahmose (Cairo, Egyptian Museum, JE4681; Smith 1981: 219, fig. 214). There are only a few previous depictions of the use of any kind of wheel at all, including siege-ladders running on solid wheels (one in the 5th-Dynasty tomb of Kaemheset at Saqqara and the other in the 11th-Dynasty tomb of Intef at Thebes: TT386; for which see Quibell and Hayter 1927 and Jaroš-Deckert 1984: 44-7; see Fig. 7.3) and a sledge with four wheels pulled by oxen (in the 13th-Dynasty tomb of Sobeknakht at Elkab, see Tylor 1896). This dearth of any real sign of development towards a sophisticated horse-drawn wheeled vehicle makes it likely that the chariot was not invented in Egypt but introduced from the outside world, almost certainly from western Asia.

As long ago as 1951, Torgny Säve-Söderbergh argued that the chariot was not introduced into Egypt by the Hyksos, but that both

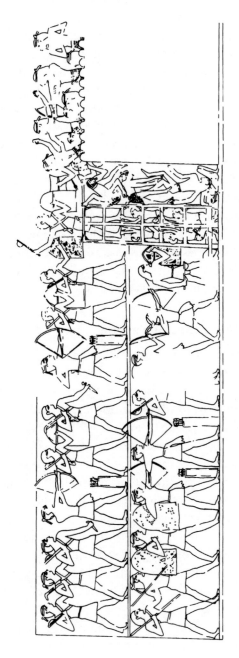

Fig. 7.3. Scene showing a mobile siege tower from the early Middle Kingdom tomb of the general Intef at Thebes.

Egyptians and Hyksos began to use it at about the same time at the end of the Second Intermediate Period (Säve-Söderbergh 1951: 60). The importance of the social and economic contexts of technological change with regard to the Egyptians' adoption of chariotry can be compared with a study of the introduction of the heavy horse-drawn plough into medieval northern Europe (White 1962). This study demonstrated that the time taken for this process of technological change lay not so much in the innovation itself but in the occurrence of the necessary changes in the social agricultural practices of the societies concerned, so that they were able to use the plough and to benefit significantly from its use. This case indicates that delays in the introduction of new technology are often to be found in social and economic processes of change rather than the ability to invent or replicate new technology. Spratt (1989: 255-6, fig. 12.5) has provided good evidence to suggest that earlier societies took longer to adopt innovations than later ones, presenting a graph that shows 'delay times' of various innovations from the bow and arrow in the 4th millennium BC to polyethylene in the 20th century AD. Another good archaeological example of this phenomenon is the delay in the appearance of techniques for casting bronze rapiers in Middle Bronze Age Britain (Rowlands 1976), although it should be mentioned, in fairness, that Stuart Piggott (1969) argues the exact opposite point of view: that no such socio-economic delay occurred in the introduction of wheeled vehicles and the plough into the cultures of Neolithic Europe.

Preconditions for the emergence of Egyptian chariotry

In order for a new piece of technology to be adopted, several basic factors need to be in place: (1) access to necessary resources or materials, (2) knowledge of methods of manufacture, (3) availability of suitably skilled craftsmen both to make and use the artefact, (4) a social need or political requirement for the technology in question, (5) a suitable social or economic context within which the technology can be deployed. If we study these in the case of the chariot and other military items supposedly introduced by the Hyksos we can get some sense of the full complexity of the situation.

In the case of Egyptian chariots, these basic factors correspond to (1) raw materials such as wood and leather, as well as live horses, (2) several

Fig. 7.4. Scene of craft workshops on a fragment of relief decoration from a 26th-Dynasty tomb at Saqqara, with chariot production at the right-hand side of the lower register.

different aspects of wood, leather, bone and metal-working technology, (3) access not only to craftsmen specialised in the manufacture of the various components of chariots, harnesses and bridles, but also to craftsmen with the necessary skills and knowledge to convert all these parts into the finished product, (4) military plans and strategies that would significantly benefit from the inclusion of chariot corps, and (5) plans for empire-building campaigns in Syria-Palestine and Nubia, as well as an increasingly militarised ruling group whose life-style and aspirations matched those of the Indo-European *maryannu* – an élite group for whom the chariot was not merely a piece of equipment but an important status symbol.

The groups of workers producing chariots must have comprised one of the most complex of all ancient workshops, both because of the diversity of materials involved and the wide range of technological skills required (see Drenkhahn 1976: 130). Several New Kingdom tombs show groups of craftsmen, such as carpenters, joiners and leather-workers working on the different parts of a chariot (see Fig. 7.4 for a 26th-Dynasty example). Drenkhahn points out that all of the six tombs containing scenes of chariot production between the reigns of Hatshepsut and Thutmose IV show the activities taking place in the workshops of the Temple of Amun at Karnak, and four of the six occupants of the tombs had been employed by the Temple of Amun. It is not clear why there should be this connection with one specific temple estate, although Drenkhahn suggests that temples – as regular recipients of foreign booty and prisoners of war – might have had more ready access to exotic timber and

7. Chariot production

Asiatic skilled craftsmen. From the late 18th Dynasty onwards, similar chariot-making scenes appear in private tombs at Saqqara, and Papyrus Anastasi I (British Museum, EA10247; Gardiner 1911: 1-34) provides an intriguing insight into the maintenance of chariotry with a description of an Egyptian charioteer's visit to a repair shop in the Levantine coastal city of Joppa.

To deal with the materials first: the principal materials used for a high quality chariot were wood, leather, rawhide, textile, bone, ivory, copper alloy, gold, gypsum plaster, faience, glass, stone and glue. The two most important materials were wood and rawhide. For the basic chassis of the vehicle, as well as its axle, wheels, pole and yoke (and sometimes, as in the case of Tutankhamun, the blinkers), various different types of wood were required – particularly ash (*Fraxinus excelsior*), imported from outside Egypt, which was used for the axle, felloes and frame. Two other imported woods were also used: field maple (*Acer campestre*) was used for the floor of the Florence chariot (see Fig. 7.5), and silver birch bark (*Betula pendula*) was used to cover an axle of a Tutankhamun chariot and also the axles of the Florence example. The purpose of the birch bark was almost certainly to waterproof the glue and rawhide holding the chariot together; it seems to have been used in the same way to waterproof composite bows. Willow (*Salix subserrata*, which *is* found in Egypt) was used for the Florence pole, and elm (*Ulmus minor*, an import) was used for its yoke, handrail and wheel spindles. Elm was also used in the chariot of Amenhotep III. Plum-wood (*Prunus domestica*, not found in Egypt) was sometimes used for the spokes. Locally available acacia was used for the front of the chassis.

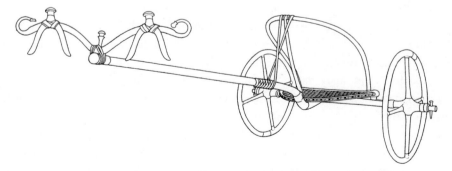

Fig. 7.5. Chariot from an 18th-Dynasty Theban tomb (Museo Archeologico, Florence).

Fig. 7.6. Depiction of steam bending for the manufacture of bows, in the tomb of Amenemhat at Beni Hasan.

The craftsmen would have needed to use the steam-bending technique to actually manufacture the chariot chassis and wheels, using strips of unseasoned timber. Egyptian carpenters were clearly already familiar with this technology at least as early as the 12th Dynasty, since there are scenes in the tombs of Amenemhat and Baket II at Beni Hasan (BH2 and BH15, see Newberry 1893: pls VII and XI) showing steam bending being used for the manufacture of bows (Fig. 7.6). In both scenes, the craftsmen are shown first holding wood over a pot of hot water to allow the steam to penetrate and soften the cellular structure, and secondly actually bending the stick into a hoop shape, with the ends buried in the ground to keep the shape. There are also 5th-Dynasty scenes in the tombs of Ptahshepses (Abusir) and Ty (Saqqara) showing the bending of dampened unseasoned poles of timber (Wild 1966: pl. CLXXIV).

Leather was used not only for the many thongs and pieces of harness but also to sheathe any surfaces likely to suffer stress or abrasion. In addition, rawhide was shrunk over the composite wheels to hold them together and provide a form of tyre, and leather traces were used to lash the central pole to the yoke. Since we know that there were few changes in leather-working technology between the Middle Kingdom and New Kingdom (see Van Driel-Murray 2000), it follows that Egyptian leather-workers would already have been capable of creating such components as tyres, traces and blinkers well before the arrival of the Hyksos.

Textiles were also used in chariots, primarily for 'kickboards', floor matting and housing. Two of the chariots from the tomb of Tutankhamun had a length of painted cloth – a kind of durable matting which would have been placed between the floors of chariots 120 and 122 and the side walls of their chassis. Vogelsang-Eastwood (2000: 276, 292) notes that one of these mats is made from a special kind of cloth involving a dense layer of long loops; she suggests that the 'springiness of the looping' would probably have helped to cushion the riders from the shaking of the vehicle.

Ivory, bone, stone, copper alloy and faience were used for the many small components holding the chariot and the harnesses together, such as copper alloy nails, stone saddle knobs, and copper alloy bits and linchpins. An important find among the pieces discovered in site Q1 at Qantir was a copper alloy 'nave cap', which prevented the linchpin from grating down on the wooden nave of the chariot. The nave cap of the Florence chariot was made from wood. Faience and glass were used for inlay on chariot bodies, as well as for yoke ends, yoke saddles and bridle bosses. Ivory was used mainly for charioteers' whip-stocks.

The net result of all this is that we can be fairly sure that the Egyptians already had access to nearly all of the necessary materials and technology for chariot production by the Middle Kingdom (see Table 7.1). They did, however, lack several important elements: first, they may not yet have had ready access to such imported woods as ash, elm and birch; secondly, they had most of the necessary skills and craftsmen to produce the components but probably did not acquire the methods and personnel to transform these into a finished chariot until the early New Kingdom; thirdly, there is very little indication of access to horses before the New Kingdom.

Technology	Imports
Steam-bending	Woods
Lathe-turning	Foreign craftsmen
Weft-loop weaving	Asiatic/Nubian horses
Increased use of leather	
Mortise and tenon joints	

Social change	Military change
Maryannu class	Emergence of 'professional' army
Appearance of 'general-kings'	Diversification of military hierarchy
Adoption of horse-riding	Use of composite bows, arm-guards and plate armour

Table 7.1. Minimum preconditions and requirements for the Egyptian adoption of chariotry in the early New Kingdom.

Chariot horses

Where did the Egyptians' chariot horses (*Equus caballus*) come from, and what evidence has survived? There are several extant examples of horses from pharaonic Egypt (see Raulwing and Clutton-Brock 2009: 40-59, Table 1 for a full discussion of examples of horses from Middle and Late Bronze Age contexts in Gaza, Sinai, Egypt and Sudan, and see Spalinger 2005: 8-13 for general discussion). The earliest horse so far found in Egypt is probably the skeleton excavated at Tell el-Dab'a in 2009, amid the stratigraphy of the palace of the Hyksos ruler Khyan. Identified as a mare between 5 and 10 years old, it appears not to have been a chariot horse but was more likely used for breeding (no further information is currently available on this horse, as it awaits full publication, see Kramar 2009; Bietak and Förstner-Müller 2009: 98-9, Taf. 8, and Bietak 2011: 40, for several brief preliminary discussions and photographs).

Previously the earliest known horse found in an Egyptian archaeological context was tentatively assumed to be the one discovered in 1958 by Bryan Emery at Buhen fortress and dated stratigraphically to around 1680-1640 BC (Emery 1960: 8-9). This horse measured 1.50m high at the withers (ridge between shoulder-bones), but the yoke measurements of surviving chariots suggest that the average Egyptian horse was probably about 1.35m high at the withers, i.e. slightly smaller than both the Buhen and the average modern Arabian horse (c. 1.45m). Clutton-Brock (1974) assigned the Buhen horse to the type defined by Bökönyi (1968) as a comparatively large and heavy-limbed type found in eastern Europe and central Asia in the Iron Age, and she also suggested that there might be 'excessive wear on the lower left first cheek premolar', perhaps indicating that it was fitted with a bit (Dixon et al. 1979: 192), making it likely to have been half of a chariot pair. Unfortunately both the stratigraphic record for this horse and a radiocarbon date taken in the 1970s have provided unclear results, making the suggested date slightly tentative. The archaeological context and historical significance of the Buhen horse have recently been reassessed by Raulwing and Clutton-Brock (2009) reaffirming doubts about the early date, and raising some uncertainties as to the existence of bit-wear on the teeth.

Another horse, with a withers height of about 1.42m, was buried beside one of the tombs of Senenmut (TT71), the well-known chief of works in the reign of Hatshepsut. Whereas the Buhen horse appears simply to have been encased in the mud-brick walling built over the spot where it died, the Senenmut horse was actually wrapped in linen bandages and placed in a 2.5m-long wooden coffin. A third horse was found in the 18th-Dynasty necropolis at Soleb in Nubia, and its height was between about 1.34m and 1.38m at the withers.

Both the Buhen and Senenmut horses appear to be basically Arabian in type, suggesting that the earliest examples were probably imported or plundered from western Asia. According to the Karnak *Annals*, Thutmose III captured more than 2000 horses after the battle of Megiddo (see Spalinger 2005: 90), and the 18th-Dynasty Theban tomb of Amunedjeh shows horses being brought by Syrians as tribute (Davies and Davies 1941: 97).

The earliest textual reference to horses in Egypt is the First Kamose Stele, which mentions those used by the Hyksos (Smith and Smith 1976: 60); the fact that the term used for a span of horses (*ḥtr*) is an Asiatic loan-word suggests that both the animals and the techniques for training and utilising them derived from western Asia. It should be noted, however, that there are also strong connections between the Nubians and horses. Although the clearest evidence for Nubia as a widely recognised international source of horses and trainers begins with the 25th Dynasty (see Dalley 1985 and Heidorn 1997), there are also earlier indications of Nubian horsemanship, therefore Nubia should not be ruled out as a possible source of horses even as early as the Second Intermediate Period, which is perhaps when the Buhen horse should be dated. It may be significant in this regard that several of our very small group of surviving early Egyptian horses were actually found in Nubia. This is particularly interesting when we bear in mind that the Thebans were perhaps as much cut off from the Kerma culture in Nubia as they were from Syria-Palestine and the Mediterranean during the Second Intermediate Period (see, for instance, Bourriau 2000: 201, although see also Bourriau 2000: 209 for Kerma Nubians as mercenaries in the late 17th-Dynasty Theban armies).

Given the evidence for the high value ascribed to Nubian horses and horsemen – and particularly their eventual use by the Assyrians for their chariotry and cavalry in the 7th century BC (see Dalley 1985), where they are specifically referred to as Kushite – the Egyptian adoption of chariotry by the end of the Second Intermediate Period might have been as much a question of Egyptians' access to suitable horses as the process of technological innovation implied in the use of chariots themselves – in other words the recognition of the need for technological change is ineffectual without access to the necessary materials and resources. Dalley (1985: 47) argues that 'the late 8th century was a time when the Assyrians were increasingly aware of the importance of equestrian technology. Suddenly during that period cavalry in particular developed into a newly powerful weapon of war. Innovation in the form of breeds of horses, methods of harnessing and of importing foreign experts, in particular from Nubia and Samaria for chariotry, from Urartu for cavalry, contributed to that development. It was a time when Nubia was ruled by kings to whom horses were one of life's chief delights ... and free trade in horses flourished. Nubia benefited enormously from an expanding market, and reached a peak of power and prosperity.' Dalley also makes the point that Samaria gained great prestige at this date from its role as entrepot supplying Nubian horses to the Assyrians for their chariotry (while the people of Urartu were supplying smaller horses, along with their trainers, for use in the Assyrian cavalry).

The transition from simple to composite bows: military technology as an integrated system

Many other innovations in Egyptian warfare seem to coincide with the immediate aftermath of the 'Hyksos period'. It is often difficult to determine the extent to which each of these changes and innovations are linked in any causal way. Probably the most significant and obvious military development apart from chariots was the adoption of the composite bow (McLeod 1970). The technique of glueing strips of horn and sinew to a wooden self bow produced the more elastic 'composite bow', which came in two types – recurved and triangular – and had a considerably greater range than the self bow (see, for instance, Miller et al. 1986). From the point of view of the overall process of military change, the adoption of chariots and composite bows must have been very closely linked, given that there is general agreement that chariots served above all as highly mobile bases from which archers could pick off the enemy from a distance (Spalinger 2005: 15-18).

Throughout the pharaonic period acacia wood was often used for bows and arrows (see Western and McLeod 1995), but the emergence of the composite bow led to a demand for different woods. The only known specimens of ash from ancient Egypt are (1) the wood of a composite bow from the tomb of Tutankhamun (see Gale et al. 2000: 341) as *F. excelsior*, rather than *F. ornus*, and (2) that used for the axle, the felloes and part of the frame of the floor of the Florence chariot. As mentioned above in the case of chariots, neither ash nor birch occur naturally in Egypt, and both of these imports were used primarily for construction, embellishment and waterproofing of chariots and composite bows. Although presumably most horn used in Egypt was derived from native – or at any rate African – species, circumstantial evidence exists to suggest that the horns of the Cretan wild goat (*agrimi*) might have been imported for making Egyptian composite bows (Warren 1995: 7 with references).

The introduction of the composite bow coincided with – and perhaps directly influenced – changes in the form of arm guards and quivers. New types of arm guards were introduced in the early New Kingdom (e.g. Berlin 15085 and Cairo JE31390, see McLeod 1982: 63), almost certainly because of the increasing use of the composite bow. The funerary depictions of the brightly coloured arm guards show them tied at both wrist and elbow. Unlike earlier guards, they cover much of the lower arm, but no actual examples seem to have survived, perhaps because they were made of something that would not have preserved well, such as padded textile.

Tapered, round-bottomed styles of quivers replaced the Middle Kingdom tubular types (McLeod 1982: 62). A red quiver in the Ägyptisches Museum, Berlin, now almost invisible under gelatinous decay, is decorated with open-work appliqués and couchwork with panels of superimposed coloured strips in red, white, green and black, with typical New-Kingdom-style green, pinked edgings. One of a pair of quivers from the 18th-Dynasty tomb of Maiherpri in the Valley of the Kings (KV36, reign of Thutmose III) is unusually well-preserved, retaining its fine, crisply executed designs in raised relief (perhaps block-stamped), revealing a quality of workmanship which has otherwise rarely survived (Cairo JE33775; see Daressy 1902: 32-3, pl. X, nos 24071-2). The new style of quiver was almost certainly the result of a change in the status of bowman and the need for both archers and their equipment to be incorporated into the design of the chariot. The arrow and javelin quivers were attached to the side-panel of the chariot in such a way and at such a precise angle that the charioteer could easily remove an arrow or javelin from the quivers when needed.

Body armour (small bronze plates riveted to linen or leather jerkins), was introduced by the early New Kingdom (see Hulit 2006), and a smaller type of shield, with a tapered lower half, began to be used. Both of these must presumably have been connected with the need to protect soldiers against the composite bow. Here we have a very clear set of cases where the form of one piece of technology was affected by the need to make it compatible with (or responsive to) another piece of technology. This phenomenon is discussed by Donald Mackenzie and Judy Wajcman in their introductory essay to *The Social Shaping of Technology* (1985), when they discuss the tendency for technology to be shaped not so much by science as by other technology: 'existing technology is more than just a precondition of new technology, but is an active shaping force in its development'. In other words, each individual weapon is part of an organic and dynamic system, so that individual pieces of military technology constantly interact with one another and adapt to the system, operating as components in a complex and slowly changing overall military strategy.

Changing systems of military reward

Turning away from military hardware to 'software', it is clear that innovations in Egyptian weaponry in the early New Kingdom were accompanied by important changes in the way that the army was organised, and indeed the role that it played in Egyptian society. Cuomo makes precisely this point in relation to the introduction of different types of catapult (and other innovations in military technology) in the Hellenistic period: 'To the extent to which there *was* a Hellenistic military revolution, it was a technical revolution not just because it saw the rise of new machines, but also because it gave wider currency and respectability to some features essential to technical knowledge. It propagated not only concrete notions about how tall a siege-tower should be or what material is best for catapult springs, but also a more general belief that one becomes a good soldier and general through training and learning, rather than being simply born a warrior and leader of men' (Cuomo 2007: 67). She therefore argues that the emergence of a new type of warfare based on technical knowledge and expertise brought about a fundamental change in the Hellenistic view of soldiery and battle – in other words the social repercussions of technical innovations are not to be underestimated.

David Lorton (1974) has suggested, on the basis of comparisons between the funerary inscriptions of the 6th-Dynasty official Weni at Abydos and the early 18th-Dynasty soldier Ahmose son of Ibana at Elkab, that there may have been no system of reward for individual soldiers in the Old Kingdom, and that complex systems of recompense might not have been introduced until *after* the Hyksos period, possibly as a direct result of the adoption of Hyksos customs of warfare. Thus, he points out that the term *sḳr ꜥnḫ* was used indiscriminately in the Old and Middle Kingdoms to refer both to enemies captured on the battlefield and to those taken while plundering defeated settlements, whereas from the late 18th Dynasty onwards it was used specifically to refer to enemy soldiers captured during the battle itself, while the term *ḥꜣḳt* was used to describe people or goods captured only in the course of post-battle plundering, taken to the king and then redistributed as rewards to individual soldiers, and finally the term *ḥꜣḳ* was used in the 18th Dynasty to designate both objects and people taken in the course of the actual battle and the subsequent plundering.

As with the weaponry, we should beware of suggesting that all changes that emerged in the early 18th Dynasty can be ascribed to contact with the Hyksos. It is equally likely – perhaps more likely – that the adoption of more complex systems of military recompense resulted from Egyptian involvement in Syria-Palestine and the consequent absorption of the 'language' of Asiatic warfare. In the same way, the Egyptians had clearly adopted Akkadian cuneiform script as the basis for international diplomatic communication by at least the middle of the 18th Dynasty (see Cohen and Westerbrook 2000), if not considerably earlier (see van Koppen and Radner 2009 and Bietak 2011: 41 for the discovery of a fragment of a cuneiform letter probably sent to Egypt by a late Old Babylonian ruler, dating to the Second Intermediate Period at Tell el-Dab'a).

Conclusions

Many innovations in Egyptian military equipment and strategies resulted directly from population movements, exchange of ideas between different ethnic and cultural groups, and processes of social change brought on both by large-scale environmental and political influences. Such innovations in military hardware went on to have significant effects on the social and political contacts between Egypt and the Levant, and between Egypt and the rest of northeastern Africa. The chronology of all this, however, suggests that the turning point for the Egyptians was not the *arrival* of the Hyksos but their *departure*.

It seems as if the Hyksos may have represented a significant barrier between the Egyptians and access to more sophisticated weaponry such as chariots, composite bows and body-armour (although see Moorey 2001 for an alternative view on this). It was only after the removal of the Hyksos that the Egyptians were able to gain access both to some of the necessary imported materials and probably also, initially at least, foreign craftsmen, so that they could begin to manufacture these new weapons. Many of the materials (such as acacia-wood, copper alloy, bone, stone, faience and rawhide) and much of the technological ability (such as steam-bending, lathe-turning and drilling) had already been available for some time within Egypt itself, but the crucial changes were the social and political ones, whereby Egyptians gained ready access to the resources of western Asia. Once they were able to import materials, craftsmen, horses and experienced charioteers, they could begin to create their own vehicles and to incorporate chariotry and horse-riding 'scout' divisions into their own military strategies.

In conclusion it is worth noting that an intriguing aspect of Egyptian chariotry – and one that is particularly evident in the Qadesh battle reliefs – is the number of ways in which Egyptian chariots appear to have differed from their Hittite and Syrian counterparts. Whereas the Egyptian chariots had a two-man crew and are shown with quivers attached for the archer, the Hittite and Syrian chariots are shown with three occupants, comprising a shield-bearer in front of the driver and a spearman behind him, and apparently no quivers for arrows or javelins. A less obvious difference between Egyptian and Hittite chariots is in the technology used to produce the 'snaffle bits' (see Herold 1999: 137-9).

If the Qadesh reliefs are a genuine reflection of differences between Egyptian and Asiatic chariot crews and their weapons, then we may have a situation comparable with that of the American and Soviet development of ballistic missiles after the war. Both sides started off with a fundamentally similar technological prototype – in the case of the

Egyptians and Hittites, the basic chariot of the 17th and 16th centuries BC, and in the case of the Americans and Soviets, the V2 rocket developed by the Germans during the Second World War. Mackenzie and Wajcman (1985: 10) describe the situation as follows: 'American and Soviet missile designers ... developed significantly different missiles, despite their shared use of the V-2 as departure point'.

In the case of both modern and ancient divergences in the use of technology, whether we are talking about chariots or missiles, there are clear indications that even cultures or ethnic groups sharing a common paradigm will find that their individual technological trajectories can vary considerably as a result of social, political and strategic factors. To take another recent example of socially determined trajectories in technology, the 20th-century dominance of the gasoline-powered car, as opposed to electrically powered vehicles, can be seen to have its origins not in decisions made on the basis of pure efficiency but in the economics of early 20th-century gender relations – thus women drivers clearly preferred electric cars, but it was primarily men who determined which car a family would have, thus leading to the virtual demise of the electric car by the 1930s, despite the fact that, for short trips, the latter was cleaner, quieter and easier to run: 'it is not some sort of simple "best" technology that always wins. It is a matter of the cultural ideals, economic relations, and social power relations that define what counts as best, for whom, and for whose preferred activities and values' (Bauchspies et al. 2006: 36).

Military hardware: the east Mediterranean knowledge economy and the emergence of the Iron Age in Egypt

The glue holding the Amarna system together was exchange – commercial, dynastic, and cultural ... while proclaiming their self-sufficiency, Great Kings in fact depended on each other for the supply of various key items, such as gold, iron and horses (Cohen and Westbrook 2000: 226).

Introduction

This chapter looks at the ways in which the surviving textual information about Egyptian and Hittite approaches to military technology and strategy in the Late Bronze Age can be enhanced and supplemented by visual evidence in the many Egyptian battle reliefs of the Late Bronze Age. It also compares the Hittite weaponry and tactics with those that appear to have been employed by the Egyptians, in order to try to gain some sense of what might be described as the 'knowledge network' of warfare in the Late Bronze Age. To what extent did two of the great empires of the Late Bronze Age differ from one another in their attitudes and approaches to battle, and, most importantly perhaps, to what extent can we see their approaches 'converging' during this period as people, ideas and artefacts flowed back and forth in the form of booty, prisoners of war and élite diplomatic exchange (see Fig. 8.1 for a map of the eastern Mediterranean and Near East in the Late Bronze Age)?

A closely related issue is the set of possible mechanisms by which war affects technology. Joel Mokyr (1990: 183) raises the question of cause and effect: 'Whether in fact innovations in military technology provided

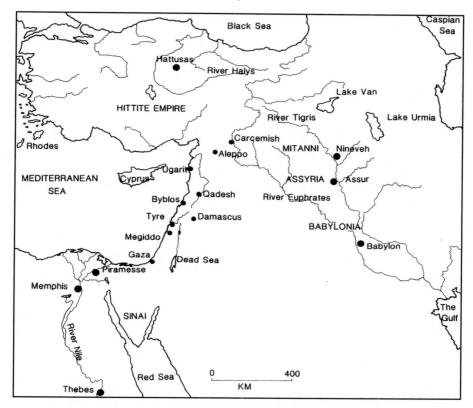

Fig. 8.1. Map of the Eastern Mediterranean and Near East in the Late Bronze Age.

substantial benefits in the production of peacetime goods and services so that war can be thought of as an agent of technical progress is far from easy to determine.' In fact Mokyr goes on to argue that 'although military needs served at times as "focusing devices" ... weapons were more often borrowers of civilian technology than sources of inspiration for it' (Mokyr 1990: 186). In the context of the development of Late Bronze Age east Mediterranean and Near Eastern military technology, there is no doubt that, as in other periods and places, we are dealing with a very complex web of social and technological factors (see Chapter 7 above).

Throughout the images depicting Near Eastern and east Mediterranean warfare there are a number of constantly repeated iconographic motifs, such as rulers smiting foreigners, the siege and capture of settlements,

111

the binding and execution of prisoners, and the offering of the spoils of war to the gods (see Heinz 2001 and Hall 1986). These acts can all be encompassed within a very simple theme in which the role of these rulers was to fight battles on behalf of the gods and then bring back the prisoners and booty to dedicate to the gods in their temples. However, a number of questions might be asked concerning such images, as well as the later paintings and reliefs documenting acts of war. One of these is equally relevant both to the question of the ancient knowledge economy of the eastern Mediterranean and to the nature of military technology and warfare in this region: to what extent were these earliest depictions of battle always an oversimplification of the real pragmatic political/ military situation, and to what extent might they misrepresent the true detail of warfare and weaponry?

The tendency in the past has been to discuss the origins of various innovations in east Mediterranean warfare in the Late Bronze Age in terms of contact between different cultural groups resulting in the transmission of military ideas and hardware. Studies have therefore concentrated on trying to find out when weapons or ideas first appear in the archaeological record, and, if they do not appear to have evolved locally, where their likely source was located. In this chapter, however, it is argued that military equipment and military strategy need to be seen as symbiotic and mutually influential – sometimes particular strategies are sparked off by the acquisition of new types of weapons, and sometimes the adoption of new methods of warfare result in the development or adoption of weapons that can enhance and facilitate such methods.

How then does the knowledge economy of military strategy and weaponry appear in the iconography of battle reliefs and in the terminology and tone of the Near Eastern diplomatic correspondence? Do the two types of source material overlap and/or correspond with one another? How are commodities (weapons), ideas (strategies) and people (e.g. mercenaries and prisoners of war) moving around the east Mediterranean in the Late Bronze Age? What do we know from Anatolian sources; what do we glean from Egyptian texts and images; and how well do these two bodies of source material correlate? The key factor here, as far as east Mediterranean technology is concerned, is 'convergence' – arguably the technologies for stone vessel-making were gradually becoming relatively homogeneous throughout the region during the Bronze Age (see Sparks 2001). Research into vitreous materials in the eastern Mediterranean also suggests that there was an extremely complex convergence of materials and techniques in this area of technology: '... the main body of Aegean Bronze Age faience, as well as Egyptian blue frit and glass fits into the general Aegean iconography and is thus considered as a characteristic Aegean product. There are, however, technical, compositional and even stylistic similarities with both the Near East and Egypt' (Panagiotaki et al. 2004: 150).

A number of scholars (e.g. Oppenheim 1978 and Moorey 1989) have discussed the likely role played by royal courts and diplomatic systems in Bronze Age processes of technological contact and exchange (see particularly Chapters 3 and 6 above, on scribes and glass-workers respectively). Moorey (2001: 4) argues that 'It was not accidental that courts were central to technological developments. Only in such places were the necessary resources in terms of labour and materials, tools and workshops readily available on an appropriate scale.' To what extent was this process of transmission via royal courts and international diplomatic correspondence also true of military technology and tactics?

Policy and strategy in the Hittite and Egyptian spheres of influence

To begin with the broadest strategic and political sphere of warfare, we can look at the evidence for Hittite and Egyptian responses to the ideas of empire-building and conquest. Trevor Bryce (2002: 100) suggests that, as far as the Hittite ruler was concerned, 'though his kingdom was geared to a state of constant military preparedness, the king himself was never the instigator of aggression, at least to his way of thinking'. In other words, even at its height, the Hittite rulers and their officials might be considered to have been in a state of denial as to their repeated undertaking of hostile acts of conquest. Interestingly, the same situation has also been argued to prevail in Egypt: Spalinger (1982: 240) argues that '... the king is the passive component of war. He acts only after he has received news of foreign unrest. His armies are dispatched only after others have stirred up trouble'. Both Bryce and Spalinger are keen to point out, however, that these were probably calculated postures deliberately evoked by both the Egyptian and Hittite texts, and that the real situation can sometimes be read, between the lines, as one of ruthless pragmatism.

Nevertheless, the fact remains that two of the major powers of the Late Bronze Age east Mediterranean share a tendency to consciously and purposefully present foreign conquests almost as accidents rather than as the result of careful *Realpolitik* strategies, whereas the latter is the clear impression given by Late Bronze Age diplomatic correspondence between the Egyptian rulers and their rivals and vassals in western Asia (see, for example, the social-psychological analysis of the Amarna Letters: Druckman and Güner 2000: 176).

How then do the Great Powers of the Late Bronze Age differ in terms of their specific military strategies? One of the most fundamental questions in the study of Egyptian warfare is whether battles were opportunist, unpredictable affairs, or whether, like Classical Greek conflicts, there was an element of ritual not merely in the depictions of the battles but in the actual confrontations between armies. There is perhaps some evidence for a tendency towards more symbolic confrontations in the whole paraphernalia of diplomacy and agreements throughout the Near East, and Yadin (1963: 100) and Goedicke (1985: 83) have both argued that the location and date of the Megiddo and Qadesh battles might have been pre-arranged by the two sides. Although many Egyptologists would certainly not agree with so radical an interpretation of the surviving reliefs and papyri documenting these events, which seem too unique and idiosyncratic to be regarded as mere large-scale rituals, there are certain recurring motifs (such as the heroism of the king in adversity and his tendency to advocate daring tactics in place of the cautious plans of his generals). Nevertheless, the course of each battle was evidently spontaneous, and there is no question of anything as predictable as the clash of hoplite phalanxes. Thus, although the time and place of crucial battles in the Late Bronze Age may at least sometimes have been pre-arranged, their forms were invariably unpredictable. Goedicke (1985: 83) is undoubtedly rather stretching the evidence when he claims that 'the notion of surprise as a legitimate strategic move is not an ancient Near Eastern concept', although he does concede that Egyptian siege warfare might have included surprise tactics.

Although the Egyptians often appear to criticise the Asiatics for their use of guerilla tactics, this does not necessarily imply that they never used such methods themselves. In *The Instruction Addressed to King Merikare*, the supposed author, a ruler of the Heracleopolitan period (*c.* 2081-1987

BC) named Khety, complains that 'the vile Asiatic ... does not announce the day of battle, like a thief whom a gang has rejected ... The Asiatic is a crocodile on its river bank that snatches from a lonely road but cannot take from the quay of a populous town' (Parkinson 1997: 223-4). Khety's criticism, however, is perhaps directed more at the Asiatics' lack of ambition or heroism than their use of unorthodox tactics.

In the various depictions of the Battle of Qadesh, Broadhurst (1992: 78) has pointed out that 'Ramesses needed assistance to defeat the vast number pitted against him. In three scenes he receives it from a chariot troop ... who trap the Hittites occupying the area behind the king, in one of the earliest examples of an ambush.' In addition, Raban (1989: 163) argues, with reference to Ramesses III's defeat of the Sea Peoples: 'The famous battle scene from his temple at Medinet Habu depicts a twin encounter: one on the land an one in the water ... From the attached texts and from the references to this battle in Papyrus Harris I, it appears as if the naval battle was much like the land battle – an ambush, or a surprise attack of combined Egyptian military units on a mass of immigrants ... .'

Iconography versus texts

If Late Bronze Age military tactics can be argued to be relatively homogeneous throughout the east Mediterranean, and perhaps only significantly influenced by differences in terrain, topography and overall political aims, what is the situation concerning soldiers and military technology? How much overlap was there between the characteristics of the troops and weaponry used by Hittites and Egyptians? As Gurney pointed out over fifty years ago, the Hittites' own depictions of their infantry warriors differ from those portrayed by the Egyptians (Gurney 1954: 88-9). Whereas the Hittites show them wearing short belted tunics only reaching down to a point above the knee, the Egyptian reliefs suggest that they wore long gowns with short sleeves. The weaponry also differs: the figure of a Hittite warrior-god from the jamb of the King's Gate at Hattuša (Boghazköy) wears a belted kilt and helmet, and is armed with an axe and short sword, whereas the typical Egyptian image of the Hittite soldier tends to show him carrying a spear, which is usually not shown by the Hittite artists until a later date. One possible answer is that many of the soldiers depicted in the Egyptian reliefs were

Fig. 8.2. Scene from the Battle of Qadesh, as depicted on an external wall of the temple of Ramesses II at Abydos, showing Egyptian chariots and charioteers – the figure in the centre wears the short kilt typical of Egyptian soldiers.

not actually Hittite but from other ethnic groups within the Hittite empire and sphere of influence. Another likely answer, however, is that the Egyptians deliberately depict the Hittites and their allies in this non-Egyptian costume in order to clearly distinguish them from the Egyptian soldiers, whose short kilt (see Fig. 8.2) would otherwise have easily been confused with that of the enemy.

Schulman (1988: 54-5) discusses some of the detailed images of Akhenaten's first campaign against the Hittites, recorded on talatat blocks from Karnak. Talatat F-1253-4 shows Hittites depicted with pigtail-style sidelocks. On two other talatat (Schulman 1988: pls 14.1-2) helmets are shown as part of the battlefield debris. This type of helmet is fairly distinctive squat, open-faced form with a neck protector and plumed crest – it appears to be the so-called *gurpisu ḫasippari suppuru* ('plumed bronze helmet') typically found in the Near East in the late 2nd millennium BC, which in fact is the kind of helmet worn by the warrior god at Boghazköy mentioned above. Here however this headgear is shown worn by both Hittites and Egyptians, suggesting further blurring of the traditionally strict boundaries of weaponry and costume. Kendall (1981: 215-21) argues that helmets of this distinctive so-called Syrian type were actually produced in Egypt.

In the 1983-4 seasons of excavation at Qantir (Piramesse), in the Egyptian eastern Delta, eight limestone 'moulds' for shields were found, each measuring around 1.25 x 1.25m (Pusch 1996: 142-4, figs 135-8).

These moulds, however, were not designed to produce the standard Egyptian rectangular shield; instead they were designed to produce typical Hittite trapezoidal or 'figure-of-eight' shields, one incorporating a stylised version of a bull's head probably referring to a Hittite weather-god. Craftsmen would have used the moulds to hammer out the sheets of copper alloy that would form the outer edges of wood and leather shields. Here we therefore have evidence of direct collaboration between Egyptian and Hittite workers, operating on Egyptian soil, to produce weaponry that would usually be considered quintessentially non-Egyptian. It is by no means clear quite why or how this technological exchange was taking place, but it places another question mark over the apparently rigid distinction between Egyptian weaponry and that of their rivals. Pusch argues that the dating of the Hittite shield moulds could theoretically relate to one or other of three events in the reign of Ramesses II: the arrival in Egypt of the deposed Hittite ruler Urhi Teshup, the year 21 peace-treaty between Ramesses and the Hittite ruler Hattusilis III, and the year 34 marriage to the Hittite princess who was given the Egyptian name of Maat-hor-neferu-ra, recorded in the 'marriage stele' at Abu Simbel. He suggests that the last of these is most likely, on the grounds of the stratigraphic position of one of the shield-moulds (linking it with pillars inscribed with the 'royal protocol of Ramesses II in regnal year 30' (Pusch 1996: 144).

Van Dijk (2000: 300) has argued that the scenario for this Egypto-Hittite technological exchange must belong to the late Ramessid period: 'Many foreigners lived in the city [of Piramesse] some of whom eventually became high-ranking officials ... As a result of the peace treaty with the Hittites, specialist craftsmen sent by Egypt's former enemy were employed in the armoury workshops of Piramesse to teach the Egyptians their latest weapons technology, including the manufacture of much-sought-after Hittite shields.'

The depiction of the year 8 battle of Ramesses III against the Sea Peoples

The principal innovations in military tactics and technology that emerged in the Egyptian battles of the New Kingdom, compared with earlier conflicts, probably stemmed from the introduction of the composite

Fig. 8.3. Scene from the battle against the Sea Peoples during the reign of the 20th-Dynasty ruler, Ramesses III, from the exterior northern wall of his mortuary temple at Medinet Habu, showing an Egyptian boat containing oarsmen, archers and foot soldiers.

bow and the chariot. The importance of the chariot was simply that it conferred mobility – it enabled archers to move around the battlefield more rapidly, but ultimately the battle, whether siege or open confrontation, was still considered to consist of two basic components: first bowmen and secondly infantry armed with spears and axes. The Medinet Habu reliefs depicting the famous naval encounter with the Sea Peoples in the reign of Ramesses III (*c.* 1182-1151 BC) show that the same situation applied even to sea battles – boats were were used as seaborne chariots containing groups of oarsmen, archers and footsoldiers (see Fig. 8.3). They allowed the Egyptians to encircle the enemy, while releasing hails of arrows, eventually closing in on the enemy's own boats, so that the infantry could engage in conventional hand-to-hand fighting.

The Medinet Habu reliefs showing the naval battle include depictions of ships that appear very similar regardless of the occupants – all of them appear to be modified versions of Aegean light galleys and Late Bronze Age Syrian merchant ships (the latter being the prototype of the Phoenician *hippos* vessel). Although those manned by Egyptian soldiers or their allies incorporate Egyptian-style aftercastles and rudders, the basic nature of each of the boats is very similar, suggesting that the emerging sea-powers of the Late Bronze Age were not necessarily employing hardware that was culturally or ethnically distinct. The boats of Sea Peoples and Egyptians, as depicted at Medinet Habu, both appear to have been very similar amalgams of east Mediterranean naval technology, and in fact, as Raban (1989: 170) suggests, 'It is therefore tempting to assume that the type of boat the Egyptian artist has selected to represent the Egyptian navy was actually a vessel introduced by the sea peoples.' Raban (1989: 171) therefore concludes that 'the specialization and the technical innovations that are shown in both types [i.e. both Sea Peoples' and Egyptians' boats] were very probably the outcome of century-long extensive naval encounters between rival parties – the sea peoples, the Canaanites and the Egyptians'. As in the case of the land-based weaponry discussed above, the development of the naval technology of the eastern Mediterranean in the Late Bronze Age seems to have involved extensive technology transfer even between supposed rivals. This may also have extended to tactics, with Ramesses III's army and navy evidently trapping the Sea Peoples by blockading the mouths of rivers, thereby 'catching the enemy like birds in a net' – this strategy may resemble 'riverine' tactics acribed to the Sea Peoples themselves in a text from Ugarit (RS.20.238, see Wachsmann 1981: 181).

The spread of military hardware and software through mercenaries, prisoners of war and diplomatic 'packages'

What then were the physical, practical mechanisms by which military technology and tactics were disseminated and shared in the Late Bronze Age knowledge economy of the east Mediterranean? Such 'mercenaries' as the Sherden brought with them their own types of weaponry and tactics (see Fig. 8.4), and this can be seen to be happening both with 'free' mercenaries and with enforced prisoner-of-war-style mercenaries. This is surely the most effective form of transmission of changes in material culture and mentalities, but diplomacy (through exchange of people and artefacts and through establishment of 'embassies') is probably the other principal mechanism.

The coincidence of several features of recent excavations at Qantir suggest that diplomatic activity and technology transfer might have been closely linked. Not only have the Hittite shield moulds, described above, been found, but in 1999, in the area of the city designated QVII,

Fig. 8.4. Scene from an external wall of the temple of Ramesses II at Abydos, showing a group of Sherden mercenaries, with their distinctive helmets, shields and swords.

part of a cuneiform tablet was unearthed (Spencer 2004: 26-7), raising the possibility that a Ramessid archive like that at Amarna might have existed in the vicinity. Even if this small fragment – only 5 x 5cm and bearing just 11 lines of text – turns out to be an isolated find, it hints at the possibility that the population of Piramesse included not only Hittite craftsmen but also perhaps a relatively permanent staff of Hittite 'embassy' officials. The finds of shield-moulds and tablet are linked by EA22, a letter in the Amarna archive that was sent by Tushratta, ruler of the western Asiatic kingdom of Mitanni, to Amenhotep III of Egypt, in which a list of élite diplomatic gifts sent to Egypt includes 'one leather shield with *urukmannu* of silver weighing ten shekels' (the Hurrian term *urukmannu* probably referring to the outer metal parts of a shield).

The excavations at Qantir have also yielded a worked boar's tusk (82/0849, see Pusch 1996: fig. 134), which may have been part of a cheek-piece from a Mycenaean-style helmet. Once again a find from Amarna provides a context both confirming the integration of 'foreign' equipment within Egyptian weaponry and the likely long-term nature of such integration and exchange: fragments of a painted papyrus excavated from building R43.2 at Amarna include two soldiers within the Egyptian army apparently depicted wearing boar's tusk helmets and cropped ox-hide tunics, which would probably identify them as Mycenaean infantry within the Egyptian army in the mid-14th century BC (British Museum EA74100, see Parkinson and Schofield 1993; Schofield and Parkinson 1994). The presence of a fragment of such a helmet at Qantir suggests that other non-Egyptian weaponry may have been used, and perhaps even manufactured, at the city of Piramesse in the Ramessid period.

The Qantir and Amarna finds, the latter dating from at least a century earlier than the former, paint a possible picture of eastern Mediterranean military technology transfer taking place within a diplomatic context for much of the New Kingdom. Table 8.1 compares the 'traditional' assumptions concerning mechanisms of Late Bronze Age technology transfer with the recent evidence concerning such processes.

Traditional assumptions	Recent evidence
Booty/spoils	'Embassies'
'High level' trade	'Low level' trade
Prisoners of war	Entourages of foreign princesses
'Mercenaries'	Technological 'packages'

Table 8.1. Technological transfer and 'convergence' in the Late Bronze Age.

The painted temple reliefs depicting some of the great battles of the Late Bronze Age have a tendency, not surprisingly, to oversimplify the situation – the Egyptian depictions accentuate the ethnic stereotypes of individual soldiers, and in order to make the battles easier to 'read' as narratives of confrontations between state armies, they use a kind of visual shorthand with which we need to deal very cautiously. However, if some of the details of these battle reliefs are interpreted sufficiently carefully – and placed in the context of the recent finds, such as the Hittite (and possible Mycenaean) material at Qantir – we can gain a strong sense of the complex reservoir of ideas and weaponry from which each of the great states of the Late Bronze Age east Mediterranean were drawing. In other words, the features which appear to be typically Hittite, Syrian, Cretan, Mycenaean or Egyptian about armies, and in particular their weaponry and tactics, need to be balanced against the *lingua franca* of warfare that undoubtedly existed. None of these armies existed in isolation from one another, and although there clearly were differences between the major armies at each point in time, such as the different style and manning of Hittite chariots compared with those of the Egyptians at Qadesh, they also had a great deal in common, and the degree to which they shared tactics, weaponry and personnel is not to be underestimated.

If there was a Late Bronze Age equivalent of the modern knowledge economy then it can be seen to have permeated the field of military technology, ensuring that soldiers, tactics and weaponry ebbed and flowed between different armies and states rather than being fixed components of ethnic groups. This also has repercussions for our approach to the study of ancient weaponry, the technology and dissemination of which may not have been so clearly delineated by cultural and ethnic boundaries as we have previously assumed. Carmen and Harding (1999: 250) argue, 'We are interested in particular types of objects – among them weapons – because we are interested in the role those objects played in a past culture, what was the nature of their social life, and not just in how they achieved their end of killing or wounding an opponent.'

Returning to Joel Mokyr's discussions of technological and economic change, his observations on medieval Europe might equally be applied to the east Mediterranean of the Late Bronze Age: 'the Europeans were willing to learn from each other. Inventions such as the spinning wheel, the windmill and the weight-driven clock recognized no boundaries' (Mokyr 1990: 188). It is also worth considering, however, that military technology – weaponry – may have existed and evolved within a particularly rich context of cultural exchange networks, which we may be severely underestimating by our tendency to stereotype them in ethnic terms.

The delayed Egyptian Iron Age: military and technological repercussions

One aspect of military technology that was already emerging during the Late Bronze Age was the introduction of iron weaponry. Throughout the Near East, iron seems to have been more frequently produced from about the mid-1st millennium BC onwards, thus suggesting that this was technically when the Iron Age began in the region as a whole. The one country where this did not happen was Egypt, and it is sometimes suggested that the Egyptians' lack of iron weapons might have played a large part in their conquest by the Assyrians (*c.* 667 BC) and Persians (*c.* 525 BC). Moorey (1994: 286), however, argues that iron weapons were not necessarily superior to their bronze equivalents, even in the Neo-Babylonian period, and that, as far as Assyrian transition from bronze to iron was concerned, 'the vital factors may have been more political than technological in the strict sense', by which he means that the expanding Assyrian empire of the 9th century BC came into contact with peoples in Syria and Anatolia who had already developed sophisticated methods of iron-working, and that this, combined with their sophisticated political organisation, pushed the Assyrians away from bronze and towards more widespread manufacture of iron weapons (the whole process being probably exacerbated by a shortage of tin): 'the Assyrian state, moreover, in the Neo-Assyrian period, had the capacity to set up the necessary industrial infrastructure for the extensive exploitation of iron' (Moorey 1994: 287).

In the mid-19th century Christian Jurgensen Thomsen invented the so-called Three Age System when he organised the prehistoric artefacts in the National Museum of Antiquities at Copenhagen into a chronological order that corresponded to a sequence of three cultural stages distinguished by the use of stone, bronze and iron respectively (Thomsen 1836, Gräslund 1981). Thomsen's work laid the foundations for the chronology of European prehistory, and the Three Age System has subsequently been applied by European historians to many other parts of the world. However, not all cultures across the world can be equally easily defined according to the use of different materials for tool-making, and the Egyptian 'Iron Age' is a good example of the problems inherent in attempting to use a material-based chronological system of this type on a world-wide basis (cf. Beaujard 2010).

The absorption of Egypt into the Achaemenid empire took place in about 600 BC, just around the time that iron became so common in Mesopotamia that it replaced copper as the cheapest metal (Haarer 2001: 264-5, Warburton 2003: 254). Why was iron not widely used in Egypt until the late 1st millennium BC, when the rest of the Near East had been experiencing a full-fledged Iron Age from at least the middle of the 1st millennium (see Moorey 1994: 289-90)? There is no cultural vacuum between the Egyptian Late Bronze Age and the early Ptolemaic period.

123

Indeed, in a sense, the Late Period corresponds to Egypt's early Iron Age, and Egyptian culture was by no means technologically moribund during this period of seven centuries. The material culture of Late Period Egypt is full of vibrant and innovative developments in the working of materials and manufacturing of artefacts. Nevertheless, there seems little doubt that iron took an unusually long time to become a core element of the Egyptian economy.

The widespread use of iron throughout the ancient world was generally delayed not by lack of access to supplies of iron ore (which is often more plentifully available than copper or tin) but by the fact that iron smelting and manufacturing techniques took some considerable time to be developed. Although iron melts at a much higher temperature than most other metals, such as copper, tin, silver and gold, it can be smelted (i.e. released from the ore) at similar temperatures to copper (1100-1150°C). The real problem is that the actual smelting techniques are much more complex, and that the subsequent stages of processing (e.g. forging, hammering and carburisation) only emerged after long periods of difficult experimentation. However, once these technological developments had appeared, the Iron Age would have had several clear advantages over the previous copper-alloy-based economies. First, the wider availability of iron ore meant that metal artefacts could be produced locally and therefore often more cheaply; secondly, the blades of iron tools and weapons usually had a tougher, sharper cutting edge than their copper alloy equivalents.

Anthony Snodgrass (1980) has outlined three basic stages in the transition from copper alloy to iron, the first being the occasional use of iron as an expensive ornamental item, the second the use of iron for standard implements (but at a less frequent level than copper), and the third the situation in which iron predominates over copper as a working metal, although not necessarily entirely displacing it. While there seems to be broad scholarly agreement with the three basic stages outlined by Snodgrass, there has been considerable criticism of the details of his theory, such as the speed with which the transition is supposed to have happened in the Mediterranean region (within about two hundred years) and the fact that the greater use of iron (and its increasing cheapness) is said to be caused at least partly by a growing shortage of copper and tin, particularly during the third stage of the transition. There has also been much debate as to whether Cyprus and the Aegean were really central to this change, as Snodgrass (1980: 338-9) argues, or whether they were peripheral to major innovations that took place first in Mesopotamia, as Peter Haarer (2001) has suggested. In other words, the problem of Egypt's late arrival in a true Iron Age is exacerbated by considerable uncertainty as to how, why and precisely when iron-working appeared elsewhere in the eastern Mediterranean.

The evidence for iron-working in the Near East during the 2nd millennium derives mainly from textual sources. It is clear from such documents that at this time iron was worth about five times as much as gold, and it was among the high prestige materials that the great kings of the region were sending to one another as gifts (Feldman 2006, Pons Mellado 2006). A few New Kingdom examples of such gifts have survived in Egypt, including the well-known golden-hilted iron dagger in the tomb of Tutankhamun, which is thought likely to have been presented to him by a contemporary Hittite ruler (Feldman 2006: 16). The most important implication of Tutankhamun's dagger is that iron was at this date (*c.* 1330 BC) still very much an exotic precious material from an Egyptian point of view. It was in fact not until the very late 1st millennium BC that iron was widely used in Egypt (i.e. Snodgrass's stage 3). It should be noted, however, that there are instances of relatively early use of iron in Egypt, at a date when it is likely to have taken the form of opportunistic use of meteoric iron – these would in a sense lie outside Snodgrass's three stages, as they tend to be utilitarian rather than prestigious ornamental uses (see Tylecote 1992: 3, 51). Ogden (2000: 166-7) points out the difficulties in securely identifying the examples of likely meteoric iron used in Egypt as early as the late 4th and early 3rd millennia BC – usually meteoric iron is assumed to be unusually high in nickel content (Lucas 1962: 237-8), but Craddock (1995: 104) has pointed out that some examples that are almost certainly meteoric in origin have no nickel in them at all. Small early pieces of iron could of course also easily have been the by-products of copper smelting (see Ogden 2000: 167).

Why did the Egyptians take some three hundred years longer to adopt iron processing technology than their neighbours in the Near East? One very practical consideration might have been the fact that hafted hammers seem not to have been introduced into Egypt until the Late

Period – this would potentially have been fairly significant in terms of the development of Egyptian iron-working, since the process of hot-working iron would have been far less comfortable with unhafted hammers (see Ogden 2000: 168).

The largest surviving set of iron artefacts that may perhaps date to the Achaemenid period in Egypt is a group of 23 wood-working tools excavated at Thebes by Petrie (1897: 18-19; 1909: 106). Petrie dated them to the 26th Dynasty, although some archaeologists have suggested that they are no earlier than the Ptolemaic period (4th to 1st century BC; see Williams and Maxwell-Hyslop 1976). It is unclear whether the mysterious lack of unhafted hammers is the only reason that can so far be suggested for Egypt's reluctance (or inability) to convert to the brave new world of iron. In the meanwhile, we can only assume that there was some as yet unidentified trend of social or economic conservatism that acted as a disincentive to metallurgical innovation in Late Period Egypt. Edgerton (2008: 9), however, makes the point that the 'failure' of a society or group to accept and adopt a technological innovation should not be dismissed as mere conservatism: 'The assumption that the new is clearly superior to what went before has an important corollary: failure to move from one to the other is to be explained by "conservatism", not to mention stupidity or straightforward ignorance. "Resistance to technology" becomes a problem to be addressed by psychologists, sociologists, even historians.'

Thus, in reality, there seem to have been many situations in which societies, ancient or modern, have chosen to reject or ignore new technologies not because they distrusted their novelty but because there were no obvious discernible problems with the existing techniques or artefacts. Just because an innovation is known to exist does not mean that it will be automatically embraced, and a failure to embrace it can stem as much from pragmatism as from 'conservatism'.

Technology embedded in urban society: finding the individual in the general

How were we to translate mounds and concentrations of artifact debris into sociological phenomena? (Sanders et al. 1979: 16).

This chapter addresses some of the questions relating to the social and economic context of technology in Egypt – in other words, the practical issues concerning the physical location of craftsmen, workshops and ateliers in ancient settlements. Where did they ply their trades and to what extent were they 'self-employed' or subject to state or temple control? The preceding chapters have discussed different areas of science and technology without directly tackling such problems as the identification of individual ancient Egyptian craft-workers and their households amid the great mass of surviving settlement data. This chapter therefore explores the ways in which Egyptian archaeological data can shed light on the pursuit of particular specialised crafts or professions.

The varieties of lifestyles and occupations in New Kingdom Egypt feature in such Ramessid texts as Papyrus Boulaq 4 (Mariette 1871: pls 15-28; Lichtheim 1976: 136-46) and Papyrus Lansing (Budge 1923; Blackman and Peet 1925). Part of the challenge of the material remains at ancient Egyptian settlement-sites such as Amarna, Memphis, Deir el-Ballas or Gurob is that of bringing to life the socio-economic abstractions of the New Kingdom texts through interpretation of the material debris of households and craft-workers.

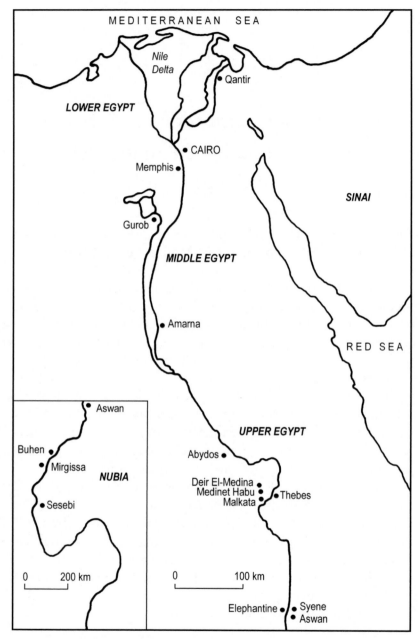

Fig. 9.1. Map showing the location of Amarna.

9. Technology embedded in urban society

The city at Amarna as a laboratory for studying social integration of technology

Despite a great deal of survey and excavation of New Kingdom settlements over the last few decades (e.g. Qantir: Pusch 1996, Deir el-Ballas: Lacovara 1990, Gurob: Shaw 2008, 2011), the Late Bronze Age city at Amarna (Figs 9.1 and 9.2) is our richest source for patterns of craftwork in New Kingdom Egyptian towns. It is possible to gain a superficial indication of the range and relative importance of activities across the city of Amarna as a whole (see the barchart in Fig. 9.3), but this kind of quantitative information can obviously be biased by many factors of preservation and archaeological visibility. It is not simply that certain activities may be altogether lost from the archaeological record but that some may, by their nature, leave more or less debris than others. It is therefore difficult to infer the relative importance of activities from barcharts recording quantities of objects, since the charts cannot be automatically 'converted' into 'hours of work' or 'numbers of craftworkers'. A higher percentage of spinning and weaving artefacts in the North Suburb than in the North City can be fairly securely interpreted as an indication of a socio-economic difference between these two sectors of the Amarna community. However, a higher percentage of carpentry artefacts than leatherwork artefacts within the North City may indicate not so much more man-hours of carpentry as the simple fact that carpentry has left more traces than leatherwork in the archaeological record.

The degree of preservation of different types of material remains can vary immensely even within a single Egyptian city such as the one at Amarna. For instance, the fact that the Amarna 'workmen's village' is situated at a greater distance from the Nile, compared with the main city at Amarna, seems to have ensured that wood, matting and textiles were much better preserved in the village than in the city. Of course some parts of a large site may also be subject to more looting or early exploration than others; thus, in his preliminary description of the site, Borchardt (1907: 18) notes three zones of differing preservation in the central city and South Suburb. The western part of the city was said to be totally excavated by either

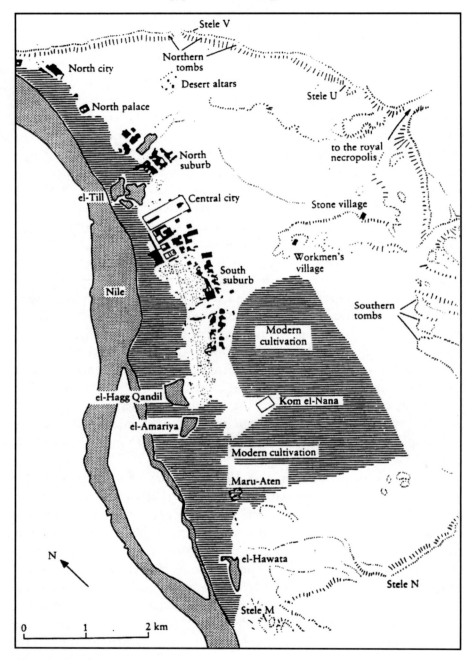

Fig. 9.2. Map of Amarna.

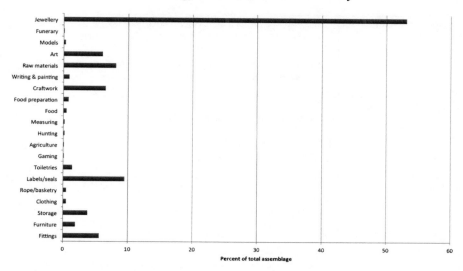

Fig. 9.3. Profile of artefact types for the whole city at Amarna, based on a sample of 6000 artefacts (proportion of jewellery = 48.3%).

Petrie or the *sebakhin* (i.e. local farmers removing mud-brick remains for use as fertiliser), while a second zone to the east, was characterised by the total destruction of a few of the houses by *sebakhin*. The third zone, where excavation was to concentrate from 1911 to 1925, was described as 'almost entirely intact'. This eastern zone had the further advantage of being at the edge of the city, so that spoil could be dumped mainly over the uninhabited desert.

When it is further considered that some crafts actually require more tools and leave greater amounts of débitage than others, then the inadequacy and complexity of the data become even more evident. The flow-chart in Table 9.1 shows how a typical set of 18th-Dynasty carpentry tools may be gradually diminished, in the archaeological record, by the various factors of preservation and inadequate excavation. As Kemp and Stevens (2010: 481) point out: 'given how few metal tools were left behind at Amarna, wood-working is a largely invisible industry. Yet ... wooden furnishings, including shrines and coffins, were prestige objects, sometimes a destination for inlays in glass and faience, and so likely to have been manufactured within the city'.

131

Systemic context	18th-Dynasty carpenter's tool-kit (see Aldred 1954, 688) **adze, axe, chisel, reamer, saw, bow-drill, mallet, awl, rubber** ↓ Removal of valuable bronze and large wooden items at abandonment of site. Potential loss of **adze**, **axe** and **saw** blades and handles. ↓
Archaeological context	Differential preservation of materials. Potential loss of wooden **mallet** and wooden handles of all other tools. ↓ Inadequate excavation. Potential loss of smaller items such as **chisel** and **drill**-head. ↓
Interpretive context	Inadequate recording, e.g. misidentifications or failure to record certain items. Potential loss of **rubber** and **adze**-handle (perhaps misidentified as grind-stone and stick respectively). ↓ Functional ambiguity, i.e. many carpenter's tools are easily confused with those of other crafts, e.g. **awl** (leather-working), **chisel**, **drill** and **mallet** (stone- and metal-working).

Table 9.1. Flow-chart showing potential loss of objects as they pass from the systemic to interpretive contexts.

Patterns of craftwork and professions at Amarna

It is useful not only to ascertain the importance of a particular occupation relative to others practised within a single residential zone at Amarna, but also to see how this relative importance varies from one zone to another. It is, for instance, interesting to note that tools associated with craft-production constitute 31% of the total artefacts in the 'South Suburb' at Amarna, but it is considerably more significant to know that this percentage is much higher than that in the 'workmen's village' (24.1%) or the 'North City' (23.9%). The numbers of craft tools from a single suburb or even a single house can only be properly assessed when they are compared both with the profiles in other parts of the city, and with the city as a whole.

In the case of the group of houses labelled P47.1-3, at Amarna, the artefactual evidence is totally dominated by tools and products relating to sculpture, leading to the unequivocal identification of this complex as a 'sculptor's workshop'. In this instance we can supplement the archaeological evidence with a scene in the tomb of Huya (Amarna Rock-tomb no.1), high steward of Queen Tiye, at Amarna, in which

Iuty, an overseer of sculptors, is shown at work in his studio (Davies 1905: pl. XVII).

Many houses at Amarna, however, have produced artefacts suggesting that a wide range of activities was being conducted, perhaps by different members of the household. The problem of interpreting such assemblages shows the potential gap between the simplistic world of textual labels and idealised images, and the complexity of the real world as presented in the form of archaeological remains (see, for instance, Eyre 1995). A few other houses in the north and south suburbs are also identifiable as workshops. House O49.14 is probably another sculptor's residence; Q46.23 was evidently occupied by a coppersmith; Q47.2 by a bead-maker; U35.2 by a painter and Q47.3 by a cobbler. The evidence, however, derives primarily from the interiors of houses (since these were the main target of pre-1970s excavators at the site), whereas the evidence of current and recent excavations confirms that much of the craftwork actually took place in courtyards and open areas (Stevens and Eccleston 2007: 153).

A group of houses (P49.3-6) were excavated by Ludwig Borchardt in his 1912 season at Amarna. The arrangement of these buildings, around a central courtyard, suggests that they may have constituted a workshop of some kind; it is clear, however, that the courtyard, covered in a surface scatter of basalt chips, was not excavated at all by Borchardt. More recent excavation at Amarna has focused on complete areas of housing and surrounding spaces, thus exploring such neglected open areas and beginning to provide a great deal more evidence concerning the plying of trades in and around individual houses at Amarna (see Kemp 1995: 1-168). It is also not clear whether it is correct to identify all the excavated domestic structures as 'houses', when in fact many might be better described as 'workshops' or 'ateliers'; Kemp and Stevens (2010: 493) remark, 'Really, the question is how fixed was the boundary between residential space and workplace in ancient Egypt; the answer being probably, not very.'

Textual sources

Another complicating factor, whether for visual or archaeological evidence, is our uncertainty as to whether 'private' patronage of professional craftsmen was a peripheral or dominant feature of the Egyptian economy. Similarly, it is difficult to tell whether the majority of skilled craftsmen plied their trades as private individuals in their own houses, or whether they were generally employed together in large state-controlled (or temple-controlled) workshops. Recent evidence probably suggesting a degree of private enterprise in the field of carpentry is provided by a group of ostraca from Deir el-Medina that are marked with illustrations of furniture types ('furniture ostraca'), and evidently constitute a detailed communication system whereby 'business transactions were drawn up showing the objects of the transaction and either the producer or the recipient, or perhaps both' (Killen and Weiss 2009: 140). The most detailed of these ostraca (O. Florence 2628) consists of concise depictions of several pieces of furniture, each associated with a sign probably representing either the carpenter or customer/recipient relating to that object (Killen and Weiss 2009: 141, 145). Using these kind of data for funerary equipment, along with other documents, Cooney (2006; 2007) has been able to reconstruct, for the very specialised royal workmen at Deir el-Medina at least, some sense of the 'formal workshop', in which the craftsmen are employed by the state to work on aspects of the royal tomb, and the 'informal workshop' which comprises tasks undertaken by loose groups of workers for private individuals. This distinction between different workshops, however, must be seen in the context of the state ownership of many of the craftsmen's valuable tools (for example O. Cairo 25509, for which see McDowell 1999: 209-10), which would almost certainly have meant that 'informal' commissions were tolerated by the state, since tools would often have needed to be made available for these non-royal purposes. This suggests an interesting socio-economic situation in the Ramessid period, in which craftsmen were perhaps officially allowed to work both to royal and private patronage, but of course our principal information derives from the highly artificial and perhaps unusually state-dominated Deir el-Medina community. As Haring (2009: 6) points out, 'It is unlikely, however, that craftsmanship was only institutional: archaeological and ethnological research suggests industry, seasonal or permanent, in peasant households and local workshops.'

When Eric Peet and Leonard Woolley were excavating parts of the city at Amarna in the early 1920s, they concluded that 'within the main area of the city there is ... no evidence of the grouping of people of various classes or trades in different quarters of the town. High-

Priest rubs shoulders with leatherworker, and Vizier with glass-maker' (Peet and Woolley 1923, 1-2). This rather intuitive quote not only suggests (incorrectly as it turns out, see Shaw 1996) that the grouping of houses of professionals and craftsmen at Amarna is largely random and unsystematic, but also indirectly raises the question of whether individuals in the city at Amarna, and other New Kingdom communities, can actually be identified socially by one specific skill or craft, or whether there were high degrees of multi-tasking by individuals (the ancient equivalents of 'portfolio' workers).

Several New Kingdom textual sources, mainly deriving from western Thebes, have the potential to shed light on the archaeological picture concerning trades and occupations. These sources may be divided into two basic types: (1) self-conscious literary and scribal documents, which can be used to explore the ancient Egyptians' own views on different trades and professions, and (2) administrative or legal records of specific individual accounts or administrative arrangements, which give some idea of the ways in which the population were divided up into different types of workers. It is the latter category that has the greatest potential from the point of view of identifying the degree to which particular craftworkers' houses were grouped together. There are two administrative documents that are particularly relevant to this kind of analysis of craftsmen and professions: the Wilbour Papyrus (Gardiner and Faulkner 1941-52) and Papyrus BM 10068 (Peet 1930: 83-102).

The Wilbour Papyrus, an administrative document dating to year 4 of Ramesses V (*c.* 1152 BC), lists (for the purpose of assessing 'tax') a large number of plots of land in Middle Egypt. Each plot is described in terms of its size, calculated yield, the name of the priest or official who owns or administers it, the name of the nearest settlement and the name and occupation of the cultivator. O'Connor (1972) used this source to plot the Middle Egyptian late New Kingdom patterns of settlements and occupation types. He distinguishes between zones with greater and lesser emphasis on agriculture and points out that different settlements have different proportions of the major types of 'occupation' listed: cultivator, priest, lady, herdsman, scribe, stable-master, soldier and 'Sherden' (east Mediterranean immigrant, see Fig. 8.4 above). The other potentially relevant administrative document is Papyrus BM 10068, one of a group of twelve 'Tomb Robbery Papyri' recording judicial inquiries at Thebes and dating to the 16th and 17th years of Ramesses IX (*c.* 1115 BC). The recto of P. BM 10068 is inscribed with a list of tomb robbers and stolen goods, while its verso comprises a list of 182 households, described as the 'town register of the West of No from the temple of King Menmaare to the settlement of Maiunehes'. Like the Wilbour Papyrus, P. BM 10068 lists the names and occupations of a series of individuals (for two different analyses of the list and its social implications, see Janssen 1992 and Shaw 2004). Peet suggests that the listed houses lay in a line between the temples of Seti I, Ramesses II and Ramesses III and then turned west towards the contemporary village of Deir el-Medina.

Both P. Wilbour and P. BM 10068 provide an indication of the relative importance of particular professions and trades (see Table 9.2). However, the high percentage of soldiers in P. Wilbour (43.7% according to Katary 1983) undoubtedly results from the nature of the document, since many military personnel would have been rewarded with plots of land. The high percentage of priests in P. BM 10068 (28%) must also be somewhat unrealistic, since, as Peet (1930: 84) cautions: 'it is important not to lose sight of the very artificial composition of the population of the West of Thebes, where there was probably little business carried on except in connection with the long line of funerary temples of the kings and the Necropolis'. On the other hand, the combination of both papyri provides an idea of the way in which urban populations might have been

Professions %		Professions %	
Priests	28.0	Herdsmen	10.0
Scribes	7.0	Fishermen	7.0
Medjay (police)	5.0	Coppersmiths	5.0
Administrators	4.0	Gardeners	4.0
Sandal-makers	4.0	Chief stablemen	3.0
Washermen	3.0	'Land-workers'	3.0
Beekeepers	2.0	Brewers	2.0
Attendants	2.0	Potters	2.0
Storemen	1.0	Porters	1.0
Incense roasters	1.0	Woodcutters	1.0
Doctors	0.6	Chief workmen	0.6
Guards	0.6	Goldworkers	0.6
Gilders	0.6	Measurers	0.6
Makers of 'w3t swi'	0.6		

Table 9.2. Table listing the percentages of different occupations mentioned in Papyrus BM 10068.

dominated by priests, soldiers, scribes and administrative officials – this equates with the evidence of the inscribed door-jambs and lintels of some of the largest houses at Amarna (Murnane 1995: 126, 130, 141-3, 166-8), since the titles of these wealthy householders imply that they would usually have been in charge of entourages of members of these four professions.

P. BM 10068 also includes many other occupations, of which the most numerous are gardeners, herdsmen, fishermen, coppersmiths and sandal-makers. Perhaps the most notable aspect of the lists is that they confirm the fact that such trades were actually considered to be full-time professions. Beekeepers, brewers and gilders are relatively familiar categories of tradesmen, but the text certainly implies that 'incense roasters' and 'measurers' were also perhaps regarded as full-time workers in the New Kingdom. Many of the types of occupation listed in P. BM 10068 might have left no trace in the archaeological record at Amarna, e.g. porter, guard, attendant or storeman.

It is possible that P. BM 10068 lists the households in their actual topographical order – if this is the case, it would be possible to gain a text-based idea of the patterning of different trades within this particular community. If the document is a true reflection of the patterning within the community – despite the fact that it seems inherently unlikely for the settlement to have been strung out in a long row as the list-form would suggest – the different professions and ranks appear to be mixed together rather than separated into specialised zones. On the other hand, the distinctive 'neighbourhoods' identified archaeologically at Amarna (see Shaw 1996: 98-100 and Kemp and Stevens 2010: 473-516) may be echoed to some extent in occasional small groups of the same type of trade spread among the other types. It is to be expected, in an evidently temple-based community, that priests might group together (particularly in the immediate vicinity of the three main royal mortuary temples of the late Ramessid period), but there are also a few concentrations of other trades, in groups of up to five in a row (such as fishermen, herdsmen and sandal-makers). Most of the 'land workers' are concentrated at the southwestern tip of the settlement. There are also occasional pairs of the same profession, such as coppersmiths, scribes and brewers. Other occupations, however, are spread relatively evenly throughout the list.

A number of conclusions can be drawn from the above discussion of visual, textual and archaeological evidence for the practising of different trades and crafts. First, it is often very difficult to reconcile textual and archaeological data concerning crafts and professions. Secondly, many publications discussing New Kingdom villages, towns and cities present only part of the picture, since streets, courtyards and 'empty' public spaces have tended not to be excavated in the past – Kemp and Stevens (2010: 495) have demonstrated eloquently, with their work on the 'grid 12' group of houses in the South Suburb at Amarna, that 'the debris of manufacture can occur indiscriminately across residential space and craft areas alike'. Thirdly, the evidence from individual households at Amarna suggests that most households contained various individuals plying a diverse range of crafts rather than simply indicating the principal 'job' of the head of the household.

This situation is often even more complicated when we consider the very large villas at Amarna, where both family members and servants would be plying different trades, and in addition surrounding small households (perhaps linked to the large ones by the need to obtain water and grain) probably have to be treated as extensions to the major 'nuclear' house. In other words, our pursuit of the houses of individual craftsmen and professionals is complicated by the fact that no working person in an urban context can be examined independently of the community within which he or she is working. Each urban household must be interpreted in terms of networks of production and consumption both on neighbourhood and city-wide levels.

Seeking the individual in the archaeological record

Janssen (1975: 159) suggested thirty-five years ago that 'the most comprehensive question seems to be whether there existed during the New Kingdom a class of free craftsmen working for a free market or not', although it might be argued that it is inappropriate to attempt to apply the definitions and terminology of such modern researchers as economists, sociologists and geographers to the study of ancient material culture. The profile of wealth-levels at Amarna, based on the architectural attributes and diversity of occupations indicated by artefactual frequencies, adds up to a picture of New Kingdom society in which individuals can be seen to be competing at different economic levels. Such competition however might exist in a redistributive economy, a free-trade economy or indeed a combination of the two, such as Cooney (2006) hypothesises. One possible strong archaeological indication of free trade might be the existence of open spaces identifiable as market areas (Kemp 1972: 674; Gledhill and Larssen 1982: 203-4), but even then there are alternative explanations for the space, such as official rationing processes (Kemp 1984: 60-80, for a description of the zir-area in the Workmen's Village) or large-scale refuse deposition.

It becomes quickly apparent that a socio-economic question, which is framed, as Janssen's is, in the abstract terms of modern economics, is not necessarily directly answerable through material remains. Excavators in the Basin of Mexico, confronted by the same basic dilemma, have asked: 'How were we to translate mounds and concentrations of artifact debris into sociological phenomena?' (Sanders et al. 1979: 16). Tietze (1986), discussing theories of the Egyptian economy put forward by Helck (1975), Morentz (1969) and Janssen (1975), suggests that the element lacking in all three models is a sense of the microcosm of daily transactions between individuals: the 'Alltag der ägyptischen Wirtschaft, der auf der Versorgung einer nach Millionen Zahlenden Bevolkerung beruhte' (Tietze 1986: 56). His detailed examination of architectural differentiation was intended to fill this gap and to give a sense of the economic structure of a specific New Kingdom city, in order to flesh out the generalisations of economic theory. He was therefore dealing with the same confrontation between, on the one hand, the essentially 'anecdotal' and site-specific data and, on the other hand, statements about the general mechanisms that may have produced and moulded the data.

The Mesoamerican archaeologist, George Cowgill, working with a huge database of artefacts from the Classic Maya urban site of Teotihuácan (300-500 AD), discusses at great length the problems of moving from the archaeological material itself (whether presented in the form of contour plans, tables or barcharts) to actual dynamic theories of political and economic organisation (Cowgill 1974; 1984). He describes the recurrent problem of the great gap between data and theory, concluding that the two can rarely be said to coincide in a definite and unambiguous way.

Spatial analysis at Amarna: converting artefacts into behavioural data

In this case-study, the first step in the conversion of Amarna artefactual patterns into socio-economic data is the collation of particular types of artefacts into general behavioural categories. This process makes the mass of statistics easier to handle and to evaluate. Table 9.3 lists the percentages of the 27 categories into which over 350+ types of artefact are collated. The 27 categories include aspects of the environment of the Amarna population, such as 'furniture' and 'clothing', as well as the activities which took place in the houses and courtyards, such as 'carpentry' and 'spinning/weaving'.

The urban activities at Amarna can therefore be divided into the broad areas of environment, subsistence, craftwork and products, excluding the categories of 'unidentified' and 'post-Amarna period' artefacts. The arrangement is almost cyclical in the sense that all of the items making up the basic static environment of the household are also, at the same time, products of the craftwork activities. Similar strategies of 'artefactual collation' have been employed by Nicholas (1981) and Tosi (1984). Nicholas's analysis of the artefactual material from a suburb of Tel el-Malyan in Iran assigns each find to a 'broad functional class of activity' and then constructs a 'functional profile' for each of three Banesh building levels in the suburb. Tosi, working with material from four sites in the Turanian basin (mainly eastern Iran), attempts to assess the 'variability in the spatial allocation of craft production' (Tosi 1984: 29). He analyses this database, within a Marxist theoretical framework, by collating artefacts with groups of particular 'archaeological indicators' that essentially correspond to Nicholas's 'functional classes'.

Environment	Subsistence	Craftwork	Products
Fittings	Agriculture	General tools	Art
Furniture	Hunting	Spinning/weaving	Funerary items
Storage	Measuring	Stone-working	Models
Clothing	Food remains	Carpentry	Jewellery
Rope/ basketry	Food preparation	Metal-working	
Labels/seals		Leather-working	
Toiletries		Writing/painting	
Gaming		Raw materials	

Table 9.3. The functional arrangement of Amarna artefactual categories into a system.

9. Technology embedded in urban society

Fig. 9.3 (p. 131) is a barchart representing the profile of behaviour for a sample of approximately 6000 non-ceramic artefacts from a large variety of parts of the city at Amarna. Three particular types of material in the barcharts (fittings, jewellery and raw materials) pose several problems. The proportions of both raw material and jewellery are particularly susceptible to distortion by the pre-1979 excavation strategies at Amarna (see Shaw 2000 for discussion of the issues presented by this kind of archaeological distortion). These two categories of material account for the largest proportion of material discarded in the spoil heaps of Eric Peet and Leonard Woolley at the Workmen's Village (Peet and Woolley 1923), and of John Pendlebury in the North City (Pendlebury 1931: 240-2; 1932: 143-5). The greater proportion of raw materials and jewellery from deposits excavated by Barry Kemp since 1979 has the effect of artificially diminishing the proportions of other activities. This is something that simply has to be borne in mind when comparing the pre-1979 artefactual data with more modern material from the Workmen's Village.

It should also be noted that elements of jewellery, such as beads, rings and amulets, are so prolific at Amarna (and at most other settlements throughout the New Kingdom) that they invariably constitute a very high proportion of the non-ceramic artefactual record. Fittings are included in the barcharts in Figs 9.3 and 9.5-9.6, but they should be treated with caution since the proportions probably derive from differences in excavators' recording techniques rather than the nature of the archaeological record itself.

During the compilation of the 6000-artefact sample that forms the basis for the various tables and charts in this chapter, it became increasingly obvious that the records of the various excavators at Amarna differ radically in their attention to those aspects of the material remains that lie midway between the spheres of 'architecture' and 'artefact'. Certain architectural features, such as column-bases and wall-plaster are consistently recorded as artefacts in the current excavations at Amarna (see Kemp's treatment of a window-frame from the Workmen's Village: Kemp 1986: 11-14). Previous excavations at the site have however been somewhat erratic in their recording of such quasi-architectural material. Ludwig Borchardt's plans, for instance, often show column-bases that are not mentioned in the find-lists. Those fittings that do appear in the find-lists of the old excavations would therefore almost certainly present a misleading picture.

The interpretation of Amarna artefactual data is also complicated by the problem of determining the relative importance of assemblages or activities at a household. Textual evidence indicates the existence of many skilled workers, such as sculptors (*gnwtyw* or *s'nḫyw*), metal-workers (*biȝtyw*) or butchers (*stfiw*), but the archaeological evidence from each household suggests that any one individual might have practised a wide range of types of craftwork. How then is the archaeologist to identify the specific aspect of the assemblage that the individual would have thought of as his 'trade' or speciality? In P. BM 10068 (Peet 1930: 95-7; Janssen 1992; Shaw 2004: 19-20) two priests are also described as being coppersmiths. Kemp (1981: 86) points out that, 'in trying to envisage the uses of various parts of the houses and estates at Tell el-Amarna we should not be inhibited by too modern a view of life, which tends to separate work from domesticity. The house of the sculptor [P47.2, i.e. Thutmose's house], unusual in its finds but not in its design, should be a constant reminder of how varied and numerous may have been the activities in and around these houses.'

The South Suburb (or 'main city') at Amarna

The large area of housing that lies south of the public and ceremonial buildings of the central city at Amarna has been excavated and analysed by many different archaeologists; it has variously been described as the 'South Suburb' and the 'main city'. Petrie's small sample of domestic buildings, excavated in 1891-2, were all in the South Suburb. These houses, however, only provided a glimpse of the basic Amarna repertoire of architectural and artefactual types. It was the work of Borchardt (in 1907 and 1911-14) that revealed the full richness and complexity of the South Suburb. The German excavations uncovered the largest area of the southern zone of housing, and this excavated zone was extended to north and west by the subsequent work of British excavators from 1921 to 1937 (see, for instance, Peet and Woolley 1923: 1-50). Judging from such dating criteria as ostraca and jewellery (bearing year-dates and cartouches respectively), the South Suburb seems to have been the earliest residential part of the city. Kemp (1981: 88) also suggests that the alignment of various South Suburb houses with the main road through the central city is an indication of their relatively early date of construction. The number of houses in the entire South Suburb (including unexcavated areas) was about 2400, covering an area of over 1.5km^2. Janssen (1983: 286) suggests that the 'southern zone' housed between 35,000 and 45,000 people, and that this was probably over half of the city's population, while Kemp (1981: 96) suggests a lower figure of about 16,000–25,000 individuals.

Both architecturally and artefactually, the South Suburb appears to have been a kind of average blend of households, perhaps constituting the original nucleus of the city. The remainder of this chapter comprises a study of four different neighbourhoods of the South Suburb: (1) gridsquare O49, which comprises four large houses surrounded by thirteen smaller buildings; (2) a tight block of nine small houses in the southeastern corner of gridsquare P46; (3) two very large houses in gridsquare R44 (belonging to a 'steward' and a high priest); and (4) a pair of houses (O47.16a and O47.20) identified as a sculptor's residence or atelier. These four neighbourhoods are widely spread out across the suburb and they were chosen to represent a range of South Suburb households primarily on the basis of architectural differences. Only the artefacts from the houses in gridsquare O49 have been published in full (Borchardt and Ricke 1980, Peet and Woolley 1923). The P46 houses were excavated by Newton in October 1923; R44.1-2 were excavated by Griffith in January 1924; and O47.16a and .20 by Waddington in January 1933 (all of the data for these derive from unpublished notebooks in the archives of the Egypt Exploration Society, London). It is not easy to assess whether this sample is actually typical, but it can at least be shown (see Fig. 9.4 below) that the architectural range in gridsquare O49 is very similar to that of the South Suburb as a whole, while the combination of the other three sections of the sample constitutes a similar (if not quite so even) architectural range.

Kemp points out that gridsquares O49, Q46 and Q47 (all excavated by Borchardt in the early 1900s) are particularly important from the point of view of the relationships between large and small houses in that 'the existence of interrelated housing groups is made most evident from the eastern margins of the city, where building petered out before maximum density was reached' (Kemp 1981: 92). Fig. 9.6 shows the percentages of

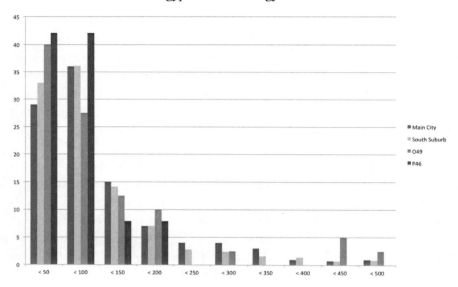

Fig. 9.4. Profile of house-sizes for O49 and P46, two different sectors of the South Suburb at Amarna.

different activities in the aggregate of artefacts from the South Suburb as a whole.

A comparison of the barchart for the South Suburb (Fig. 9.5) with that for the whole city (Fig. 9.3) is probably the best starting point for a discussion of the character of the South Suburb itself. There are a few activities in which the South Suburb seems relatively lacking – furniture, toiletries, basketry and agriculture – but generally it echoes the character of the city as a whole in that the same range of activities is present in roughly the same proportions. The most obvious aspect of the South Suburb barchart is the large quantity and variety of craftwork practised. At 17%, the proportion of craftwork is higher than in any other part of the site, justifying Fairman's description of this zone as the 'industrial centre' (Fairman 1949: 37). The percentages of art (paintings and sculptures), writing and painting are also much higher than elsewhere. These proportions present a picture of a sector of the population that was, on average, more literate, more productive and more likely to possess items of sculpture. An important aspect of the South Suburb, however, is its great internal diversity: the architectural evidence shows that the population of the suburb embraced both the highest and lowest levels

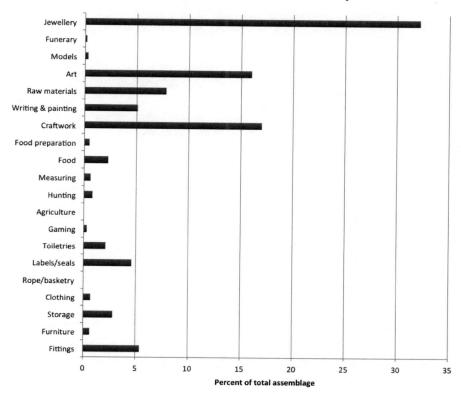

Fig. 9.5. Profile of artefact types in the South Suburb at Amarna.

of the Amarna economy, from the mansions of the high priests Pawah and Panehsy to the cramped houses of anonymous leather-workers and potters.

Fig. 9.6 compares the architecturally poorer households of gridsquare P46 with the mixture of rich and poor in gridsquare O49. The difference between the two must partially be a result of the sample-sizes (500 artefacts from O49 compared with only 64 from P46), particularly with regard to the lack of activities within the spheres of 'domestic environment' and 'subsistence' which are usually present in small numbers throughout the city. However, the relative proportions of types of craftwork and products are more telling. Both O49 and P46 have a high proportion of craftwork (23% and 25.1% respectively), but whereas in O49 the evidence of craftwork is spread evenly across a range of activities including spinning and weaving, faience-production, leather-working, sculpting and metal-

145

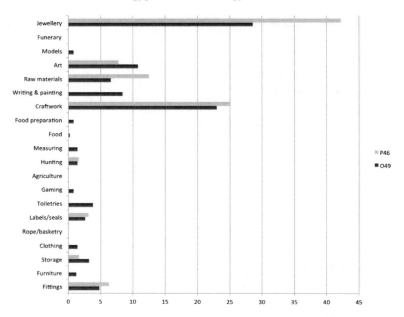

Fig. 9.6. Profile of artefact types in O49 and P46, two different sectors of the South Suburb at Amarna.

working, the P46 craft debris is largely dominated by evidence of faience production, which comprises 18.8% of the total artefactual assemblage from P46.

The total lack of evidence of artefacts relating to writing and painting in P46 houses contrasts sharply with a percentage of 8.4% in O49. If the poor families of P46 were illiterate, they were by no means alone in this, for the barchart showing evidence of writing across the city as a whole (Fig. 9.7) indicates that it is gridsquare O49 that is relatively unusual in having such a high proportion of artefacts relating to literacy. The lack of writing among the P46 households must undoubtedly have been the norm. It is surprising, however, to note that they possessed a considerably higher proportion of artistic products (7.8%) than any residential area outside the South Suburb (apart from the so-called 'palace servants' quarters'). Since the craft tools from P46 include none of the metal-, stone- or wood-working implements that usually indicate the presence of sculptors, it seems likely that the art in P46 houses was actually owned rather than being produced for others (as in such ateliers as O49.14 and O47.16a-20).

9. Technology embedded in urban society

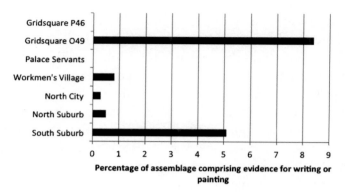

Fig. 9.7. Proportions of writing and painting artefacts in different parts of the city at Amarna.

The 1987 excavations in the main city at Amarna (Kemp 1988) confirm the importance of figurative art throughout the whole of the South Suburb, with finds of female figurines from the debris of a pottery and glaze 'factory' in the courtyard of building Q48.4. Figurines at Amarna must have been essential to the domestic cults centred around such deities as Bes and Taweret, who were associated with childbirth and the security of the family (Kemp 1979, Pinch 1983). Large scale stone and wood statuary, on the other hand, were much more closely associated with the richer houses, where the courtyards or gardens often contained shrines, incorporating sculptures and stelae, dedicated to the official god, Aten, and to the royal family. The excavations of New Kingdom houses at Memphis (Giddy 1999) have revealed similarly high proportions of figurines (6.9% of the total artefacts), showing that the phenomenon extends well beyond the confines of Amarna.

The barchart of activities at P46 probably also presents a view of the South Suburb pared down to the most basic parameters of life. As far as subsistence is concerned, there are only a few flint tools but no indication of food or cooking implements. Compared with the Amarna Workmen's Village, for instance, the inhabitants of the small housing block of P46 seem to have been much more reliant on other sections of the community; this interdependence is a clue to the nature of the South Suburb as a whole.

In some ways the statistical breakdown of types of activity in the South Suburb and the Workmen's Village contradicts the traditional view of these two zones. Usually the Workmen's Village is characterised as an

147

isolated outpost only surviving through its dependency on the main city, as opposed to the thriving 'industrial' community in the southern part of the city. The South Suburb as a whole is certainly as self-sufficient as any other part of Amarna: the artefactual evidence indicates a strong cycle of localised production and consumption, against a background of higher proportions of domestic and food-related artefacts than in the North Suburb or North City. The great difference between the South Suburb and the Workmen's Village, however, is that the South Suburb is split up into many smaller units, such as neighbourhoods or single households, which are much more specialised than either the Village as a whole or even individual houses within the Village.

The patterning of the artefacts in the South Suburb indicates that a group of poor households, such as those in P46 might have devoted themselves to large amounts of faience production, while relying on other households to provide them with basic necessities. Kemp and Stevens (2010: 496) seem to reach a similar conclusion with regard to faience production, on the basis of their detailed excavation of 'grid 12' in the South Suburb: 'Certainly there is little obvious sign of state imprint on the organisation of manufacturing facilities for faience'. Similarly, in the sculptor's atelier O47.16a-20 there is a high proportion of artefacts relating to sculpture (metal-working, stone-working and miscellaneous tools comprising 7.8% of the total assemblage) but relatively low proportions of artefacts relating to subsistence (1.9%) and faience production (1.9%).

Conclusions and discussion

If the patterning of artefacts in the South Suburb at Amarna is a true expression of the Egyptian New Kingdom economic system, then the emphasis is on the interdependence of specialists, exchanging goods and services among themselves, rather than the still commonly held view of a homogeneous mass of workers sustained by an apparatus of temple and state redistribution (Janssen 1975; 1983). Undoubtedly there was a large amount of work done for the state alone – such pictorial evidence as the paintings in the 18th-dynasty tomb of Rekhmira at Thebes (Davies 1943) appear to show large groups of craftsmen employed in royal workshops – but the inhabitants of cities such as Amarna and Memphis were probably also involved in production for private consumption.

9. Technology embedded in urban society

The patterning of houses and objects in the South Suburb shows an intricate patchwork of production and consumption, involving individual families and neighbourhoods specialising in particular forms of manufacture. Such houses as O47.16a-20 and P47.1-3 seem oriented towards more large-scale production (for royal or priestly patrons) but in most of the households of the South Suburb the artefacts suggest small-scale domestic production that can only have realistically functioned within a tight interdependent network of families, supplying one another's needs from carpentry to spinning and weaving. It is possible (but difficult to prove from the archaeological record alone) that specialists at this lowest level of production could have been compelled to hand over their products (whether textiles or furniture) in return for state rations. Kemp and Stevens (2010: 499) argue that the overall socio-economic situation at Amarna is one involving 'an intricate balance between the communal and the individualistic that varied all the time from one small part of the site to another'. Clearly there was, to some degree, a spectrum of economic possibilities, from the relatively tight state control and provisioning of the Workmen's Village to the looser scenarios in different neighbourhoods of the South Suburb, where some households may have enjoyed a degree of relative autonomy.

Both Kemp's analyses of granaries across Amarna as a whole (Kemp 1972: 670-72; Kemp 1986), and Christian Tietze's study of Amarna architecture (Tietze 1986) suggest that the smaller households may have supplied labour and finished products to the inhabitants of wealthy houses (such as O49.1 and R44.1) in return for supplies of grain. Such a situation is borne out by the tendency of smaller houses to cluster around the perimeters of large houses' courtyards. This single redistributive facet of the economy of the South Suburb is understandable, given the fact that the average inhabitant of Amarna would have been unable to grow enough food locally to survive. Only the richer members of the community could have had the resources to grow crops on the western side of the river, transport the produce across the river, and store it in large silos. Textual evidence shows that the wealthy occupants of the cities of the New Kingdom probably also owned country-estates (bḥnw) which would have helped to fuel the urban economy (O'Connor 1972: 693-5).

James (1985: 201) points out that 'the craftsmen shown in Rekhmira's

149

tomb are, as should be expected, working on royal commissions, but many are engaged in simple activities that are not seen to be concerned necessarily with the manufacture of specifically royal objects'. This modified view of Egyptian urban society in the Late Bronze Age, as a socio-economic system in which 'state employees' might co-exist with large numbers of specialists working both for the state and for themselves, has been long argued by Smith (1972: 710-11) and Kemp (1972; 1977; 1986), and has more recently been argued – primarily on the basis of Theban textual data – by Cooney (2006, 2007). The archaeological data discussed above, with regard to the South Suburb, suggest that this scenario is still the most convincing.

10

Conclusions

We will sometimes use the word technosocial to direct attention to the mutual interpenetration of technology and society. We want to highlight how technology affects social relationships, how social relationships affect technology, and how this changes over time and place (Bauchspies, Croissant and Restivo 2006: 9).

As the preface to this book has already indicated, the coverage of ancient Egyptian materials, technologies and innovations here could not hope to be all-embracing (see Nicholson and Shaw 2000 for at least an attempt at such comprehensiveness, although even this work omits numerous areas of technology, such as boat-building, hydrology, sculpture, stone masonry, painting, mining etc.). Instead, I have focused on case-studies that can provide certain insights into the various ways in which the material culture of the pharaonic period was moulded, formed, and propelled in certain directions by diverse human, environmental, social and historical factors. Just as Kubler (1962: 1) argues that 'man's native inertia is overcome only by desire, and nothing gets made unless it is desirable', so studies of innovation and transmission of material culture in the Nile valley suggest that the ancient Egyptians were no more or less guilty of inherent conservatism than any other Bronze Age cultures in north Africa and the Near East. Not all Egyptian technological choices were necessarily optimal (in modern terms), but the case-studies discussed in each of the chapters above demonstrate that, within their own cultural and economic contexts, these decisions are usually at least clearly explicable.

General mechanisms of innovation

Rogers (1983) outlines a sequence of stages by which innovations diffused via such phases as knowledge, persuasion, implementation etc., and also various factors that were considered to accelerate or retard the process by which an innovation might spread through a culture or from one culture to another. Whether the detail of such a process can be regarded as genuinely applicable to ancient cultures – as Shortland (2004: 5-8) has argued – or whether it in fact derives too much of its essentials from relatively modern cultural scenarios, it nevertheless indicates, as some of the chapters above have attempted to do, that the process of adopting or evolving a new form of technology is rarely straightforward or simple.

Boyd and Richerson (1985) demonstrate just how complex processes of transmission of cultural phenomena can be: they analyse a number of ethnographic situations in which groups of people have either (1) opted to maintain particular cultural traditions, artefacts, and materials, or (2) adopted new ones, perhaps specifically because they see some local advantage (even if that advantage is not inherent in the 'original' nature or use of the cultural phenonomen in question). They distinguish between a number of different forms of cultural transmission, arguing that something like the adoption of the snowmobile by the Cree people of northern Canada, in place of the snowshoe, is an example of 'directly biased transmission', which can be regarded as a situation in which human decision-making acts as a form of natural selection on cultural attributes. Boyd and Richerson, however, also outline the situation in which two individuals within a specific group tend to have far more cultural similarities than two individuals that each belong to quite ethnically or geographical distinct populations – this they define as 'conformist tradition', i.e. in this scenario, people tend to conform culturally with their immediate surroundings. It is not necessary to go into the full detail of this application of evolutionary ideas to processes of cultural change to appreciate that the decision to adopt an innovation is generally neither as straightforward nor as inevitable as it may sometimes seem in retrospect. This situation was particularly stressed above in the case of the adoption by the Egyptians of such diverse technological entities as the hieroglyphic writing system and the process of mummification

152

– each of these major innovations emerged from a very specific social context. Both writing and the embalming of bodies emerged in many other cultures, but their idiosyncratic characteristics in the Nile valley derive from the very particular social and environmental features of early Egypt. As Sillar and Tite (2000: 11) have reasoned: 'There can be no simple formulation for the identification of the particular mixture of environmental, physical, economic, social, and ideological influences that affect technological choices.'

The shaping of technology

Technology of course not only has distinct over-arching contexts, such as society, ideology and economics, but also tends to be significantly 'shaped' and affected by other contemporaneous technologies (see Mackenzie and Wajcman 1985 for many examples of this trend). In the conclusion to a discussion of Egyptian and Near Eastern glazing technologies, Paynter and Tite (2001) make the point that 'glazing technology did not develop in isolation but was influenced by developments in other crafts ... artisans were expected to be skilled with many materials and might work in close proximity to other artisans in royal workshops'. Chapter 6, above, includes examination of the ways in which pyrotechnological artisans, such as glass, metal and stone-workers, might well have influenced one another technologically, while Chapter 7 includes several examples of the related phenomenon, whereby different types of Egyptian military technology emerge or evolve primarily in response to one another, particularly in the early New Kingdom. Another case-study could also have been added on the possible links between stone vessel-making and faience production (see Stocks 1997; 2003a: 225-34), whereby the waste powders of ground quartz and copper (resulting from the process of drilling stone beads or vessels) might have been re-used as the cores of faience artefacts. Thus technicians/artisans, techniques and products can often be seen to be interlinked and systemically related.

Two other factors are particularly significant in ancient Egyptian technology: first, the interplay of archaism and conservatism, and secondly the frequently related role of ritual as an integral element. The elements of archaism and conservatism have been particularly discussed above in the chapters devoted to mummification, stone-working and medicine, and in all three cases the technological skills are combined with utterances and performances drawing on magical and ritualistic resources, from embalmers using fishtail knives to Egyptian *ḫarṭibē* in the Assyrian court. As Trigger (1986: 6) points out, in an analysis of Gordon Childe's attitudes to technology in archaeology, 'production is carried out, and scientific knowledge is applied, within an institutional framework that consists of social and religious as well as economic factors' – in other words, the religious and ritualistic components of ancient Egyptian technology are vital parts of the technological packages, and can no more be dissociated from the 'practical' technical aspects than political or legal factors can be detached from modern industrial production.

Reconstructing the economic contexts

Our understanding of the variety of types of technological strategies and skills that make up the whole system of production and consumption in ancient Egypt, gradually evolving from the Predynastic through to the end of the pharaonic period, need to be seen within a dynamic and developing economic framework, which is still only sketchily understood, even in the Late Bronze Age. One reason that the economic scenario is still so inadequately documented in Egypt is because so much of the discussion to date has tended to be based on textual data rather than on the archaeological material that constitutes the nuts and bolts of the economy – it is only now that proper material-culture based accounts of the economics of ancient Egypt are beginning to be created through synthesis of data from the growing number of settlement sites being excavated (see, for instance, Werschkun 2011, for economic analysis of the Old Kingdom, and Hodgkinson 2010, 2011 for archaeologically oriented New Kingdom socio-economics). As Haring (2009: 2) has pointed out, in a summary of the current position of ancient Egyptian economics, 'More integrative approaches that include archaeological data may well add significantly to our present state of knowledge.'

Just as Cuomo (2007: 165) highlights the need to explore the specificity of Greek and Roman technology and economics, on the basis that 'neither economy nor technology follow absolute laws, and thus have to be seen as deeply embedded in a certain time and place', so some of the case studies presented above have demonstrated that such materials as glass and iron began to be used in particular ways and for particular reasons in Egypt (as opposed to Mesopotamia or Cyprus for instance), rather than there being one single process of technological diffusion that broadly applied to all of the societies and economies of western Asia and the east Mediterranean.

If we are to fully understand the nature of Egyptian technological developments, we need to analyse and understand the cultural and economic contexts within which such processes of material-culture change and transmission take place.

Appendix 1. Measuring space

The development of the ability to measure both space and time was essential to the emergence of many different forms and aspects of Egyptian science and technology. The measuring and surveying of distances was clearly central to the construction of stone monuments, and the knowledge of weights, measures and calculus was fundamental to the smooth running of the Egyptian bureaucracy. The latter is evident not only from surviving texts but also from tomb scenes showing scribes recording the amount of grain or counting cattle, and from the measured rations and weights of copper issued at the New Kingdom workmen's village at Deir el-Medina (see Davies 1999: 141 for the monitoring of laundry and copper worktools).

Early systems of measuring were based primarily on the lengths of different parts of the human body, particularly fingers, hands, arms and feet. The principal unit of measurement was the royal cubit (52.4cm), approximately the length of a man's forearm and represented by the hieroglyph in the form of a forearm. The royal cubit comprised 7 palm widths each of 4 digits of thumb width (thus 28 digits to the cubit). Artists generally used a grid to lay out their drawings, and until the end of the Third Intermediate Period (1070-712 BC) they used the 'short cubit' of 6 palms (44.9cm) which was roughly the length from elbow to thumb tip, conventionally 45cm. From the Saite period (664-525 BC) onwards, however, the royal cubit was used by artists. During the Persian occupation, on the other hand, the royal Persian cubit of 64.2cm was sometimes used. The length of the double *rmn* was equal to that of the diagonal of a square with sides of 1 royal cubit (74.07cm). The double *rmn*, divided into 40 smaller units of 1.85cm each, was the measurement used in land surveying, along with the *t3* (or *mḥ-tʿ*) of 100 royal cubits. Area was measured in *st3t* (100 cubits square), later called the *aroura*.

A number of measuring rods, including the wooden examples used by craftsmen and surveyors have survived (see Scott 1942 for a general discussion of cubit rods). The most detailed knowledge of the cubit derives not from workaday measures, which could vary considerably, but from ceremonial cubit-rods cut in stone and deposited in temples, or occasionally buried with officials. These were also inscribed with other useful information such as inundation levels or references to nomes (provinces), forming a kind of compendium of the sort once found in school exercise books. Scenes of land surveying are portrayed in several Theban tombs of the 18th Dynasty (TT38, TT57, TT69, TT75, and a fragment in the British Museum from an unknown tomb: BM EA37982; see Berger 1934). A knotted rope was used in surveying land, the boundaries of which could be marked with stones, as portrayed in the tomb of Menna (TT69, *c.* 1400 BC; see Campbell 1910: 85, Maher-Taha 2002).

A large number of Egyptian weights – in stone, pottery and bronze – have survived (see Weigall 1908, Skinner 1954); the earliest, excavated at Naqada, date to the Predynastic period (*c.* 3500-3000 BC, see Petrie 1926: 4). Many weights in the Dynastic period are inscribed, while others are in the shape of cattle or bulls' heads or other animals (see Doll 1982: 60-2). Weights were traditionally made in units known as *dbn*, weighing approximately 93.3g, but after the 12th Dynasty (1991-1783 BC) this unit was supplemented by the *kitĕ* (*ḳdt*) of 9-10g, and the *dbn* itself was increased to weigh 10 *kitĕ*. The *dbn* was a measure of copper, silver or gold, whereas the *kitĕ* measured silver or gold only. They were used to describe the equivalent value of a wide variety of non-metallic goods, thus forming a rudimentary price system in the non-monetary economy of the pharaonic period (see Černy 1954).

The so-called 'equal arm balance' was used by the Egyptians. If a balance is to be stable, its potential energy must be minimal when the beam is horizontal, therefore the centre of mass must be below the fulcrum point (but not too far below it). For the balance to be sensitive, the angle of declination must be as large as possible: this can be improved if the beam is made longer. Although there are depictions of small balances used by the ancient Egyptians, there are also many depictions of very large balances with beams longer than 1.5m. It is necessary to have an element of the scales which shows when the beam is in balance (i.e. horizontal);

this can be achieved by a plummet hanging by three strings (often shown being steadied by the person doing the weighing), although it is not clear exactly why this was hung from three strings.

Measures of capacity also existed, notably the *hin* (about 0.47 litres), ten *hin* making one *ḥḳꜣt* of about 4.77 litres, and the *ḫꜣr* of 160 *hin* (75.2 litres). The *hin* could be sub-divided into units as small as 1/32, as well as into thirds. Scribes measuring grain are depicted in the late 18th-Dynasty Theban tomb of the 'estate inspector' Menna (TT69, see Campbell 1910: 85-106, Maher-Taha 2002).

Appendix 2. Measuring time

The earliest Egyptian calendars were based on lunar observations combined with the annual cycle of the Nile inundation, measured with Nilometers (Heilporn 1989). On this basis the Egyptians divided the year into twelve months and three seasons: *ȝḥt* (the inundation itself), *prt* (spring-time, when the crops began to emerge) and *šmw* (harvest-time). Each season consisted of four thirty-day months (*ȝbdw*), and each month comprised three ten-day weeks. This was an admirably simple system, compared with the modern European calendar of unequal months, and in fact it was briefly revived in France at the time of the French Revolution (Zerubavel 1977).

The division of the day and night into twelve hours each appears to have been initiated by the Egyptians, probably by simple analogy with the twelve months of the year, but the division of the hour into sixty minutes was introduced by the Babylonians (Smith 1969). The smallest unit of time recognised in ancient Egypt was the *ʿt*, usually translated as 'moment' and having no definite length.

The Egyptian year was considered to begin on 19 July (according to the later Julian calendar), which was the date of the heliacal rising of the dog-star Sirius (Krauss 1985). The Egyptian goddess Sopdet, known as Sothis in the Greco-Roman period (332 BC-395 AD), was the personification of the 'dog-star', which the Greeks called Seirios (Sirius). She was usually represented as a woman with a star poised on her head, although the earliest depiction, on an ivory tablet of the 1st-Dynasty king Djer (*c.* 3000 BC) from Abydos, appears to show her as a seated cow with a plant between her horns (Vandier 1952: 842-3). It has been pointed out that, since the plant is symbolic of the year, the Egyptians may have already been correlating the rising of the dog-star with the beginning of the solar year, even in the early 3rd millennium BC.

Surviving textual accounts of the observation of the heliacal rising of the dog-star form the lynch-pin of the traditional chronology of Egypt. However, even with the addition of five intercalary 'epagomenal' days (corresponding to the birthdays of the deities Osiris, Isis, Horus, Seth and Nepthys, see Spalinger 1995), a discrepancy gradually developed between the lunar year of 365 days and the real solar year, which was about six hours longer. This effectively meant that the civil year and the genuine seasonal year were only synchronised once every 1460 years, although this does not seem to have been regarded as a fatal flaw until the Ptolemaic period, when the concept of the 'leap year' was introduced in the Alexandrian calendar, later forming the basis for the Julian and Gregorian calendars. As well as the civil calendar there were also separate religious calendars consisting of festivals and ceremonies associated with particular deities and temples (e.g. the Feast of Opet at Thebes, celebrated in the second month of *ȝḥt*). The priests often calculated the dates of these according to the lunar month of about 29.5 days rather than according to the civil calendar, since it was essential that many of them should coincide with particular phases of the agricultural or astronomical cycle.

The clepsydra ('water clock') was a device for measuring time, consisting of a water-filled vessel (usually of stone, copper or pottery) with a hole in the base through which the water gradually drained away (Cotterell et al. 1986, Couchoud 1988). The earliest surviving examples, in the Egyptian Museum, Cairo, date to the 18th Dynasty (1550-1307 BC), and the oldest of these is a vessel dating to the reign of Amenhotep III found in fragments at Karnak in 1905. Each of the hours in the Karnak clock is marked by a row of small 5mm-diameter depressions, therefore time could only have been read to an accuracy of about 10 minutes. All pharaonic-period clocks are of the type in which the velocity of the water flow decreases as the water-level drops, therefore the bottom of the vessel has a smaller diameter than the top. An official of Amenhotep I called Amenemhat (*c.* 1520 BC) claims, in an inscription in his Theban tomb, to have invented the water clock.

The design of the clocks was complicated by the fact that the length of each of the 12 hours of the night changed from one part of the year to another, as the overall period of darkness grew shorter or longer. Water-clocks therefore had to have 12 different scales, one for each month of the year. Amenemhat gives the lengths of the scale for midwinter: 12 digits (225mm), and the scale length on the Karnak clock almost exactly corresponds to this. This means, however, that the clock would have needed another scale, perhaps painted on the rim, since these scales would have no longer corresponded to the correct months by the reign of Amenhotep III. This conservatism is also the case with the astronomical ceilings of Seti I and Ramesses IV, which are almost identical, despite one being about 150 years earlier than the other. Cotterell et al. (1986) have calculated that the Karnak clock is more likely to have been geared up to the civil rather than astronomical night, on the basis that its scales tie in with a particular water temperature (given that the viscosity of water decreases as the temperature rises). In the Ptolemaic period the 'inflow' clock was introduced. There are a variety of fragments of stone clepsydrae in the collection of the British Museum, incuding part of a basalt vessel dating to the reign of Philip Arrhidaeus (EA938, *c.* 320 BC), which is marked with vertical lines of small holes relating to the twelve hours of the night. Part of a chert cubit rod in the Metropolitan Museum, New York, bears the words 'The hour according to the cubit: a jar(?) of copper filled with water ...', thus implying that the rod was dipped into a copper vessel in order to read the time as the water level fell (Hayes 1959: 412-13).

There were two types of 'shadow-clock' (see Clagett 1995: 84, 93, Krupp 1979: 195) and a tablet dating to the reign of the 19th-Dynasty ruler Merenptah may have been an early sun-dial (Clagett 1995: 97); it has a central hole (presumably for a gnomon) and inscribed radiating lines for reading off the hours. It has been suggested that the *wȝs*-sceptre, consisting of a straight shaft with its handle in the form of the head of a canine animal, and its base ending in two prongs, may have originally been used as a gnomon, perhaps representing the divine measurement of time.

Appendix 3. Astronomy and astrology

The first indications of astronomical knowledge in Egypt perhaps take the form of circular and linear arrangements of small upright sandstone slabs identified in 1992 at the Neolithic site of Nabta Playa, *c.* 100km west of Abu Simbel (Wendorf et al. 1996). It has been argued that this Late Neolithic monument, dating to *c.* 4000 BC, is oriented to such astronomical phenomena as the cardinal points and the summer solstice (Wendorf and Schild 2001: 463-502), although there is some debate as to whether this is genuinely the case, both in terms of date and proposed function (e.g. Wengrow 2006: 57, Spence 2010: 176).

Certainly, by the early pharaonic period textual and visual evidence for astronomical observations and understanding begin to appear, particularly with reference to the orientation of monuments and the measurement of time. The ceilings of ancient Egyptian temples, tombs and coffins were frequently decorated with depictions of the heavens, since most funerary and religious entities were regarded as microcosms of the universe itself (see, for instance, Kamrin 1999). Just as the sky-goddess Nut was thought to spread her star-studded body over the earth, so she was also considered to stretch herself protectively over mummies and the houses of the gods. In the Old Kingdom, from the reign of the 5th-Dynasty pharaoh Unas (2356-2323 BC) onwards, the belief that mortals could be reborn in the form of the circumpolar stars led to the depiction of large numbers of stars on the ceilings of the corridors and chambers of pyramids. Indeed, Utterance 432 in the Pyramid Texts was a request for Nut to spread herself over the deceased so that he might be 'placed among the imperishable stars' and have eternal life (see Faulkner 1969: 142).

The astronomical knowledge of the Egyptian priests and architects at this time is indicated by early examples of the ceremony of *pḏ šs* ('stretching

163

the cord'), first attested on a granite door-jamb from Hierakonpolis, dating to the reign of the 2nd-Dynasty king Khasekhemwy (Cairo, JE 33896; *c.* 2650 BC, see Engelbach 1934). This method relied – at least initially – on the process of sighting on the Great Bear and Orion constellations, using a *mrḫt* (literally, 'instrument of knowing'), which was similar to a primitive astrolabe, and the *bꜣy*, a sighting tool made from the central rib of a palm leaf, thus aligning the foundations of the pyramids and sun temples with the cardinal points, usually achieving an error of less than half a degree (see Žába 1953, Arnold 1991: 15-16). Although the texts and reliefs in temples of later periods continued to describe the enactment of this procedure (as in the temple of Horus at Edfu) it appears to have become primarily a foundation ceremony and in practice many monuments may simply have been aligned in relation to the river (most frequently at right angles to the river). Shaltout and Belmonte (2008), however, have recently argued, on the basis of fresh survey data at 330 temples throughout Egypt, that many Egyptian temples appear to have stellar or solar orientations (e.g. towards the stars Sirius and Canopus or towards the winter solstice sun).

The earliest detailed texts relating to astronomy are the 'diagonal calendars' or 'star clocks' (Neugebauer and Parker 1964, Mengoli 1988, Leitz 1995) painted on wooden coffin lids of the 9th-12th Dynasties and also of the Late Period. These calendars consisted of 36 columns, listing the 36 groups of stars ('decans') into which the night-sky was divided (Neugebauer and Parker 1969). Each specific decan rose above the horizon at dawn for an annual period of ten days. The brightest of these was the dog-star Sirius (known to the Egyptians as the goddess Sopdet), whose 'heliacal rising' on about 19 July coincided with the annual Nile inundation and therefore appears to have been regarded as an astronomical event of some importance (see Krauss 1985 on Sothic risings, and see Janssen 1987 on the significance of the inundation). The god Sah, the mythical consort of Sopdet, was the personification of another decan, the constellation of Orion.

The calendrical system based on decans was flawed by its failure to take into account the fact that the Egyptian year was always about six hours short, adding up to a slippage of ten days every 40 years. It is therefore unlikely that the Middle Kingdom 'star clocks' were ever regarded as a practical means of measuring time. Nevertheless, the decans were later depicted on the ceilings of tombs and temples, starting with the 18th-Dynasty tomb of Senenmut in western Thebes (TT353, *c.* 1460 BC; see Dorman 1991: 138-46). The 'astronomical ceilings' in the Osireion of Sety I at Abydos (*c.* 1300 BC) and the tomb of Ramesses IV (*c.* 1160 BC) in the Valley of the Kings, include cosmological texts (from the *Book of Nut*) describing the period of seventy days spent in the underworld by each decan.

From at least as early as the Middle Kingdom the Egyptians recognised five of the planets, portraying them as deities sailing across the heavens in barks. These 'stars that know no rest' were Jupiter (Horus who limits the two lands), Mars (Horus of the horizon or Horus the red), Mercury (Sebegu, a god associated with Seth), Saturn (Horus, bull of the sky) and Venus ('the one who crosses' or 'god of the morning'). The ceilings of many royal tombs in the Valley of the Kings were decorated with depictions of the heavens. In the tombs of Ramesses VI, VII and IX (KV9, KV1 and KV6 respectively), dating to the second half of the 12th century BC, a set of 24 seated figures representing stars were transected by grids of horizontal and vertical lines, allowing the passage of time to be measured in terms of the transits of stars through the sky.

The concept of the horoscope (including the belief that the stars could influence human destiny) does not seem to have reached Egypt until at least the 2nd century BC, by which time the Babylonian zodiac, represented on the ceiling of the chapel of Osiris on the roof of the temple of Hathor at Dendera, had been adopted – as Evans (2004: 2) puts it: 'the story of the emergence of astrology in Egypt is complex and is only imperfectly understood: Mesopotamian doctrines were elaborated and embellished in a bilingual culture of Greeks and Egyptians ... astrology expanded into a partial vacuum left by the decline of the traditional temple oracle'. It is interesting to note, however, that in Egypt the old system of decans was simply absorbed into the new astrological texts and images, and that astrological activity seems to have been closely associated with temples of Sarapis (Evans 2004: 35). A number of Demotic horoscopes, inscribed on ostraca, have survived, indicating that the new astrology was embraced not only by Greeks but also by native Egyptians (see Neugebauer 1943). The surviving lists of lucky and unlucky days – the earliest surviving example of such a 'hemerology' dates to the Middle Kingdom (P. Kahun XVII, 3; UC32192; see Griffith 1898: 62 and Collier and Quirke 2004:

26-7) – appear to have had no connection with astrology, deriving instead from the intricacies of religious festivals and mythological events, and, according to recent analyses of the main papyri, heavily influenced by the calculation of lunar cycles (see Porceddu et al. 2008).

Abbreviations

BAR = *British Archaeological Repo*rts
BIFAO = *Bulletin de l'Institut Français d'Archéologie Oriental*
BMP = British Museum Press
CdE = *Chronique d'Egypte*
CUP = Cambridge University Press
EA = *Egyptian Archaeology: The Bulletin of the Egypt Exploration Society*
EES = Egypt Exploration Society
HUP = Harvard University Press
IFAO = Institut Français d'Archéologie Oriental
JARCE = *Journal of the American Research Center in Egypt*
JEA = *Journal of Egyptian Archaeology*
JNES = *Journal of Near Eastern Studies*
KPI = Kegan Paul International
MDAIK = *Mitteilungen des Deutschen Archäologischen Instituts, Abteilung Kairo*
MMA = Metropolitan Museum of Art, New York
OUP = Oxford University Press
YUP = Yale University Press
ZÄS = *Zeitschrift der für Ägyptische Sprache und Altertumskunde*

Bibliography

Allen, J.R., 1988. *Genesis in Egypt: The Philosophy of Ancient Egyptian Creation Accounts*, New Haven: YUP.

Amiet, P., 1966. 'Il y a 5000 ans les Elamites inventaient l'écriture', *Archeologia* 12: 20-2.

Andrassy, P., Budka, J. and F. Kammerzell (eds) 2009. *Non-textual Marking Systems, Writing and Pseudo Script from Prehistory to Present Times*, Lingua Aegyptia – Studia Monographica No. 8, Göttingen: Lingua Aegyptia.

Anthes, R., 1928. *Die Felseninschriften von Hatnub*, Leipzig: J.C. Hinrichs.

Arnold, D., 1991. *Building in Egypt: Pharaonic Stone Masonry*, New York and Oxford: OUP.

Arnold, D., 1999. *Temples of the Last Pharaohs*, New York and Oxford: OUP.

Arnold, D. and Pischikova, E.1999. 'Stone vessels: luxury items with manifold implications', *Egyptian Art in the Age of the Pyramids. Catalogue of an exhibition held at the Metropolitan Museum of Art, Sept. 16, 1999-Jan. 9, 2000*, ed. C. Ziegler, New York: MMA, 121-32.

Assmann, J., 2001. *The Search for God in Ancient Egypt*, tr. D. Lorton, Ithaca and London: Cornell University Press.

Assmann, J., 2002. *The Mind of Egypt: History and Meaning in the Time of the Pharaohs*, tr. A. Jenkins, Cambridge MA and London: HUP.

Aston, D., 2009. 'Theban potmarks – nothing other than funny signs? Potmarks from Deir el-Medineh and the Valley of the Kings', *Pictograms or Pseudo Script? Non-textual Identity Marks in Practical Use in Ancient Egypt and Elsewhere*, ed. B.J.J. Haring and O.E. Kaper, Leuven, Peeters, 49-65.

Aufderheide, A.C., 2003. *The Scientific Study of Mummies*, Cambridge: CUP.

Badawy, A., 1963. 'The transport of the colossus of Djehutihetep', *MIO* 8: 325-32.

Baines, J., 1983. 'Literacy and ancient Egyptian society', *Man*, NS 18/3: 572-99.

Baines, J., 1989. 'Communication and display: the integration of early Egyptian art and writing', *Antiquity* 63: 471-82.

Baines, J., 2007. *Visual and Written Culture in Ancient Egypt*, Oxford: OUP.

Baines, J. and Eyre, C.J. 1983. 'Four notes on literacy', *GM* 61: 65-96.

Bard, K., 1992. 'Origins of Egyptian writing', *The Followers of Horus*, ed. R. Friedman and B. Adams, Oxford: Archaeopress, 297-306.

Bardinet, T., 1995. *Les papyrus médicaux de l'Egypte pharaonique: traduction intégrale et commentaire*, Paris: Fayard.

Bass, G.F., 1967. *Cape Gelidonya: A Bronze Age Shipwreck*, Philadelphia.

Bibliography

Bass, G.F., Pulak, C., Collon, D. and Weinstein, J., 1989. 'The Bronze Age shipwreck at Ulu Burun: 1986 campaign', *American Journal of Archaeology* 93: 1-29.

Bauchspies, W.K., Croissant, J. and Restivo, S., 2006. *Science, Technology and Society: A Sociological Approach*, Oxford: Blackwell.

Baumgartel, E.J., 1970. *Petrie's Naqada Excavation: A Supplement*, London: Bernard Quaritch.

Beaujard, P., 2010. 'From three possible Iron-Age world-systems to a single Afro-Eurasian world-system', *Journal of World History* 21/1: 1-43.

Berger, S., 1934. 'A note on some scenes of land-measurement', *JEA* 20: 54-6.

Bietak, M., 2011. 'A Hyksos palace at Avaris', *EA* 38: 38-41.

Bietak, M. and Förstner-Müller, I., 2009. 'Der Hyksospalast bei Tell el-Dabca. Zweite und Dritte Grabungskampagne (Frühling 2008 und Frühling 2009)', *Ägypten und Levante* 19: 91-120.

Blackman, A.M., 1953. *The Rock Tombs of Meir* V, London: EES.

Blackman, A.M., 1988. *The Story of King Kheops and the Magicians Transcribed from Papyrus Westcar* (Berlin *Papyrus* 3033), ed. W.V. Davies, Reading: J.V. Books.

Blackman, A.M. and Peet, T.E. 1925. 'Papyrus Lansing: a translation with notes', *JEA* 11: 284-98.

Boehmer, R.M., Dreyer, G. and Kromer, B., 1993. 'Einiger frühzeitliche 14C-Datierungen aus Abydos und Uruk', *MDAIK* 49: 63-8.

Bökönyi, S., 1968. 'Mecklenburg collection, part 1: data on Iron Age horses of central and eastern Europe', *Bulletin of the American School of Prehistoric Research* 25: 3-71.

Borchardt, L., 1907. 'Voruntersuchung von Tell el-Amarna im Januar 1907', *Mitteilungen der Deutschen Orient-Gesellschaft* 34: 14-31.

Borchardt, L. and Ricke, H., 1980. *Die Wohnhäuser in Tell el-Amarna*, Berlin: Mann.

Boulu, G., 1990. *Le médecin dans la civilization de l'Égypte pharaonique*, unpublished PhD thesis, University of Amiens.

Bourriau, J., 2000. 'The Second Intermediate Period (*c.* 1650-1550 BC)', *Oxford History of Ancient Egypt*, ed. I. Shaw, Oxford: OUP, 184-217.

Bourriau, J. and J. Phillips (eds) 2004. *Invention and Innovation: The Social Context of Technological Change*, Oxford: Oxbow.

Boyd, R. and Richerson, P.J., 1985. *Culture and the Evolutionary Process*, Chicago: University of Chicago Press.

Brandt-Rauf, P.W. and Brandt-Rauf, S.I. 1987. 'History of occupational medicine: relevance of Imhotep and the Edwin Smith papyrus', *British Journal of Industrial Medicine* 44: 68-70.

Bréand, G., 2005. 'Les marques et graffiti sur poteries de l'Egypte pré- et protodynastique: perspectives de recherches à partir de l'exemple d'Adaïma', *Archéo-Nil* 15: 17-30.

Bréand, G., 2009. 'The corpus of pre-firing potmarks from Adaïma (Upper Egypt)', *British Museum Studies in Ancient Egypt and Sudan* 13: 49-72.

Breasted, J.H., 1930. *The Edwin Smith Surgical Papyrus, published in facsimile and hieroglyphic transliteration with translation and commentary in two volumes*, Chicago: University of Chicago Press.

Bibliography

Brier, B. and Houdin, J.-P., 2008. *The Secret of the Great Pyramid*, London: Harper Collins.

Brill, R.H., 1970. 'The chemical interpretation of the texts', *Glass and Glassmaking in Ancient Mesopotamia: An Edition of the Cuneiform Texts which contain Instructions for Glassmakers with a Catalogue of Surviving Objects*, ed. L. Oppenheim, R.H. Brill, D. Barag and A. von Saldern, Corning NY: Corning Museum of Glass Press, 105-28.

Brisson, L., 2000. 'Myth and knowledge', *Greek Thought: A Guide to Classical Knowledge*, ed. J. Brunschwig and G.E.R. Lloyd, Cambridge MA: HUP, 39-50.

Broadhurst, C., 1992. 'Religious considerations at Qadesh', *Studies in Pharaonic Religion and Society in Honour of J. Gwyn Griffiths*, ed. A.B. Lloyd, London: KPI, 77-81.

Bryan, B., 1992. 'Royal and divine statuary', *Egypt's Dazzling Sun: Amenhotep III and his World*, ed. A. Kozloff and B. Bryan, Bloomington IN: Indiana University Press, 125-92.

Bryce, T., 2002. *Life and Society in the Hittite World*, Oxford: OUP.

Budge, E.A.W., 1923. *Facsimiles of Egyptian Hieratic Papyri in the British Museum*, London: British Museum [pls XV-XXX: Papyrus Lansing].

Caminos, R.A., 1954. *Late Egyptian Miscellanies*, Oxford: OUP.

Campbell, C., 1910. *Two Theban Princes Kha-em-Uast & Amen-Khepeshf, sons of Rameses III, Menna, a Land-Steward, and Their Tombs*, London: Oliver and Boyd.

Carmen, J. and Harding, A. (eds), 1999. *Ancient Warfare: Archaeological Perspectives*, Stroud: Sutton.

Černy, J., 1954. 'Prices and wages in Egypt in the Ramesside period', *Cahiers d'histoire mondiale* 1: 903-21.

Chace, A.B., Bull, L. and Manning, H.P., 1929. *The Rhind Mathematical Papyrus*, Oberlin: Mathematical Association of America.

Chafe, W.L., 1982. 'Integration and involvement in speaking, writing, and oral literature', *Spoken and Written Language: Exploring Orality and Literacy*, ed. Deborah Tannen, Norwood, NJ: Ablex.

Chandler, R., 1976. *The Notebooks of Raymond Chandler and English Summer: a Gothic Romance*, New York: Ecco Press.

Cialowicz, K., Slaboński, R. and Debowska, J., 2007. *Kość i zloto: poczatki sztuki egipskiej: z wykopalisk Instytutu Archeologii Uniwersytetu Jagiellońskiego I Muzeum Archeologicznego w Poznaniu*. Poznań: Poznańskie Towarzystwo Prehistoryczne.

Clagett, M., 1995. *Ancient Egyptian Science II: Calendars, Clocks and Astronomy*, Philadelphia: American Philosophical Society.

Cline, E.H. and Yasur-Landau, A., 2007. 'Musings from a distant shore: the nature and destination of the Uluburun ship and its cargo', *Tel Aviv* 34/2: 125-41.

Clutton-Brock, J., 1974. 'The Buhen horse', *Journal of Archaeological Science* 1: 89-100.

Cohen, R. and Westerbrook, R., 2000. *Amarna Diplomacy: The Beginnings of International Relations*, Baltimore and London: Johns Hopkins University Press.

Collier, M. and Quirke, S., 2004. *The UCL Lahun Papyri: Religious, Literary, Legal, Mathematical and Medical*, Oxford: BAR.

Cooney, K.M., 2006. 'An informal workshop: textual evidence for private funerary art production in the Ramesside period', *Living and Writing in Deir el-Medina: Socio-historical Embodiment of Deir el-Medina Texts*, ed. A. Dorn and T. Hofmann, Basel: Aegyptiaca Helvetica, 43-55.

Cooney, K.M., 2007. *The Cost of Death, The Social and Economic Value of Ancient Egyptian Funerary Art in the Ramesside Period*, Leiden: Egyptologische Uitgaven.

Cotterell, B., Dickson, F.P. and Kamminga, J., 1986. 'Ancient Egyptian water-clocks: a reappraisal', *Journal of Archaeological Science* 13: 31-50.

Couchoud, S., 1988. 'Calcul d'un horloge à eau', *Bulletin de la Société d'Egyptologie de Genève* 12: 25-34.

Craddock, P., 1995. *Early Metal Mining and Production*, Edinburgh: Edinburgh University Press.

Cunningham, A. and Wilson, P., 1993. 'De-centring the "Big Picture": the origins of modern science and the modern origins of science', *British Journal for the History of Science* 26: 407-32.

Cuomo, S., 2007. *Technology and Culture in Greek and Roman Antiquity*, Cambridge: CUP.

Dalley, S., 1985. 'Foreign chariotry and cavalry in the armies of Tiglath-Pileser III and Sargon II', *Iraq* 47: 31-48.

Daressy, M.G., 1902. *Fouilles de la Vallée des Rois (1898-1899)*, Cairo: Service des Antiquités de l'Egypte.

Daumas, F., 1956. 'Le sanatorium de Dendara', *BIFAO* 56: 35-57.

David, R., 2008. 'Egyptian mummies: an overview', *Egyptian Mummies and Modern Science*, ed. R. David, Cambridge: CUP, 10-20.

Davies, B.G., 1999. *Who's Who at Deir el-Medina: A Prosopographic Study of the Royal Workmen's Community*, Leiden: Nederlands Instituut voor het Nabije Oosten.

Davies, N. de G., 1901. *The Mastaba of Ptahhetep and Akhethetep at Saqqareh II: The Mastaba*, London: EEF.

Davies, N. de G., 1905. *The Rock Tombs of el Amarna* II, London: EES.

Davies, N. de G., 1929. 'The town house in ancient Egypt', *Metropolitan Museum Studies* 1/2: 233-55.

Davies, N. de G., 1930. *The Tomb of Ken-Amun at Thebes*, New York: MMA.

Davies, N. de G., 1943. *The Tomb of Rekh-Mi-Re at Thebes*, New York: MMA.

Davies, N.M. and Davies, N. de G., 1941. 'Syrians in the tomb of Amunedjeh', *JEA* 27: 96-8.

Davis, W., 1976. 'The origins of register composition in Predynastic Egyptian art', *Journal of the American Oriental Society* 96: 404-18.

Dawson, W.R. and Peet, T.E., 1933. 'The so-called Poem on the King's Chariot', *JEA* 19: 167-74.

Debono, F. 1993-4. 'Un atelier d'artisans au Ramesseum', *Memnonia* IV-V, Cairo: IFAO, 37-53.

de Morgan, J., 1897. *Recherches sur les origins de l'Egypte* II, Paris: E. Leroux.

Dixon, D.M., Clutton-Brock, J. and Burleigh, R. 1979. 'The Buhen horse', *Excavations at Buhen 1: The Archaeological Report*, ed. W.B. Emery, London: EES, 191-5.

Bibliography

Dodson, A., 1994. *The Canopic Equipment of the Kings of Egypt*, London: KPI.

Doll, S.K., 1982. 'Weights and measures', *Egypt's Golden Age: the Art of Living in the New Kingdom 1558-1085 BC*, ed. Brovarski, Doll and Freed, Boston MA: Boston Museum of Fine Arts, 58-62.

Dorman, P., 1991. *The Tombs of Senenmut: The Architecture and Decoration of Tombs 71 and 353*, New York: MMA.

Drenkhahn, R., 1976. *Die Handwerker und ihre Tätigkeiten im alter Ägypten*, Wiesbaden: Otto Harrassowitz.

Drenkhahn, R., 1995. 'Artisans and artists in pharaonic Egypt', *Civilizations of the Ancient Near East*, ed. J. Sasson, New York: Simon and Schuster, 331-43.

Dreyer, G., 1993. 'Umm el-Qaab: Nachuntersuchungen im frühzeitlichen Königsfriedhof. 5./6. Vorbericht', *MDAIK* 49: 23-62.

Dreyer, G., 1998. *Umm el-Qaab I. Das prädynastische Königsgrab U-j und seine frühen Schriftzeugnisse, AV 86*, Mainz: Philipp von Zabern.

Dreyer, G. and Swelim, N., 1982. 'Die Kleine Stufenpyramide von Abydos-Süd (Sinki) Grabungsbericht', *MDAIK* 38: 83-93.

Druckman, D. and Güner, S., 2000. 'A social psychological analysis of Amarna diplomacy', *Amarna Diplomacy: The Beginnings of International Relations*, ed. R. Cohen and R. Westbrook, Baltimore and London: Johns Hopkins University Press, 174-90.

Duell, P., 1938. *The Mastaba of Mereruka*, 2 vols, Chicago: Oriental Institute.

Dunham, D., 1947. 'Four Kushite colossi in the Sudan', *JEA*, 33: 63-5.

Dunham, D., 1965. ' Building an Egyptian pyramid', *Archaeology* 9: 159-65.

Ebbell, B., 1937. *The Papyrus Ebers: The Greatest Egyptian Medical Document*, London: OUP.

Edgerton, D., 2006. *The Shock of the Old: Technology and Global History since 1900*, London: Profile.

Edwards, I.E.S., 1993. *The Pyramids of Egypt*, 5th edn, Harmondsworth: Penguin.

Edwards, J.F., 2003. 'Building the Great Pyramid: probable construction methods employed at Giza', *Technology and Culture* 44/ 2: 340-54.

Ehret, C., 1978. 'Historical inference from transformations in cultural vocabularies', *Sprache und Geschichte in Africa* 2: 189-218.

Ehret, C., 2006. 'Linguistic stratigraphies and Holocene history in northeastern Africa', *Archaeology of Early Northeastern Africa. In memory of Lech Krzyzaniak*, ed. M. Chlodnicki and K. Kroeper, Poznan: Poznan Archaeological Museum, 1019-55.

Emery, W.B., 1960. 'Preliminary report on the excavations of the Egypt Exploration Society at Buhen, 1958-59', *Kush* 8: 7-10.

Engelbach, R., 1934. 'A foundation scene of the Second Dynasty', *JEA* 20: 183-4.

Evans, J., 2004. 'The astrologer's apparatus: a picture of professional practice in Greco-Roman Egypt', *Journal for the History of Astronomy* 35: 1-44.

Eyre, C., 1987. 'Work and organization of work in the Old Kingdom and New Kingdom', *Labor in the Ancient Near East*, ed. M.A. Powell, New Haven CT: American Oriental Society, 5-48, 167-222.

Eyre, C., 1995. 'Symbol and reality in everyday life', Abstracts of the 7th International Congress of Egyptologists, Cambridge, 3-9 September 1995, ed. C. Eyre, London, 55-6.

Fairman, H.W., 1949. 'Town planning in pharaonic Egypt', *Town Planning Review* 20: 32-51.

Fairman, H.W., 1954. 'Worship and festivals in an Egyptian temple', *Bulletin of the John Rylands Library* 37: 165-203.

Faulkner, R.O., 1969. *The Ancient Egyptian Pyramid Texts*, Warminster: Aris and Phillips.

Feldman, M.H., 2006. *Diplomacy by Design: Luxury Arts and an 'International Style' in the Ancient Near East, 1400-1200 BCE*, Chicago: University of Chicago Press.

Figueiredo, A., 2004. 'Locality HK6 at Hierakonpolis: results of the 2000 field season', *Egypt at its Origins: Studies in Memory of Barbara Adams*, ed. S. Hendrickx, R.F. Friedman, K.M. Cialowicz and M. Chlodnicki, Leuven: Peeters, 1-24.

Finkel, I.L. and Reade, J.E., 1996. 'Assyrian hieroglyphs', *Zeitschrift für Assyriologie und Vorderasiatische Archäologie* 86: 244-68.

Fischer-Elfert, H., 1986. *Die Satirische Streitschrift der Papyrus Anastasi I: Übersetzung und Kommentar*, Ägyptologische Abhandlungen 44, Wiesbaden: Otto Harrassowitz.

Fitchen, J., 1978. 'Building Cheops' pyramid', *Journal of the Society of Architectural Historians* 37/1 (Mar. 1978), 3-12.

Foley, J.M. 1980. 'Oral literature: premises and problems', *Choice* 18: 487-96.

Friedman, R., 2000. 'Figures in flint', *Nekhen News* 12: 14-17.

Friedman, R.F., Maish, A., Fahmy, A.G., Darnell, J.C. and Johnson, E.D., 1999. 'Preliminary report on field work at Hierakonpolis: 1996-1998', *JARCE* 36: 1-35.

Friedman, R.F., Watrell, E., Jones, J., Fahmy, A.G., Van Neer, W. and Linseele, V., 2002. 'Excavations at Hierakonpolis', *Archéonil* 12: 55-68.

Fukagawa, S., 2011. *Investigation into Dynamics of Ancient Egyptian Pharmacology: A Statistical Analysis of Papyrus Ebers and Cross-cultural Medical Thinking*, Oxford: Archaeopress.

Gale, R., Gasson, P., Hepper, N. and Killen, G., 2000. 'Wood', *Ancient Egyptian Materials and Technology*, ed. P.T. Nicholson and I. Shaw, Cambridge: CUP, 334-71.

Gallorini, C., 2009. 'Incised marks on pottery and other objects from Kahun', *Pictograms or Pseudo Script? Non-textual Identity Marks in Practical Use in Ancient Egypt and Elsewhere*, ed. B.J.J. Haring and O.E. Kaper, Leuven, Peeters, 107-42.

Gardiner, A.H., 1911. *Egyptian Hieratic Texts, Transcribed, Translated and Annotated*, Leipzig: Hinrichs.

Gardiner, A.H., 1947. *Ancient Egyptian Onomastica*, 3 vols, Oxford: Clarendon Press.

Gardiner, A.H., 1955. *The Ramesseum Papyri*, Oxford: OUP.

Gardiner, A.H. and Faulkner, R.O., 1941-52. *The Wilbour Papyrus*, 4 vols, Oxford: OUP.

Garstang, J., 1903. *Mahasna and Bet Khallaf*, London: Bernard Quaritch.

Ghalioungui, P., 1973. *The House of Life (Per Ankh): Magic and Medical Science in Ancient Egypt*, Amsterdam: B.M. Israel.

Ghalioungui, P., 1983. *The Physicians of Pharaonic Egypt*, Cairo: Al-Ahram Center for Scientific Translation.

Ghalioungui, P., 1987. *The Ebers Papyrus: A New English Translation, Commentaries and Glossaries*. Cairo: Al-Ahram Center for Scientific Translation.

Gille, B., 1980. *Les mécaniciens grecs: la naissance de la technologie*. Paris: Gallimard.

Gillings, R.J., 1972. *Mathematics in the Time of the Pharaohs*, Cambridge MA: Massachusetts Institute of Technology.

Glanville, S.R.K., 1927. 'The mathematical leather roll in the British Museum', *JEA* 13: 232-8.

Gledhill, J. and Larssen, M.T., 1982. 'The Polanyi paradigm and the dynamics of archaic states: Mesopotamia and Mesoamerica', *Theory and Explanation in Archaeology: The Southampton Conference*, ed. C. Renfrew, M.J. Rowlands and B.A. Segraves, New York and London: Academic Press, 197-230.

Goedicke, H. (ed.), 1985. *Perspectives on the Battle of Kadesh*, Baltimore MD: Halgo.

Goneim, M.Z., 1957. *Horus Sekhem-Khet: The Unfinished Step Pyramid at Saqqara*, Cairo: IFAO.

Goody, J., 1968. *Literacy in Traditional Societies*, Cambridge: CUP.

Goody, J., 1977. *The Domestication of the Savage Mind*, Cambridge: CUP.

Goody, J., 1986. *The Logic of Writing and the Organization of Society*, Cambridge: CUP.

Goody, J., 1987. *The Interface between the Written and the Oral*, Cambridge: CUP.

Goren, Y., Finkelstein, I. and Na'aman, N. (eds) 2004. *Inscribed in Clay: Provenance Study of the Amarna Tablets and Other Ancient Near Eastern Texts*, Tel Aviv: Emery and Claire Yass Publications in Archaeology.

Goyon, J.C., 1972. *Rituels funéraires de l'ancienne Égypte*, Paris: Éditions du Cerf.

Grapow, H., von Deines, H. and Westendorf, W., 1954-73. *Grundriss der Medizin der alten Ägypter*, 9 vols, Berlin: Akademie Verlag.

Gräslund, B., 1981. 'The background to C.J. Thomsen's Three-Age system', *Towards a History of Archaeology*, ed. G. Daniel, London: Thames and Hudson, 45-50.

Griffith, F.Ll., 1896. *Beni Hasan* III, London: EEF.

Griffith, F.Ll., 1898. *The Petrie Papyri: Hieratic Papyri from Kahun and Gurob (Principally of the Middle Kingdom)*, 2 vols, London: Bernard Quaritch.

Gurney, O.R. 1954. *The Hittites*, Harmondsworth: Penguin.

Haarer, P., 2001. 'Problematising the transition from bronze to iron', *The Social Context of Technological Change*, ed. A.J. Shortland, Oxford: Oxbow, 255-73.

Habachi, L., 1960. 'Notes on the unfinished obelisk of Aswan and another smaller one in Gharb Aswan', *Drevni i Egipet*, ed. V.V. Struve, Moscow: Institut Vostokovedeni i a, Akademi i a Nauk USSR, 216-35.

Habachi, L., 1972. *The Second Stela of Kamose and his Struggle against the Hyksos Ruler and his Capital*, Glückstadt: Verlag JJ Augustin.

Halioua, B. and Ziskind, B., 2005. *Medicine in the Days of the Pharaohs*, Cambridge MA: HUP.

Hall, E.S., 1986. *The Pharaoh Smites his Enemies: A Comparative Study*, Munich: Deutscher Kunstverlag.

Bibliography

Harer, W.B., 1994. 'Peseshkef: the first special-purpose surgical instrument', *Obstetrics and Gynecology* 83: 1053-5.

Haring, B.J.J. 2009. 'Economy', *UCLA Encyclopedia of Egyptology*, ed. W. Wendrich, Los Angeles: UCLA. [http://escholarship.org/uc/item/2t01s4qj]

Haring, B.J.J. and Kaper, O.E.(eds), 2009. *Pictograms or Pseudo Script? Non-textual Identity Marks in Practical Use in Ancient Egypt and Elsewhere*, Leuven, Peeters.

Harvey, S., 1988. 'Fish-tail knife', *Mummies and Magic: The Funerary Arts in Ancient Egypt*, ed. S. D'Auria, P. Lacovara and C.H. Roehrig, Cambridge MA: Boston Museum of Fine Arts, 73.

Havelock, E.A. 1963. *Preface to Plato*, Oxford: Blackwell.

Hawass, Z., 2003. *Secrets from the Sand: My Search for Egypt's Past*, London: Thames and Hudson.

Hayes, W.C., 1959. *Scepter of Egypt II: The Hyksos Period and the New Kingdom*, New York: MMA.

Heidorn, L.A., 1997. 'The horses of Kush', *JNES* 56/2: 105-14.

Heilporn, P., 1989. 'Les nilomètres d'Elephantine et la date de la crue', *CdE* 64: 283-5.

Heinz, S.C., 2001. *Die Feldzugdarstellungen des Neuen Reiches*, Vienna: Österreichische Akademie der Wissenschaften.

Helck, W., 1975. *Wirtschaftsgeschichte des Alten Ägypten im 3. und 2. Jahrtausend vor Chr*, Leiden: Brill.

Helck, W., 1990. *Thinitische Töpfmarken,* ÄA 50, Wiesbaden: Otto Harrassowitz.

Henderson, J., 2000. *The Science and Archaeology of Materials: An Investigation of Inorganic Materials*, London: Routledge.

Hendrickx, S. and Vermeersch, P., 2000. 'Prehistory: from the Palaeolithic to the Badarian culture (*c.* 700,000-4000 BC)', *Oxford History of Ancient Egypt*, ed. I. Shaw, Oxford: OUP.

Herold, A., 1999. *Streitwagentechnologie in der Ramses-Stadt: Bronze an Pferd und Wagen*, Mainz: Philipp von Zabern.

Herold, A., 2007. *Streitwagentechnologie in der Ramses-Stadt: Knäufe, Knöpfe und Scheiben aus Stein*, Mainz: Philipp von Zabern.

Hester, T.R. and Heizer, R.F., 1981. *Making Stone Vases: Ethnoarchaeological Studies at an Alabaster Workshop in Upper Egypt*, Monographic Journals of the Near East, Malibu CA: Undena Publications.

Hikade, T., 1997. 'Ein außergewöhnliches Silexmesser aus Abydos', *MDAIK* 53: 85-9.

Hikade, T., 2002. 'Die lithischen Industrien des Alten Reiches auf Elephantine', *MDAIK* 58: 305-22.

Hikade, T., 2003. 'Getting the ritual right – fishtail knives in Predynastic Egypt', *Egypt – Temple of the Whole World: Studies in Honour of Jan Assmann*, Studies in the History of Religions 97, ed. S. Meyer, Leiden and Boston: Brill, 137-51.

Hikade, T., 2004. 'Some thoughts on Chalcolithic and Early Bronze Age flint scrapers in Egypt', *MDAIK* 60: 57-68.

Hikade, T., 2010. 'Stone tool production', *UCLA Encyclopedia of Egyptology*, ed.

W. Wendrich, Los Angeles: UCLA. http://digital2.library.ucla.edu/viewItem. do?ark=21198/zz0025h6kk

Hodgkinson, A., 2010. 'High-status industries in the capital and royal cities of the New Kingdom', *Commerce and Economy in Ancient Egypt*, ed. A. Hudecz and M. Petrik, Oxford: Archaeopress, 71-9.

Hodgkinson, A., 2011. 'Mass production in New Kingdom Egypt: the industries of Amarna and Piramesse', *Current Research in Egyptology 2009: Proceedings of the Tenth Annual Symposium*, ed. D. Boatright, J. Corbelli and C. Malleson, Oxford: Oxbow, 81-98.

Hoffman, M.A., 1980. 'A rectangular Amratian house from Hierakonpolis and its significance for predynastic research', *JNES* 39: 119-37.

Holmes, D.L., 1992. 'Chipped stone-working craftsmen, Hierakonpolis and the rise of civilization in Egypt', *The Followers of Horus; Studies Dedicated to Michael Allen Hoffman 1944-1990*, ed. R. Friedman and B. Adams, Oxford: Oxbow Books, 37-44.

Hornung, E., 1999. *The Ancient Egyptian Books of the Afterlife*, Ithaca and London: Cornell University Press.

Hulit, T., 2006. 'Tut'Ankhamun's body armour: materials, construction, and the implications for the military industry', *Current Research in Egyptology 2004*, ed. R. Dann, Oxford: Oxbow, 100-11.

Imhausen, A., 2007. 'Egyptian mathematics', *The Mathematics of Egypt, Mesopotamia, China, India and Islam: A Sourcebook*, ed. V.J. Katz, Princeton: Princeton University Press, 7-57.

Imhausen, A. and Ritter, J., 2004. 'Mathematical fragments: UC21114B, UC32118B, UC32134A+B, UC32159-UC32162', *The UCL Lahun Papyri: Religious, Literary, Legal, Mathematical and Medical*, ed. M. Collier and S. Quirke, Oxford: BAR, 71-98.

Iversen, E. (ed.), 1939. *Papyrus Carlsberg No. VIII, With Some Remarks on the Egyptian Origin of Some Popular Birth Prognoses*, Copenhagen: Munksgaard.

Izre'el, S., 1995. 'The Amarna letters from Canaan', *Civilizations of the Ancient Near East*, ed. J.M. Sasson, New York: Scribners, 2411-19.

Izre'el, S., 1997. *The Amarna Scholarly Tablets*, Groningen: Styx.

Janssen, J.J., 1975. *Commodity Prices from the Ramessid Period: An Economic Study of the Village of Necropolis Workmen at Thebes*, Leiden: Brill.

Janssen, J.J., 1987. 'The day the inundation began', *JNES* 46: 129-36.

Janssen, J.J., 1992. 'A New Kingdom settlement: the verso of P.BM10068', *Altorientalische Forschungen* 19: 8-23.

Jaroš-Deckert, B., 1984. *Grabung in Assasif, V: Das Grab des Jnj-jtj.f. Die Wandmalereien der XI. Dynastie*, Cairo: DAIK.

Jelinkova-Reymond, E., 1956. *Les inscriptions de la statue guérisseuse de Djed-her-le-Sauveur*, Cairo: IFAO.

Johnston, K.J., 2001. 'Classic Maya scribe capture', *Antiquity* 75: 373-81.

Jonckheere, F., 1951. 'La place du prêtre de Sekhmet dans le corps médical de l'ancienne Égypte', *Archives internationals d'histoire des sciences* 4: 915-24.

Bibliography

Jones, J., 2002. 'Towards mummification: new evidence for early developments', *EA* 21: 5-7.

Jórdeczka, M., Królik, H., Masojć, M. and Schild, R., 2011. 'Early Holocene pottery in the Western Desert of Egypt: new data from Nabta Playa', *Antiquity* 85: 99-115.

Junker, H., 1928. 'Die Stele des Hofarztes Irj', *ZÄS* 63: 53-70.

Junker, H., 1953. *Grabungen auf dem Friedhof des Alten Reiches bei den Pyramiden von Giza 11*. Vienna: Rohrer.

Kahl, J., 2002-4. *Frühägyptisches Wörterbuch*, 2 vols, Wiesbaden: Harassowitz.

Kaiser, W., Arnold, F., Bommas, M., Hikade, T., Hoffmanm, F., Jaritz, H., Kopp, P., Niederburger, W., Paetznick, J.-P., von Pilgrim, B., von Pilgrim, C., Raue, D., Rzeuska, T., Schaten, S., Seiler, A., Stalder, L. and Ziermann, M., 1999. 'Stadt und Tempel von Elephantine. 25./ 26./ 27. Grabungsbericht', *MDAIK* 55: 63-236.

Kamrin, J., 1999. *The Cosmos of Khnumhotep II at Beni Hasan*, London and New York: KPI.

Känel, F. von, 1984. *Les prêtres-ouâb de Sekhmet et les conjurateurs de Serket*, Paris: Presses Universitaires de France.

Kaplony, P., 1963. *Die Inschriften der ägyptischen Frühzeit*, 3 vols, Wiesbaden: Harassowitz.

Kemp, B.J., 1972. 'Temple and town in ancient Egypt', *Man, Settlement and Urbanism*, ed. P.J. Ucko, R. Tringham, and G.W. Dimbleby, London: Duckworth, 57-80.

Kemp, B.J., 1977. 'The city of el-Amarna as a source for study of urban society in ancient Egypt', *WA* 9: 123-39.

Kemp, B.J., 1979. 'Preliminary report on the el-Amarna survey, 1978', *JEA* 65: 5-12.

Kemp, B.J., 1981. 'The character of the South Suburb at el-Amarna', *MDOG* 113: 81-97.

Kemp, B.J. (ed.), 1984. *Amarna Reports* I, London: EES.

Kemp, B.J. (ed.), 1986. *Amarna Reports* III, London: EES.

Kemp, B.J. (ed.), 1988. *Amarna Reports* V, London: EES.

Kemp, B.J. (ed.), 1995. *Amarna Reports* VI, London: EES.

Kemp, B.J., 2000. 'Soil (including mud-brick architecture)', *Ancient Egyptian Materials and Technology*, ed. P.T. Nicholson and I. Shaw, Cambridge: CUP, 78-103.

Kemp, B.J., 2006. *Ancient Egypt: Anatomy of a Civilisation*, 2nd edn, London: Routledge.

Kemp, B., and Stevens, A., 2010. *Busy Lives at Amarna: Excavations in the Main City (Grid 12 and the House of Ranefer, N49.18), I: The Excavations, Architecture and Environmental Remains*, London: EES.

Kendall, T., 1981. 'Gurpiša ša aweli: the helmets of the warriors at Nuzi', *Studies on the Civilization and Culture of Nuzi and the Hurrians in Honour of Ernest R. Lacheman on his Seventy-Fifth Birthday, April 29, 1981*, ed. M.A. Morrison and D.J. Owen, Winona Lake: Eisenbrauns, 201-31.

Killen, G. and Weiss, L., 2009. 'Markings on objects of daily use from Deir el-Medina: ownership marks or administrative aids?', *Non-Textual Marking Systems, Writing and Pseudo Script from Prehistory to Modern Times*, ed. P. Andrássy, J. Budka and F. Kammerzell, Göttingen: Lingua Aegyptian.

Bibliography

Kinnier Wilson, J.V., 1972. *The Nimrud Wine Lists: A Study of Men and Administration at the Assyrian Capital in the Eighth Century BC*, London: British School of Archaeology in Iraq.

Kobusiewicz, M., 1996. 'Technology, goals and efficiency of quartz exploitation in the Khartoum Neolithic: the case of Kadero', *Interregional Contacts in the Later Prehistory of Northeastern Africa*, Studies in African Archaeology 5, ed. L. Krzyzaniak, K. Kroeper and M. Kobusiewicz, Poznan: Poznan Archaeological Museum, 347-54.

Kossmann, M., 1994. 'Amarna-Akkadian as a mixed language', *Mixed Languages*, ed. P. Bakker and M. Mous, Amsterdam: IFOTT, 169-73.

Kramar, T., 2009. 'Archäologie: älteste Keilschrift aus Ägypten', *Die Press.com*, 28 June 2009, http://diepresse.com/home/science/482083/index.do?_vl_backlink.

Krauss, R., 1985. *Sothis- und Monddaten: Studien zur astronomischen und technischen Chronologie Altägyptens*, Hildesheim: Gerstenberg Verlag.

Krupp, E.C., 1979. *In Search of Ancient Astronomies*, New York: Doubleday.

Kubler, G., 1962. *The Shape of Time: Remarks on the History of Things*, New Haven: YUP.

Lacovara, P., 1990. *Deir el-Ballas: Preliminary Report on the Deir el-Ballas Expedition, 1980-1986*. Cairo: ARCE.

Lehner, M., 1985a. 'The development of the Giza necropolis: the Khufu Project', *MDAIK* 41: 109-43.

Lehner, M., 1985b. 'A contextual approach to the Giza Pyramids', *Archiv für Orientforschung* 31: 136-58.

Lehner, M., 1997. *The Complete Pyramids*, London: Thames and Hudson.

Lehner, M., Kamel, M., and Tavares, A., 2009. *Giza Plateau Mapping Project Seasons 2006-2007: Preliminary Report*, Boston MA: AERA.

Leitz, C., 1995. *Altägyptische Sternuhren*, Leuven: Peeters.

Lemonnier, P., 1993. *Technological Choices: Transformation in Material Cultures since the Neolithic*, London: Routledge.

Lichtheim, M., 1976. *Ancient Egyptian Literature II: The New Kingdom*, Los Angeles: UCLA Press.

Lichtheim, M., 1980. *Ancient Egyptian Literature III: The Late Period*, Los Angeles: UCLA Press.

Lilyquist, C. and Brill, R.H., 1993. *Studies in Early Egyptian Glass*, New York: MMA.

Littauer, M.A. and Crouwel, J.H., 1979. *Wheeled Vehicles and Ridden Animals in the Ancient Near East*, Leiden and Cologne: E.J. Brill.

Littauer, M.A. and Crouwel, J.H., 1985. *Chariots and Related Equipment from the Tomb of Tut'ankhamun*, Oxford: Griffith Institute.

Lloyd, G.E.R., 1975. 'A note on Erasistratus of Ceos', *Journal of Hellenic Studies* 95: 172-5.

Lloyd, G.E.R., 2004. *Ancient Worlds, Modern Reflections: Philosophical Perspectives on Greek and Chinese Science and Culture*, Oxford: OUP.

Longrigg, J., 1998. *Greek Medicine from the Heroic to the Hellenistic Age: A Source Book*, London: Duckworth.

Lorton, D., 1974. 'Terminology related to the laws of warfare in Dynasty XVIII', *JARCE* 11: 53-68.

Lucas, A., 1926. *Ancient Egyptian Materials and Industries*, 1st edn, London: Edward Arnold.

Lucas, A., 1932. 'The use of natron in mummification', *JEA* 18: 125-40.

Lucas, A., 1962. *Ancient Egyptian Materials and Industries*, 4th edn, rev. J.R. Harris, London: Edward Arnold.

Lyons, J., 1995. 'Colour in language', *Colour: Art and Science*, ed. T. Lamb and J. Bourriau, Cambridge: CUP, 194-224.

Lythgoe, A.M. and Dunham, D., 1965. *The Predynastic Cemetery N7000, Naga ed-Dêr Part IV*, Berkeley and Los Angeles: University of California Press.

Mackenzie D. and Judy Wajcman, J. (eds), 1985. *The Social Shaping of Technology*, Milton Keynes: Open University Press.

Maher-Taha, M., 2002. *Le tombeau de Menna (TT69)*, Cairo: Centre de Documentation et d'Etudes sur l'Ancienne Egypte (CEDAE).

Mariette, A., 1871. *Les papyrus égyptiens du musée de Boulaq I*, Paris: Franck.

Mathieu, B., Meeks, D. and Wissa, M. (eds) 2006. *L'Apport de l'Egypte à l'Histoire des Techniques: Méthodes*, Chronologie et Comparaisons, Cairo: IFAO.

McDowell, A.G., 1993. *Hieratic Ostraca in the Hunterian Museum (the Colin Campbell Ostraca)*, Glasgow and Oxford: Griffith Institute.

McDowell, A.G., 1999. *Village Life in Ancient Egypt: Laundry Lists and Love Songs*, Oxford: OUP.

McLeod, W.E., 1970. *Composite Bows from the Tomb of Tut'ankhamun*, Oxford: Griffith Institute.

McLeod, W.E., 1982. *Self Bows and Other Archery Tackle from the Tomb of Tut'ankhamun*, Oxford, Griffith Institute.

Mengoli, P., 1988. 'Some considerations of Egyptian star clocks', *Archiv der Geschichte der Naturwissenschaften* 22/4: 1127-50.

Meskell, L. and Joyce, R.A., 2003. *Embodied Lives: Figuring Ancient Maya and Egyptian Experience*, London: Routledge.

Miatello, L., 2010. 'The nb.t in the Moscow mathematical papyrus, and a tomb model from Beni Hasan', *JEA* 96: 228-32.

Midant-Reynes, B., 1987. 'Contribution à l'étude de la société prédynastique: le cas du couteau "ripple-flake"', *SAK* 14: 185-224.

Miller, R., McEwen, E. and Bergman, C.A., 1986. 'Experimental approaches to ancient Near Eastern archery', *World Archaeology*, 18/2: 178-95.

Mokhtar, G., Riad, H. and Iskander, Z., 1973. *Mummification in Ancient Egypt*, Cairo: Cairo Museum.

Mokyr, J., 1990. *The Lever of Riches: Technological Creativity and Economic Progress*, New York and Oxford: OUP.

Moorey, P.R.S., 1986. 'The emergence of the light, horse-drawn chariot in the Near East *c.* 2000-1500 BC', *World Archaeology* 18/2: 196-215.

Moorey, P.R.S., 1989. 'The Hurrians, the Mitanni and technological innovation',

Archaeologica Iranica and Orientalis: Miscellanea in Honorem Louis Vanden Berghe, ed. L. de Meyer and E. Haerinck. Ghent: Peters, 273-86.

Moorey, P.R.S., 1994. *Ancient Mesopotamian Materials and Industries*, Oxford: Clarendon Press.

Moorey, P.R.S., 2001. 'The mobility of artisans and opportunities for technology transfer', *The Social Context of Technological Change: Egypt and the Near East, 1650-1550 BC*, ed. A.J. Shortland. Oxford: Oxbow, 1-14.

Moran, W.L., 1992. *The Amarna Letters*, London and Baltimore: Johns Hopkins University Press.

Morenz, L., 2004. *Bild-Buchstaben und symbolische Zeichen. Die Herausbildung der Schrift in der hohen Kultur Altägyptens, OBO 205*, Fribourg and Göttingen: Saint-Paul.

Moussa, A.M. and Altenmüller, H. 1971. *The Tomb of Nefer and Ka-Hay: Old Kingdom Tombs at the Causeway of King Unas at Saqqara*, Mainz: Philipp von Zabern.

Murnane, W.J., 1995. *Texts from the Amarna Period in Egypt*, Atlanta GA: Scholars Press.

Naville, E., 1908. *The Temple of Deir el Bahari VI*, London: EEF.

Needler, W., 1956. 'A flint knife of King Djer', *JEA* 42: 41-4.

Neugebauer, O., 1943. 'Demotic horoscopes', *Journal of the American Oriental Society* 63: 115-27.

Neugebauer, O. and Parker, R.A., 1964. *Egyptian Astronomical Texts II: The Ramesside Star Clocks*, Providence RI: Brown University.

Neugebauer, O. and Parker, R.A., 1969. *Egyptian Astronomical Texts III: Decans, Planets, and Zodiacs*, Providence RI: Brown University.

Newberry, P.E., 1893. *Beni Hassan* II, London: EES.

Newton, R.G., 1980. 'Recent views on ancient glasses', *Glass Technology*, 21/4: 173-83.

Nicholson, P.T., 1993. *Ancient Egyptian Faience and Glass*, Aylesbury: Shire.

Nicholson, P.T., 2006. 'Glass vessels from the reign of Thutmose III and a hitherto unknown glass chalice', *Journal of Glass Studies* 48: 11-21.

Nicholson, P.T., 2007. *Brilliant Things for Akhenaten: The Production of Glass, Vitreous Materials and Pottery at Amarna Site O45.1*, London: EES.

Nicholson, P.T. and Henderson, J., 2000. 'Glass', *Ancient Egyptian Materials and Technology*, ed. P.T. Nicholson and I. Shaw, Cambridge: CUP, 195-226.

Nicholson, P.T., Jackson, C.M. and Trott, K.M. 1997. 'The Ulu Burun glass ingots, cylindrical vessels and Egyptian glass', *JEA* 83: 143-53.

Nicholson, P.T. and Shaw, I. (eds), 2000. *Ancient Egyptian Materials and Technology*, Cambridge: CUP.

Nims, C.F., 1950. 'Egyptian catalogues of things', *JNES* 9: 253-62.

Nissen, H.J., 1986. 'The archaic texts from Uruk', *World Archaeology* 17: 317-34.

Nunn, J., 1996. *Ancient Egyptian Medicine*, London: BMP.

O'Connor, D., 1972. 'The geography of settlement in ancient Egypt', *Man, Settlement and Urbanism*, ed. P.J. Ucko, R. Tringham and G.W. Dimbleby, London: Duckworth, 681-98.

Ogden, J., 2000. 'Metals', *Ancient Egyptian Materials and Technology*, ed. P.T. Nicholson and I. Shaw, Cambridge: CUP, 148-76.

Bibliography

Onasch, H.-U., 1994. *Die assyrischen Eroberungen Ägyptens*, Ägypten und Altes Testament 27, Wiesbaden: Harrassowitz.

Ong, W.J., 2002. *Orality and Literacy: The Technologizing of the Word*, London: Routledge.

Oppenheim, L., 1978. 'Man and nature in Mesopotamian civilization', *Dictionary of Scientific Biography 15, Supplement 1*. New York: Scribner, 634-66.

Oppenheim, L., Brill, R.H., Barag, D. and von Saldern, A., 1970. *Glass and Glassmaking in Ancient Mesopotamia: An Edition of the Cuneiform Texts which Contain Instructions for Glassmakers with a Catalogue of Surviving Objects*, Corning NY: Corning Museum of Glass Press.

Osing, J., 1981. 'Onomastika', *Lexikon der Ägyptologie* IV, ed. W. Helck, E. Otto and W. Westendorf, Wiesbaden: Harrasowitz, 572.

Panagiotaki, M., Maniatis, Y., Kavoussanaki, D., Hatton, G. and Tite, M., 2004. 'The production technology of Aegean Bronze Age vitreous materials', *Invention and Innovation: The Social Context of Technological Change 2, Egypt, the Aegean and the Near East 1650-1150 BC*, ed. J. Bourriau and J. Phillips. Oxford: Oxbow, 149-75.

Parker, R.A., 1972. *Demotic Mathematical Papyri*, Providence: Brown University Press.

Parkinson, R., 1997. *The Tale of Sinuhe and Other Ancient Egyptian Poems, 1940-1640 BC*, Oxford: OUP.

Parkinson, R. and Schofield, L., 1993. 'Akhenaten's army', *EA* 3: 34-5.

Parry, D., 2004. *Engineering the Pyramids*, Stroud: Sutton.

Pearce, L.E., 1999. 'Sepiru and luaba: scribes of the late first millennium', *Languages and Cultures in Contact: At the Crossroads of Civilizations in the Syro-Mesopotamian Realm*, ed. K. van Lerberghe and G. Voet, Leuven: Peeters, 355-68.

Peet, T.E., 1930. *The Great Tomb-Robberies of the 20th Egyptian Dynasty*, Oxford: Clarendon Press.

Peet, T.E., 1931. 'A problem in Egyptian geometry', *JEA* 17: 100-6.

Peet, T.E. and Woolley, C.L., 1923. *City of Akhenaten I*, London: EES.

Pellegrin, P., 2000. 'Medicine', *Greek Thought: A Guide to Classical Knowledge*, ed. J. Brunschwig and G.E.R. Lloyd, Cambridge MA: Belknap Press, 387-414.

Peltenburg, E.J., 1987. 'Early faience: recent studies, origins, and relations with glass', *Early Vitreous Materials*, ed. M. Bimson and I. Freestone, London: BMP, 5-29.

Pendlebury, J.D.S., 1931. 'Preliminary report of excavations at Tell el-Amarnah 1930-31', *JEA* 17: 240-3.

Pendlebury, J.D.S., 1932. 'Preliminary report of excavations at Tell el-Amarnah 1931-32', *JEA* 18: 143-9.

Petrie, W.M.F., 1883. *The Pyramids and Temples of Gizeh*, London: Field and Tuer.

Petrie, W.M.F., 1892. *Medum*, London: Nutt.

Petrie, W.M.F., 1894. *Tell el Amarna*, London: EEF.

Petrie, W.M.F., 1897. *Six Temples at Thebes*, London: Bernard Quaritch.

Petrie, W.M.F., 1909. *The Arts and Crafts of Egypt*, Edinburgh: Foulis.

Petrie, W.M.F., Wainwright, G.A. and Mackay, E., 1912. *The Labyrinth, Gerzeh and Mazghunah*, London: ERA.

Bibliography

Petrie, W.M.F., 1917. *Tools and Weapons*, London: Egyptian Research Account.

Petrie, W.M.F., 1926. *Weights and Measures*, London: Egyptian Research Account.

Petrie, W.M.F. and Quibell, J.E., 1896. *Naqada and Ballas*, London: British School of Archaeology in Egypt.

Pfaffenberger, B., 1988. 'Fetishized objects and humanized nature: towards a social anthropology of technology', *Man* (n.s.) 23: 236-52.

Piggott, S., 1969. 'The first wagons and carts: twenty-five years later', *Bulletin of the Institute of Archaeology* 16: 3-18.

Pinch, G., 1983. 'Childbirth and female figurines at Deir el-Medina and el-Amarna', *Orientalia* 52: 405-14.

Pinch, G., 1994. *Magic in Ancient Egypt*, London: BMP.

Podzorski, P.V., 1990. *Their Bones Shall Not Perish: An Examination of Predynastic Human Skeletal Remains from Naga-ed-Dêr in Egypt*, New Malden: SIA.

Pons Mellado, E., 2006. 'Trade of metals between Egypt and other countries from the Old until the New Kingdom', *Chronique d'Egypte* 81: 7-16.

Porceddu, S., Jetsu, L., Tapio, M. and Toivari-Viitala, J., 2008. 'Evidence of periodicity in ancient Egyptian calendars of lucky and unlucky days', *CAJ* 18: 327-39.

Postgate, N., Wang, T. and Wilkinson, T., 1995. 'The evidence for early writing: utilitarian or ceremonial?', *Antiquity* 69: 459-80.

Pusch, E., 1996. ' "Pi-Ramesses-beloved-of-Amun, headquarters of they chariotry": Egyptians and Hittites in the Delta residence of the Ramessides', *Pelizaeus Museum Hildesheim: the Egyptian Collection*, ed. A. Eggebrecht, Mainz: Philipp von Zabern, 126-45.

Pusch, E. and Rehren, T., 2007. *Hochtemperatur-Technologie in der Ramses-Stadt: Rubinglas für den Pharao*, Hildesheim: Gerstenberg.

Quibell, J.E., 1898. *The Ramesseum*, London: EEF.

Quibell, J.E., 1913. *The Tomb of Hesy: Excavations at Saqqara*, Cairo: Service des Antiquités.

Quibell, J.E. and Hayter, A.G.K., 1927. *Teti Pyramid: North Side*, Cairo: Institut. Français d'Archéologie Orientale.

Raban, A., 1989. 'The Medinet Habu ships: another interpretation', *International Journal of Nautical Archaeology and Underwater Exploration* 18/2: 163-71.

Radner, K., 2009. 'The Assyrian king and his scholars: the Syro-Anatolian and the Egyptian schools', *Of God(s), Trees, Kings and Scholars: Neo-Assyrian and Related Studies in Honour of Simo Parpola*, Studia Orientalia 106, ed. M. Luukko, S. Svärd, and R. Mattila, Helsinki: Finnish Oriental Society, 221-38.

Raulwing, P. and Clutton-Brock, J., 2009. 'The Buhen horse fifty years after its discovery (1958-2008)', *Journal of Egyptian History* 2: 1-106.

Rautman, A.E. (ed.), 2000. *Reading the Body: Representations and Remains in the Archaeological Record*, Philadelphia: University of Pennsylvania Press.

Rawlins D. and Pickering, K., 2001. 'Astronomical orientation of the pyramids', *Nature* 412: 699.

Ray, J.D., 1986. 'The emergence of writing in Egypt', *WA* 17/3: 307-16.

Rehren, T., Pusch, E.B. and Herold, A., 2001. 'Qantir-Piramesses and the organization of the Egyptian glass industry', *The Social Context of Technological Change: Egypt and the Near East, 1650-1550 BC*, ed. A.J. Shortland. Oxford: Oxbow, 223-8.

Reisner, G.A., 1928. 'The empty sarcophagus of the mother of Cheops', *Bulletin of the Museum of Fine Arts* 26: 75-89.

Reisner, G.A., 1931. *Mycerinus: The Temples of the Third Pyramid*, Cambridge MA: HUP.

Renfrew, C.A., 1986. 'Varna and the emergence of wealth in prehistoric Europe', *The Social Life of Things: Commodities in Cultural Perspective*, ed. A. Appadurai, Cambridge, CUP, 141-68.

Reymond, E.A.E., 1976. *A Medical Book from Crocodilopolis*, Vienna: Verlag Brüder Hollinek.

Rice, M., 1990. *Egypt's Making: The Origins of Ancient Egypt 5000-2000 BC*, London: Routledge.

Ritner, R.K., 1989. 'Horus on the crocodiles: a juncture of religion and magic in late dynastic Egypt', *Religion and Philosophy in Ancient Egypt*, ed. W.K. Simpson, New Haven: Yale Egyptological Seminar, 103-16.

Ritner, R.K., 1993. *The Mechanics of Ancient Egyptian Magical Practice*, Studies in Ancient Oriental Civilizations 54, Chicago: Oriental Institute.

Ritner, R.K., 2000. 'Innovations and adaptations in ancient Egyptian medicine', *JNES* 59/2: 107-17.

Ritner, R.K., 2001. 'Magic in medicine', *The Oxford Encyclopedia of Ancient Egypt*, ed. D.B. Redford, Oxford and New York: OUP, 326-9.

Robins, G. and Shute, C.C., 1987. *The Rhind Mathematical Papyrus*, London, BMP.

Robson, E., 2001. 'Technology in society: three textual case studies from Late Bronze Age Mesopotamia', *The Social Context of Technological Change: Egypt and the Near East, 1650-1550 BC*, ed. A.J. Shortland, Oxford: Oxbow, 39-57.

Roehrig, C.H., 2005. 'Glass', *Hatshepsut from Queen to Pharaoh*, ed. C.H. Roehrig, R. Dreyfuss and C.A. Keller, New York: MMA, 67-9.

Rogers, E.M., 1983. *Diffusion of Innovations*, 3rd edn, New York: The Free Press.

Romer, J., 2007. *The Great Pyramid: Ancient Egypt Revisited*, Cambridge, CUP.

Rossi, C., 2004. *Architecture and Mathematics in Ancient Egypt*, Cambridge, CUP.

Roth, A.M., 1992. 'The psS-kf and the "opening of the mouth" ceremony: a ritual of birth and rebirth', *JEA* 78: 113-47.

Roth, A.M., 1993. 'Fingers, stars and the "opening of the mouth"', *JEA* 79: 57-80.

Rowlands, M.J., 1976. *The Organization of Middle Bronze Age Metalworking*, Oxford: BAR.

Sauneron, S., 1989. *Un traité égyptien d'ophiologie: papyrus du Brooklyn Museum no 47.218.48 et .85*, Cairo: IFAO.

Säve-Söderbergh, T., 1951. 'The Hyksos rule in Egypt', *JEA* 37: 59-60.

Scarre, C., 1994. 'The meaning of death: funerary beliefs and the prehistorian', *The Ancient Mind: Elements of Cognitive Archaeology*, ed. C. Renfrew and E. Zubrow. Cambridge: CUP, 75-82.

Bibliography

Schmandt-Besserat, D., 1978. 'An early recording system in Egypt and the ancient Near East', *Immortal Egypt*, ed. D. Schmandt-Besserat, Malibu: Undena, 5-12.

Schmandt-Besserat, D., 1981. 'From tokens to tablets: a re-evaluation of the so-called "numerical tablets"', *Visible Language* 15/4: 321-44.

Schmandt-Besserat, D., 1992. *Before Writing: from Counting to Cuneiform*, Austin TX: University of Texas Press.

Schmandt-Besserat, D., 1996. *How Writing Came About*, Austin TX: University of Texas Press.

Schofield, L. and Parkinson, R., 1994. 'Of helmets and heretics: a possible Egyptian representation of Mycenaean warriors on a papyrus from el-Amarna', *Annual of the British School at Athens* 89: 157-70.

Schulman, A.R., 1980. 'Chariots, chariotry and the Hyksos', *Journal of the Society for the Study of Egyptian Antiquities* 10: 105-53.

Schulman, A., 1988. 'Hittites, helmets and Amarna: Akhenaten's first Hittite war', *Akhenaten Temple Project II*, ed. D. Redford, Toronto: Akhenaten Temple Project, 54-79.

Scott, N.E., 1942. 'Egyptian cubit rods', *Metropolitan Museum of Art Bulletin* n.s. 1: 70-5.

de Selincourt, A. (tr.), 1954. *Herodotus: The Histories*, rev. J. Marincola, Harmondsworth: Penguin.

Serpico, M. and White, R., 2000. 'Oil, fat and wax', *Ancient Egyptian Materials and Technology*, ed. P.T. Nicholson and I. Shaw, Cambridge: CUP, 390-429.

Sethe, K., 1902. *Imhotep, der Asklepios der Aegypter*, Leipzig: Hinrichs.

Shaltout, M. and Belmonte, J.A., 2008. 'On the orientation of ancient Egyptian temples (4) Epilogue in Serabit el-Khadim and overview', *Journal for the History of Astronomy* 39: 182-211.

Shaw, I., 1996. 'Akhetaton – the city of one god', *Royal Cities of the Biblical World*, ed. J. Goodnick Westenholz, Jerusalem: Bible Lands Museum, 83-112.

Shaw, I., 2000. 'Sifting the spoil heaps: excavation techniques from Peet to Pendlebury at el-Amarna', *Studies dedicated to Prof. H.S. Smith*, ed. M.A. Leahy and J. Tait, London: EES, 273-82.

Shaw, I., 2001. 'Egyptians, Hyksos and military technology: causes, effects or catalysts?', *The Social Context of Technological Change: Egypt and the Near East, 1650-1550 BC*, ed. A. Shortland, Oxford: Oxbow, 59-72.

Shaw, I., 2004. 'Identity and occupation: how did individuals define themselves and their work in the Egyptian New Kingdom?', *Invention and Innovation: The Social Context of Technological Change*, ed. J. Bourriau and J. Phillips, Oxford: Oxbow, 12-24.

Shaw, I., 2008. 'A royal harem town of the New Kingdom: new fieldwork at Medinet el-Gurob', *Queens of Egypt*, ed. C. Ziegler, Paris: Somogy Art Publishers, 104-15.

Shaw, I., 2009. 'Non-textual marks and the Twelfth-Dynasty dynamics of centre and periphery: a case-study of potmarks at the Gebel el-Asr gneiss quarries', *Non-textual Marking Systems, Writing and Pseudo Script from Prehistory to Present Times*, ed. P. Andrassy, J. Budka and F. Kammerzell, Lingua Aegyptia – Studia Monographica No. 8, Göttingen: Lingua Aegyptia, 69-82.

Shaw, I., 2010a. *Hatnub: Quarrying Travertine in Ancient Egypt*, London: EES.

Shaw, I., 2010b. 'Socio-economic and iconographic contexts for Egyptian military technology in the east Mediterranean: the knowledge economy and "technology transfer" in Late Bronze Age warfare', *The Knowledge Economy and Technological Capabilities: Egypt, the Near East and the Mediterranean 2nd Millennium BC-1st Millennium AD. Proceedings of a Conference held at the Maison de la Chimie Paris, France 9-10 December 2005*, ed. M. Wissa, Barcelona: Aula Orientalis, 77-85.

Shaw, I., 2011. 'New fieldwork at the Medinet el-Gurob New Kingdom settlement: investigating a harem palace town in the Faiyum (summary of the 2009-10 seasons)', *Achievements and Problems of Modern Egyptology, Moscow 29 September-2 October 2009*, ed. G. Belova, Moscow: Russian Academy of Sciences.

Shennan, S., 2002. *Genes, Memes and Human History: Darwinian Archaeology and Cultural Evolution*, London and New York: Thames and Hudson.

Shirakawa, E., 2006. 'Choice of vocabularies: wordplay in ancient Egypt', *Current Research in Egyptology 2004*, ed. R.J. Dann, Oxford: Oxbow.

Shorter, A.W., 1936. 'A magical ostracon', *JEA* 22: 165-8.

Shortland, A.J., 2001. *The Social Context of Technological Change: Egypt and the Near East, 1650-1550 BC*, Oxford: Oxbow.

Shortland, A.J., 2004. 'Hopeful monsters: invention and innovation in the archaeological record', *Invention and Innovation: The Social Context of Technological Change 2, Egypt, the Aegean and the Near East 1650-1150 BC*, ed. J. Bourriau and J. Phillips, Oxford: Oxbow, 1-11.

Shortland, A.J., 2007. 'Who were the glassmakers? Status, theory and method in mid-second millennium glass production', *Oxford Journal of Archaeology* 26: 261-74.

Shute, C., 2001. 'Mathematics', *The Oxford Encyclopedia of Ancient Egypt* II, ed. D.B. Redford, Oxford and New York: OUP, 348-51.

Sillar, B. and Tite, M., 2000. 'The challenge of "technological choices" for materials science approaches in archaeology', *Archaeometry* 42/1: 2-20.

Silverman, D., 1991. 'Divinity and deities in ancient Egypt', in *Religion in Ancient Egypt*, ed. B.E. Shafer, Ithaca and London: Cornell University Press, 7-87.

Skinner, F.G., 1954. 'Measures and weights', *A History of Technology* I, ed. C. Singer, E.J. Holmyard and A.R. Hall, Oxford: OUP, 774-84.

Smith, H.S., 1972. 'Society and settlement in ancient Egypt', *Man, Settlement and Urbanism*, ed. P. Ucko, R. Tringham and G.W. Dimbleby, London: Duckworth, 705-19.

Smith, H.S. and Smith, A., 1976. 'A reconsideration of the Kamose texts', *ZÄS* 103: 48-76.

Smith, S., 1969. 'Babylonian time reckoning', *Iraq* 31: 74-81.

Smith, W.S., 1981. *The Art and Architecture of Ancient Egypt*, 2nd edn, Harmondsworth: Pelican.

Snape, S.R. and Tyldesley, J., 1983. 'Two Egyptian flint knapping scenes', *Lithics* 4: 46-7.

Snodgrass, A.M., 1980. 'Iron and early metallurgy in the Mediterranean', *The Coming of the Age of Iron*, ed. T.A. Wertime and J.D. Muhly, New Haven, CN: Yale University Press, 335-74.

Soukiassian, G., 1997. 'A governor's palace at 'Ayn Asil, Dakhla Oasis', *Egyptian Archaeology* 11: 15-17.

Spalinger, A.J., 1982. *Aspects of the Military Documents of the Ancient Egyptians*, New Haven and London: YUP.

Spalinger, A.J., 1995. 'Some remarks on the epagomenal days in ancient Egypt', *JNES* 54: 33-47.

Spalinger, A.J., 2005. *War in Ancient Egypt: The New Kingdom*, Oxford: Blackwell.

Sparks, R., 2001. 'Stone vessel workshops in the Levant: luxury products of a cosmopolitan age', *The Social Context of Technological Change: Egypt and the Near East, 1650-1550 BC*, ed. A.J. Shortland, Oxford: Oxbow Books, 93-112.

Spence, K., 2000. 'Ancient Egyptian chronology and the *astronomical orientation* of pyramids', *Nature* 408: 320-4.

Spence, K., 2010. 'Establishing direction in early Egyptian burials and monumental architecture: "measurement" and the spatial link with the "other"', *The Archaeology of Measurement: Comprehending Heaven, Earth and Time in Ancient Societies*, ed. I. Morley and C. Renfrew, Cambridge: CUP, 170-9.

Spencer, P., 2004. 'Digging diary 2003', *EA* 24: 25-9.

Spratt, D.A., 1989. 'Innovation theory made plain', *What's New? A Closer Look at The Process of Innovation*, ed. S.E. van der Leeuw and R. Torrence, London: Unwin Hyman, 245-57.

Steiner, R.C., 1992. 'Northwest Semitic incantations in an Egyptian medical papyrus of the fourteenth century BCE', *JNES* 51: 191-200.

Sternberg-el-Hotabi, H., 1988. 'Balamierungsritual pBoulaq 3', *Rituale und Beschwörungen 2*, ed. C. Butterweck, Gütersloh: Gütersloher Verlagshaus Mohn.

Stevens, A. and Ecclestone, M., 2007. 'Craft production and technology', *The Egyptian World*, ed. T. Wilkinson, London and New York: Routledge, 146-59.

Stevenson, A., 2009. 'Palettes', *UCLA Encyclopedia of Egyptology*, ed. W. Wendrich, Los Angeles. http://digital2.library.ucla.edu/viewItem.do?ark=21198/zz001nf6c0

Stocks, D., 1986. 'Egyptian technology II: stone vessel manufacture', *Popular Archaeology*, May 1986: 14-18.

Stocks, D., 1993. 'Making stone vessels in ancient Mesopotamia and Egypt', *Antiquity* 67: 596-603.

Stocks, D., 1997. 'Derivation of ancient Egyptian faience core and glaze materials', *Antiquity* 71: 179-82.

Stocks, D., 2003a. *Experiments in Egyptian Archaeology: Stoneworking Technology in Ancient Egypt*. London: Routledge.

Stocks, D., 2003b. 'Immutable laws of friction: preparing and fitting stone blocks into the Great Pyramid at Giza', *Antiquity* 77: 572-8.

Struve, W.W., 1930. *Mathematischer Papyrus des Staatlichen Museums der schönen Künste in Moskau*, Studien und Quellen zur Geschichte der Mathematik, Astronomie und Physik, part A, vol. 1, Berlin: Springer.

Bibliography

Thomsen, C.J., 1836. *Ledetraad til Nordisk Oldkyndighed*, Copenhagen: Royal Danish Society of Antiquities (tr. Lord Ellesmere, 1848, *A Guide to Northern Archaeology*, London: James Bain).

Tillmann, A., 1992. *Die Steinartefakte des dynastischen Ägypten, dargestellt am Beispiel der Inventare aus Tell el-Dab'a und Qantir*, Tübingen: unpublished PhD thesis.

Tiradritti, F., (ed.), 1998. *Egyptian Treasures from the Egyptian Museum in Cairo*, Vercelli: White Star.

Tylecote, R.F., 1992. *A History of Metallurgy*, London: Institute of Materials.

Tylor, J.J., 1896. *Wall Drawings and Monuments of El Kab: The Tomb of Sebeknekht*, London: Bernard Quaritch.

Vallance, J., 2000. 'Doctors in the library: the strange tale of Apollonius the bookworm and other stories', *The Library of Alexandria: Centre of Learning in the Ancient World*, ed. R. MacLeod, London and New York: I.B. Tauris, 95-113.

van den Brink, E.C.M., 1992. 'Corpus and numerical evaluation of the "Thinite" potmarks', *The Followers of Horus: Studies Dedicated to Michael Allen Hoffman, 1944-1990*, ed. R. Friedman and B. Adams, Oxford: Oxbow, 265-96.

Vandier, J., 1952. *Manuel d'archeologie egyptienne I: Les époques de formation*, Paris: Picard.

Van Dijk, J., 2000. 'The Amarna period and the later New Kingdom', *The Oxford History of Ancient Egypt*, ed. I. Shaw, Oxford: OUP, 265-307.

Van Driel-Murray, C., 2000. 'Leatherwork and skin products', *Ancient Egyptian Materials and Technology*, ed. P.T. Nicholson and I. Shaw, Cambridge: CUP, 299-319.

van Koppen, F. and Radner, K., 2009. 'Ein Tontafelfragment aus der diplomatischen Korrespondenz der Hyksosherrscher mit Babylonien', *Ägypten und Levante* 19: 115-19.

van Walsem, R., 1978-79. 'The psS-kf: an investigation of an ancient Egyptian funerary instrument', *OMRO* 59: 193-249.

Velde, H. te, 1970. 'The god Heka in Egyptian theology', *Jaarbericht van het Voorasiatisch-Egyptisch Genootschap 'Ex Oriente Lux'* 21: 175-86.

Vermeersch, P. and Paulissen, E., 1997. 'Extensive Middle Palaeolithic chert extraction in the Qena area (Egypt)', *Man and Flint, Proceedings of the VIIth International Flint Symposium, Warsaw, September 1995*, Warsaw: Institute of Archaeology and Ethnology, Polish Academy of Sciences, 133-42.

Vogelsang-Eastwood, G., 2000. 'Textiles', *Ancient Egyptian Materials and Technology*, ed. P.T. Nicholson and I. Shaw, Cambridge: CUP, 268-98.

Von Damow, E., 2004. 'Canaanite in cuneiform', *Journal of the American Oriental Society* 124/4: 641-74.

von Staden, H., 1989. *Herophilus: The Art of Medicine in Early Alexandria*, Cambridge: CUP.

Wachsmann, S., 1981. 'The ships of the Sea Peoples', *International Journal of Nautical Archaeology* 10: 187-220.

Warburton, D., 2003. *Macroeconomics from the Beginning: The General Theory, Ancient Markets, and the Role of Interest*, Neuchâtel, Switzerland: Recherches et Publications.

Bibliography

Warren, P., 1995. 'Minoan Crete and Pharaonic Egypt', *Egypt, the Aegean and the Levant: Interconnections in the Second Millennium BC*, ed. W.V. Davies and L. Schofield, London: BMP, 1-18.

Weeks, K., 1976-8. 'Studies of Papyrus Ebers', *Bulletin de l'Institut d'Egypte* 58-9: 292-9.

Weigall, A.E.P., 1908. *Weights and Balances, Catalogue général des antiquités égyptiennes du Musée du Caire*, Cairo: IFAO.

Wendorf, F., 1968. 'Site 117: a Nubian final paleolithic graveyard near Jebel Sahaba, Sudan', *The Prehistory of Nubia*, ed. F. Wendorf, Dallas: Fort Bergwin Research Center and SMU Press, 954-95.

Wendorf, F. and Schild, R., 2001. *Holocene Settlement of the Egyptian Sahara I: The Archaeology of Nabta Playa*, New York: Kluwer Academic.

Wendorf, F., Schild, R. and Zedeno, N., 1996. 'A late Neolithic megalith complex in the Eastern Sahara: a preliminary report', *Interregional Contacts in the Later Prehistory of Northeastern Africa*, ed. L. Krzyzaniak, K. Kroeper and M. Kobusiewicz, Poznan: Poznan Archaeological Museum, 125-32.

Wengrow, D., 2006. *The Archaeology of Early Egypt: Social Transformations in North-East Africa, 10,000 to 2650 BC*, Cambridge: CUP.

Werschkun, C., 2011. *Resource Procurement and Management in Egyptian Settlements of the Old Kingdom*, unpublished PhD thesis, University of Liverpool.

Westendorf, W., 1966. *Papyrus Edwin Smith: Ein medizinisches Lehrbuch aus dem Alten Ägypten*, Berne and Stuttgart: Hans Huber.

Western, A.C. and McLeod, W., 1995. 'Woods used in Egyptian bows and arrows', *JEA* 81: 77-94.

Wheeler, N.F., 1935. 'Pyramids and their purpose III: pyramid mysticism and mystification', *Antiquity* 9: 5-21.

White, L., 1962. *Medieval Archaeology and Social Change*, Oxford, OUP.

Wiebach-Koepke, S., 2003. *Phänomenologie der Bewegungsabläufe im Jenseitskonzept der Unterweltbücher Amduat und Pfortenbuch und der liturgischen 'Sonnenlitanei', Ägypten und Altes Testament 55*, Wiesbaden: Harassowitz.

Wild, H., 1966. *Le tombeau de Ti*, fasc. III. Cairo: IFAO.

Wildung, D., 1977. *Egyptian Saints: Deification in Pharaonic Egypt*, New York: New York University Press.

Wilhelm, G., 1984. 'Zur Paläographie der in Ägypten geschribenen Keilschriftbriefe', *SAK* 11: 643-53.

Wilkinson, C. (ed.), 2008. *The Observer Book of Invention*, London, Observer Books.

Williams, A.R. and Maxwell-Hyslop, K.R., 1976. 'Ancient steel from Egypt', *Journal of Archaeological Science* 3: 283-305.

Wiseman, D.J., 1955. 'Assyrian writing-boards', *Iraq* 17: 3-15.

Wreszinski, W., 1909. *Der grosse medizinische Papyrus des Berliner Museums (Pap. Berl. 3038)*, Leipzig: J.C. Hinrichs.

Wreszinski, W., 1912. *Der Londoner medizinische Papyrus (Brit. Museum nr. 10,059) und der Papyrus Hearst in Transkription: Übersetzung und Kommentar*, Leipzig: J.C. Hinrichs.

Bibliography

Wreszinski, W., 1913. *Der Papyrus Ebers: Umschrift, Übersetzung und Kommentar*, Leipzig: J.C. Hinrichs.

Wreszinski, W., 1935. *Atlas zur altägyptischen Kulturgeschichte* II, Leipzig: J.C. Hinrichs.

Yadin, Y., 1963. *The Art of Warfare in Biblical Lands* I, New York, Toronto and London: McGraw-Hill.

Yoffee, N., 1995. 'Political economy in early Mesopotamian states', *Annual Review of Anthropology* 24: 281-311.

Žába, Z., 1953. *L'orientation astronomique dans l'ancienne Egyptee, et la precession de l'axe du monde*, Prague: xx.

Zaccagnini, C., 1983. 'Patterns of mobility among ancient Near Eastern craftsmen', *JNES* 42: 245-64.

Zerubavel, E., 1977. 'The French Republican calendar: a case study in the sociology of time', *American Sociological Review* 42: 868-77.

Index

References to pages with illustrations are in italic.

191

Index

Index

Index

Index

Index

Ancient Egyptian terms

Index

Assyrian terms